Routledge Revivals

Habib Bourguiba, Islam and the Creation of Tunisia

First published in 1984, *Habib Bourguiba, Islam and the Creation of Tunisia* is a study of Habib Bourguiba, the founder of independent Tunisia, that argues that Islam played a vital role in the development of the Tunisian nationalist movement. This book is therefore both a biography of the Tunisian leader and a discussion of the role of Islam as the key to legitimacy throughout the Arab world. The author argues that Islam was such a fundamental component in defining the specificity of the Tunisian nation that even Bourguiba, the most secular of Arab leaders, could not shed the Arab-Islamic heritage of Tunisia. Instead, he used Islam as a principle mode of communication to mobilise the Tunisian masses. This book will be of interest to students of African studies, history, political science and religion.

Habib Bourguiba, Islam and the Creation of Tunisia

Norma Salem

Routledge
Taylor & Francis Group
Routledge Revivals

First published in 1984
By Croom Helm Ltd.

This edition first published in 2024 by Routledge
4 Park Square, Milton Park, Abingdon, Oxon, OX14 4RN
and by Routledge
605 Third Avenue, New York, NY 10017

Routledge is an imprint of the Taylor & Francis Group, an informa business

Publisher's Note
The publisher has gone to great lengths to ensure the quality of this reprint but points out that some imperfections in the original copies may be apparent.

Disclaimer
The publisher has made every effort to trace copyright holders and welcomes correspondence from those they have been unable to contact.

A Library of Congress record exists under ISBN: 0709933193

ISBN: 978-1-032-66778-2 (hbk)
ISBN: 978-1-032-66778-2 (ebk)
ISBN: 978-1-032-66818-5 (pbk)

Book DOI 10.4324/9781032667782

Habib Bourguiba, Islam and the Creation of Tunisia

Norma Salem

CROOM HELM
London • Sydney • Dover, New Hampshire

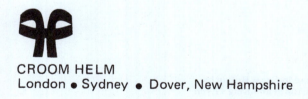

Croom Helm Ltd, Provident House, Burrell Row,
Beckenham, Kent BR3 1AT
Croom Helm Australia Pty Ltd, GPO Box 5097,
Sydney, NSW 2001, Australia
Croom Helm, 51 Washington Street,
Dover, New Hampshire, 03820 USA

British Library Cataloguing in Publication Data

Salem, Norma
Habib Bourguiba, Islam and
the creation of Tunisia
1. Salem, Norma. 2. Tunisia
Presidents – Biography
I. Title
961'.104'0924 DT264.49.B6

ISBN 0-7099-3319-3

Printed and bound in Great Britain by
Biddles Ltd, Guildford and King's Lynn

CONTENTS

FOREWORD i

NOTES ON TRANSLITERATION, TRANSLATION and CHAPTER NOTES iv

CHAPTER I: Introduction 1

CHAPTER II: The Formative Years (1903-1920) 20

Historical Background (1861-1907) 20
Time and the Family 29
Space and the Family 34
Emigration and the School 39
Formulation of Tunisian Nationalism 42

CHAPTER III: Between Two Cultures (1920-1934) ... 52

Re-enactment of the Formulated Reaction 52
Cultural Immersion 66
Re-immersion in Tunisia 74
The Issue of Naturalization 81
The Neo-Destour 93

CHAPTER IV: "L'Interlocuteur Valable" (1934-1955) 98

Language and Religion 98
The First Test of Strength 101
The First Dialogue 105
The Second Test of Strength 109
The War Interregnum 112
Criss-Crossing Dialogues 116
Quest in the East 118
A Renewed Dialogue 122
The Third Test of Strength 127
Fruitful Dialogue 129

CHAPTER V: Anatomy of Legitimacy 132

The Legal Dimension 133
The Historical Dimension 145
The Charismatic Dimension 150
The Construction of a Legitimate State :
From Protectorate to Sovereignty 151

CHAPTER VI: Conclusion 167

A Question of Biography and History 167
Religion and Politics 171
Personality and Time 179
Two Answers 181
Islam and Legitimacy: No New Question 188

NOTES 195

BIBLIOGRAPHY 235

TRANSLITERATION APPENDICES 255

Common Usage to Transliterated form 255
Transliterated Form to Common Usage 258

INDEX 263

To my family

FOREWORD

This study is largely based on my doctoral dissertation, written between December 1980 and August 1982. It was undertaken as an indirect continuation of previous work on Michel ʿAflaq and Anwar Al-Sâdât as I was and continue to be fascinated by the pervasive presence of Islam in the political discourse of the Arab world, despite the attractions of modernization and secularization.

The objectives of the research are focused on one man and, thus, are much more specific than most studies on contemporary political thought in the Arab world. The main claim to originality is in placing the evolution of Bourguiba, as representative of the Tunisian nationalist movement, within proper perspective with respect to intellectual influences both from the West, mainly through France, and from the Arab-Islamic heritage of Tunisia. The central question focused upon through the prism of Bourguiba's life-story is: How does Islam play a role in the process of legitimation in the Arab world? As a result, the biographical study strikes a balance between the narrative approach, using psychological and sociological analyses, and the topical approach.

I owe a debt of gratitude to many teachers, colleagues and friends, in Montreal and overseas. Professor Niyazi Berkes was instrumental in laying the foundations of my intellectual venture, through the short time we were in contact at the Institute of Islamic Studies. Abdallah Laroui, through his several books, has had tremendous influence on the formation of my critical attitude. The work of Clifford Geertz, relating religion and culture to ideology, has influenced some of my thinking as well.

Foreword

My initial interest in the Maghreb in general was encouraged by Kenneth Perkins and by Charles J. Adams, both of whom were supportive and always willing to listen to my woes. L. Carl Brown and his many books and articles led me to focus on Tunisia in particular while Hichem Djait encouraged me to work on the Tunisian history of the twentieth century. Hichem Djait, Myron Echenberg, Elbaki Hermassi, Michael Hudson, James Petras and John Sigler read various parts of my work. My sincere thanks for the time they gave and for the encouragement they offered. Many Tunisians donated generously of their time and energy in many ways and I owe special thanks to those who opened their homes and their hearts to my inquisitive questions.

Rachad Antonius, Benson Brown, Ali Dessouki, Nels Johnson, Thoraya Tlatli and Harold Weaver, whose intelligent conversations were always a pleasure, provided me with the means to hold in equilibrium the scepticism that continues to plague my thinking. They are, however, innocent of any errors of fact or interpretation which remain mine. I owe special gratitude to my uncle, Raymond Raad, without whose support I might not have been able to complete this work. Dr. Issa J. Boullata was the first to encourage me to publish my previous work. was advisor of my dissertation.

The Ministere de l'Education du Quebec, McGill University and the Institute of Islamic Studies provided scholarships while I was working on my doctoral research. The Institute of Arab Studies (Belmont, Massachusetts), the Ministère des Affaires Intergouvernementales, Québec, and the Entraide Universitaire du Canada allowed the wherewithal to undertake three trips to Tunisia, where I collected written material and interviewed several Tunisian figures. The Département d'Histoire and the Programme d'Études Arabes at the Université de Montréal offered me the opportunity to teach Arab history from the beginnings of Islam; thus enabling me to maintain the historical depth so necessary to understand the relationship between Islam and politics in the Arab world.

The Centre for Developing-Area Studies, McGill University, provided me with a pleasant working environment for a number of years. Thomas Bruneau and Thomas Eisemon, the Center Co-Directors, were also kind enough to encourage me to use the word processor and made special efforts to help me obtain computer time. Wendy Campbell, a colleague in history, was kind enough to teach me some of the secrets of the new art of word processing and to share in the task of typing in the final draft. In general, the Centre for Developing-Area Studies made it possible to be in contact with many researchers interested in a wide spectrum of problems touching upon the Third World. Such contact encouraged further reading in the social sciences and exploring the comparative approach. It also demonstrated, only too clearly, how rarely Islamic history is taken into account in the development of general theories in the social sciences and how far studies on the Islamic areas of the Third World lag behind.

NOTES ON TRANSLITERATION, TRANSLATION and CHAPTER NOTES

In principle, the Institute of Islamic Studies system of transliteration is followed except that the alif maqşûrah is indicated as an alif, the superscript dash is indicated as ^ and the subscript dot is indicated by ̦. Transliteration for topics dealing with the Maghrib poses a double problem. Many of the sources are in French and authors writing in French have not followed a consistent system of transliteration. They have usually transliterated from spoken rather than from written Arabic. Often, this has made the reconstruction of the original Arabic practically impossible. The problem is particularly acute in the case of names of persons and of geographical places. The latter pose an additional problem since quite a few were translated rather than transliterated into French.

Whenever the correct Arabic is known, the systematic transliteration is given in a separate appendix. The Index provides a cross-reference from the transliterated form to the commonly accepted form. Arab authors, writing in languages other than Arabic, are indicated as they themselves write their names in Latin script, and again the systematic transcription is given in the Appendix and a cross-reference in the Index. Quotations from Arabic texts are translated into English but quotations from French texts are given as such.

The traditional system of numbered notes for each chapter has been adhered to, but in shortened form. The full entry is given in the notes either when the source is first referred to or when publication data are pertinent to the argument being developed. Otherwise, only the author's last name and the first substantive in the book's title are given. This compromise avoids the *op. cit.* formula but *ibid.* is maintained since it is believed that the reader would have no trouble tracing the reference to the one immediately before.

Chapter 1

INTRODUCTION

The aim of this study is to discover how religion plays a role in politics, at least to the extent that Islamic themes are used in Arab political discourse. I try to approach this goal by means of a biographical study of how Habib Bourguiba, a leader of the Tunisian nationalist movement, expressed himself on the relationship between religion and politics.

The pursuit of this goal posed a number of theoretical questions: Can the categories derived from "Western" social studies be applied to the study of Arab-Islamic history? How are "religion" and "politics" to be defined? How relevant is semantic analysis to the study of religious themes in political discourse? What is the relationship of biography to history in general? What is the role of the individual in history?

These questions have been treated to various degrees of depth in a multiplicity of ways, within the framework of several disciplines from "sociology of religion" through "political science" to "linguistics". Faced with the enormity of the task, I do not attempt to formulate an epistemology synthesizing or exhausting all the possible solutions proffered by these disciplines, but simply present the general frame of mind in which I worked to derive meaning from the relationship between Islam and Habib Bourguiba.

It is true that most categories developed by modern social sciences are Eurocentric. For example, a basic category of sociology, "class", developed by studying the changes occurring in Europe during the transition from a feudal to a capitalist system, has not been re-examined in the light of the historical experience of the Arab-Islamic Middle East and North Africa so as to broaden its meaning and relevance.[1] The Eurocentric bias of such categories is made worse when they are shorn of the complex of issues they are connected to and are applied simplistically to a different cultural field without any consciousness of their underlying assumptions. For example, no consideration is made for the fact that even with regard to European history, social scientists have widely disagreed on the very nature and meaning of "class". As a consequence, class analysis is applied in the realm of Middle East studies without making explicit the specific theoretical framework being used. Students of Africa, Latin America or Asia differentiate classes in relation to the modes of production (Marxists in general), others in relation to occupation (functionalists), still others differentiate classes according to political criteria with respect to the exercise of power (élite studies). Certain anthropologists view economics and politics as secondary variables, and conceptualize classes in terms of cultural values or status. Finally, a few social scientists hold that classes do not exist as social realities but are simply convenient mental constructs. Unfortunately students of the Middle East and North Africa do not differentiate but assume a consensus.

Another example of the careless application of sociological categories is the fact that few students of the Middle East and North Africa distinguish between the objective existence of "social classes" and "class consciousness", as if the objective existence of a social class were a sufficient as well as necessary condition for class consciousness and class action. Perhaps such confusion is part of the explanation for such puzzling phenomena as "religious confessionalism" or "tribal solidarity" or "regionalism" which are used as substitutes for a serious effort in widening the original sociological categories to include the historical experience of the Arabs. Hermassi holds that it would be a mistake to attempt to construct universal paradigms for the analysis of the different solutions proposed by different societies to the problem of progress. He proposes that the historical experience of Third World countries is so different from historical developments of Europe and industrialized countries that new categories should be created.[2] When such sociological categories are translated into a non-European language, they are usually placed within a different semantic field dependent upon the historical background of that language. For example, Duvignaud points out that the Arabic term for "class", "ţabaqah" (pl. ţabaqât) does not have the precise meaning of "class" nor the connotations of the European historical experiences with which "class" is associated.[3] In contrast, I have not given up on the project of discovering universal principles but believe that these universal principles could become truly "universal" only by being broadened in the light of the historical experiences of all peoples and not simply of Europeans.

Time is not taken into consideration as an independent factor; in other words, it is usually assumed that there is no historic gap between the creation of a specific social formation, which itself had taken time to be brought forth by the social relations dependent on specific modes of production, the production of an ideology legitimizing that social formation and the reflection of that ideology upon the individual's consciousness. This study seems to point towards some possibility of alliances between classes or, rather, between what I called "class-fractions". Perhaps one could propose the idea that a variety of factors, other than the simple objective existence of a class, interfere with the historical process of class conflict. For example, a consciousness of the need to resist colonialism might be achieved by fractions of two or more classes at the same moment, leading them to form alliances despite their objectively conflicting class interests. The above discussion of the concept of "class" as it applies to Arab society can only be presented apologetically in the light of the primitiveness of social analyses concerning the history of the Arabs.

These considerations lead us to the problem of how to define elementary categories in such a way as to be able to use them cross-culturally. The following attempt at defining the two elementary categories, "religion" and "politics", is an illustration of the possibility of consciously shearing them from their specific historical background providing the basis of unconscious assumptions which trap the observer.

"Religion", and its Arabic equivalent "dîn", are commonly understood to mean a set of ideas and institutions premised on the belief in the supranatural. "Politics", and its Arabic equivalent "siyâsah", commonly mean a set of ideas and institutions dealing with power, or "who gets what, when and how".[4] It is usually assumed that in the

"West", as opposed to the Islamic "East", the two categories are inherently unrelated both as theoretical concepts and as phenomena in terms of both ideas and institutions. Historically, this is not true - as the long struggle between Church and State in Europe and the continued language of the various churches indicate (e.g. the "kingdom" of God on earth). Without delving into the philosophical aspects of whether "religion" and "politics" should or should not be related, it may be noted that, as an interested observer, I am distinguishing between operational categories and linguistic phenomena; in other words, between the "emic" and the "etic". These distinctions are derived from the linguistic categories, "phonemic" and "phonetic" where the first refers to the changes in sound that an informant perceives to differentiate between word meanings (e.g. bit and pit) while the second refers to the systems elaborated by observers to distinguish sounds according to criteria external to the culture being studied and, hopefully, culture-free sufficiently to allow their use cross-culturally.[5] In sum, I use "religion" and "politics" defined above, as "etic" categories, created by an observer in order to relate phenomena cross-culturally, without prejudice to the "emic" categories produced by the culture or cultures being studied. Thus, I do not assume that Bourguiba himself understands "religion" and "politics" as defined above nor do I assume that he held they should or should not be related. On the contrary, an aim of this study is to discover how he himself understood each category and how he himself understood their relationship.

Actually, since Bourguiba was under the influence of two cultures, the Arab-Islamic and the French-Western, what he understood by each category cannot be taken for granted as reflecting the general meaning within one or the other culture. A deeper study is necessary in order to clarify how the two cultural meanings affected each other in the process of the "active-syncretic acculturation"[6] experienced by Bourguiba. By attempting to analyze what Bourguiba actually meant, whether in French or in Arabic, in the context of the historic conditions limiting his thought and action, we might approach some understanding of the dynamic process by which Islam affects politics in the Arab world of modern times.

In his classic study, The Elementary Forms of Religious Life, Emile Durkheim views religion as a complex of symbols expressing the effort to give meaning to social realities. Durkheim, along with Weber and Freud, followed the Kantian tradition in distinguishing between the substance of society, as a legitimate phenomenal unit, and its form, which he called "collective representation".[7] Such "collective representations" include religion as a major component. Whether the distinction itself is real or simply conceptual is not relevant to the issue since no one paradigm has yet been developed to cover the meaning of these "collective representations", and even less has been achieved in relating them to society[8] despite the observation that "... without symbolism human behavior would be segmental and impoverished and man unable to make full contact with reality and therefore with himself."[9] Since societies have "symbolic codes" or "systems of signs" (necessary instruments for the construction of "collective representations"), the study of language has given us some "techniques with which to unravel these codes and thereby enable us to see belief, the elaboration of belief, and the development of belief, in action."[10]

Generally speaking, two functions of "collective representations" are usually distinguished: (1) the integrative function whereby disparate parts of the social system are placed together into a meaningful whole, and (2) the generative function whereby changes in the system are adapted to. The first function is related to Durkheim's concept of social "solidarity" which Weber broadens to the consensus of values at the base of the social order or, in other words, legitimacy.

Viewed in historical perspective, where time is considered as an independent factor, the dynamics of the symbolic and of the social systems must be relativized in order to understand the "generative" function of collective representations. In other words, time could have a different effect upon each system so that the relationship between the systems themselves is not always in phase. To solve the problem of the effect of time, any new theory

> ...must...refuse to give absolute primacy in symbolic action to either the formal structures of collective representation or the individual processes of understanding, interpretation, adjustment and expression. It must, indeed, focus on the social processes in which these two sorts of force interact: the social

> relations of communication and interpretation, and those properties of the symbolic system itself, and of the social system of which the symbolic system is a part, which give coherence to communication: which either stabilize or which make change in it regular.[11]

The raw materials for this case-study of the social relations of communication and interpretation which may be considered as means for analyzing the role of religion in politics, are Bourguiba's speeches and essays. In the first place, these speeches and essays are situated within the biography of Bourguiba which is itself framed within the social system of Tunisia as it developed during his lifetime. In the second place, the speeches and essays are analyzed using a methodology I had previously worked with in studies on other political leaders of the Arab world - namely ʿAflaq and Sâdât - where I reconstructed how each political leader modulated religious terms, so that they denoted secular concepts, while still carrying the persuasive powers of religious connotations.

There exists a need to find new approaches to the study of the relationship between religion and politics, in general, and between Islam and Middle Eastern politics, in particular. Only three members of the American scholarly community had pointed out and written about the importance of the religious element in Iran, before the Islamic revolution.[12] On the one hand, social scientists are ill equipped to deal with the problem. An intellectual block seems to hinder them, as they are not trained to consider the social reality of such a religious phenomenon as the return to the sacred in Islamic areas. On the other hand, it is very difficult to find Orientalists, specialists of the classical Islamic discourse, who bother to study the contemporary phenomenon.[13]

My attempt at a new approach is inspired by Izutsu's use of semantic analysis in his several works on the Qurʾân but with a number of fundamental differences.[14] First, these studies - on ʿAflaq, Sâdât and Bourguiba - transcend the limits of linguistics in attempting a linkage between religion and politics through language. Second, they are not textual analyses and do not attempt to make the material at hand interpret its own concepts or speak for itself. On the contrary, since they focus on the mutual transformations of religious and secular/political themes, the double heritage conveyed in the two languages Bourguiba used, French and Arabic, is drawn upon. This approach is particularly adapted to men of action such as ʿAflaq, Sâdât and Bourguiba. In fact, the methods of source criticism are insufficient in their case since they are not primarily men of letters and do not have the time to care for, attend to or control their sources. Using this approach permits us to identify key terms in their political discourse which open the doors of the intellectual influences under which such political leaders undertook their action.

Political discourse is intrinsically linked to the issue of legitimacy since its primary objective is to obtain the consent of the community (polis) for the socio-economic and political options of those in power or, the other side of the coin, for the aspirations of those in opposition.[15] In the case of Bourguiba, the key terms which have been found to lend meaning to his political behavior are "réalisme", "dialogue", "personnalité" and "action". It will be argued that some phases of the process of "active-syncretic acculturation" had been achieved already during the nineteenth century in Tunisia as represented by, in particular, Béchir Sfar; that Bourguiba continued this process; that the major dimensions of the first three concepts were derived from the "West" mainly through the French stream of that intellectual heritage; that the fourth concept, "action", has deep roots in the Arab-Islamic heritage; and that Bourguiba does not represent a culmination of the process of "acculturation" which is continuing in all the Arab world in general and in Tunisia in particular.

The problem of how to link "collective representations" to the individual process of communication is, of course, parallelled by the problem of how to relate biography to history. Some fifty years ago, biography was very much considered an integral part of history since one of the main schools of history was the "great man" theory claiming that great individuals were the main causative factors in historical development.[16] But, strangely enough, "... there is general recognition today that history and biography are quite distinct forms of literature."[17]

The basic reason is that biography continues to admit, to some extent, the subjectivity of the biographer. In contrast, history has been the victim of late nineteenth and early twentieth century positivism which confused objectivity with "scientificity" and denied any relationship between the subject (become object) and its student. With subjectivity as criterion, biography may then be classified into a spectrum:[18] (1) the "informative" or "objective" where the author avoids all comment or structure; (2) "scholarly" or historical with "some selection of evidence, but no unacknowledged guesswork, no fictional devices, and no attempt to interpret the subject's personality and actions psychologically"; (3) "artistic-scholarly" where the biographer not only selects evidence but also uses fictional devices and attempts to interpret the subject and thus "thinks of himself as more than a historian"; (4) "narrative" where some subjective imagination is allowed although it is not pure fiction; (5) "fictional" where "the imagination is given full rein". Although the use of literary tools leaves the biographer open to literary criticism yet, except for the fictional type, a biographer must first be judged as a historian before sentence is passed on his artistry. Consequently, this conflict between evidence and interpretation is the central difficulty of biography. Nonetheless, it is only by admitting to a spectrum of measures of subjectivity, of identification with the "hero", that a biographer may uphold the asymptotic search for truth.[19]

Actually, this is the position to which history has come as well, since history is also a matter of <u>selection</u> and <u>reconstruction</u> in order to recreate the illusion of events never to be relived again. In sum, the first types of biography are clearly allied to history in their search, asymptotic as it may be, for a "true" representation of the past. To the extent that this search for the true places limits on the literary methods that may be used in writing history, it also limits the literary tools permitted a biographer.

Of course, the measure of the author's subjectivity is not the only criterion by which biography is classified. The types, primary or secondary, and the respective amounts of sources used also distinguish biography into several kinds. Here the historians' tools for the evaluation of sources are indispensable and, consequently, biography and history are similar in their treatment of their sources, particularly of written material.[20] Finally, in terms of substance, both biography and history deal with the past or, in other words, their unit of study is the fourth dimension, Time with a capital "T" as it relates to the three dimensions of space.

Biography comes even closer to history when it is topical, rather than chronological or narrative. Where narrative biography focuses on the life-story of the subject for its own sake, topical biography examines wider issues through the reconstruction of the subject's experience. This study falls into the category of "critical" biography in terms of subjectivity and is partly narrative (Chapters II, III, IV) and partly topical (Chapters V, VI) where Bourguiba's life-story becomes the means of elucidating the central issue of political legitimacy which, I believe, forms the crux of the relationship between religion and politics.

> Quels que soient les thèmes qui font l'objet des recherches et du débat d'idées en pays d'Islam, le problème central demeure - dans tous les cas - celui de la légitimation...[21]

The validity of the biographical approach in the historical study of various issues poses a particular problem since this approach might create a special optical effect where the motives, principles and attitudes of a single individual appear as determinant over and above "deeper" social forces. There is a dangerous tendency, in biographical studies, to fall back on a psychology of influences and on a micro-sociology of the conflict of ideas among leaders as the necessary causes in history.

The problem of the "uniqueness" of the subject and the "uniqueness" of the chain of events he/she has the ability to create is linked to the rejection of historical laws, as inapplicable to unrepeatable phenomena. Perhaps the myths surrounding the "pure sciences" are partly to blame, such as the myth of Galileo throwing a feather and a stone from the top of the leaning tower of Pisa in order to "prove" the law of gravity by which the feather and the stone are supposed to reach the ground simultaneously. If Galileo had actually tried that "experiment", the law of gravity would most definitely have been proved a lie since friction, air currents, and other contingent factors, would not have been abstracted in reality and the stone would have reached the ground first. In fact, the specificity of each stone/feather throwing event could overwhelm any observer unless he/she abstracted the circumstantial from the fundamental factors. In sum, the law of gravity is <u>necessary</u> to explain the fall of any body on earth but it is not sufficient, by itself, to explain the actual fall of any specific body. Moreover, it is only within the limiting conditions of Newtonian physics that the above considerations of stone/feather throwing events is made. Beyond these limits, the new physics of relativity becomes operative.

The thrust of the argument is that the uniqueness of a life or of an event lies in the inability of historians to distinguish between the circumstantial and the fundamental factors and in their inability to assess the limiting conditions for the relevance of these factors rather than in the nature of the beast itself. Perhaps the solution lies in the combination of the deductive and the inductive methods; general propositions about social development may be accepted as hypotheses to be tested through a careful reconstruction of history. A process of extrapolation for deriving meaning from similar events and biographies might eventually permit the separation between necessary and contingent causes and the determination of limiting conditions in the continually renewed search for general propositions.

Since the distinction between necessary and contingent was not usually drawn in historical studies, the question was usually posed in "either/or" terms: either an individual was determined by historical laws or he/she had the margin of freedom to affect the course of history.[22] It is at the level of necessary causes that I would place economic, social and political developments. But necessary causes are not in themselves sufficient to explain either a particular event or a particular subject's behavior, even within the boundary conditions proposed. It is at the level of contingencies that psychological influences are brought in to complement the explanation. Beyond limiting conditions, yet to be discovered in the social sciences, a measure of uncertainty also enters as the process of studying a life or an event interferes with that life or event. The responsibility of the historian for his/her own role cannot then be shifted to the "fact" as he/she becomes aware of his/her own interference and its consequences.

History itself has been called upon to play a role in the legitimization of the contemporary political order in Tunisia. In fact, Bourguiba claimed the role of "maker of the history of that country" (i'tibârî şâni' târîkh hâdhâ al-balad).[23]

Thus, history has become part of political discourse in Tunisia,[24] and the history of Tunisia has become, therefore, subject to political vicissitudes. A student of Tunisian history must bear a sense of responsibility for his/her role in writing that history.

This subjection to political vicissitudes is particularly true of the series Histoire du Mouvement National Tunisien. The series was begun by Chedli Klibi, presently Secretary General of the League of Arab States, in 1967 with a volume entitled Habib Bourguiba: Articles de Presse, 1929-1934, obviously as a homage to Bourguiba. The subsequent volumes were edited by Mohamed Sayah (then Director of the Socialist Destour Party, 1964-69, and presently Minister of Equipment) and consist of fifteen volumes covering the period up to independence in 1956.

The translation into Arabic of this series was begun in 1979 under the general title of Târîkh al-ḩarakah al-waţaniyyah al-tûnisiyyah History of the Tunisian Patriotic Movement'. Note that national" has been translated as "patriotic", thus changing the frame of reference from a narrow Tunisian entity to an implicit larger-than-Tunisia framework. Volumes II, III, IV, VII, and VIII were prepared by Moncef Dellagi of the National Archives but were then taken over by Mohamed Sayah within the framework of the "Section d'Orientation et de Formation des Cadres du Parti Socialiste Destourien".[25]

The fact that the series, Histoire du Mouvement National Tunisien, was first written in French, and an Arabic translation only recently begun, is already indicative of a certain political option.; In its foreign policy, Tunisia attempts to maintain a balance between openness to the "West" and continued contact with the Arab-Islamic "East". Using French as the language of the first documented history of the Tunisian nationalist movement indicates either a tipping of the balance towards the "West" or, at the very least, an emphasis upon the distinctness of a Tunisian rather than an Arab-Islamic "personnalité".[26]

The series contains a collection of edited documents considered part of the records of the Tunisian nationalist movement. Since it was not my purpose to write a definitive history of the Tunisian nationalist movement but to understand the significance of Bourguiba who epitomized a mode of thought and a strategy of action in the mutual transformation of religion and politics, there was no need to check these documents by means of direct comparison with archival material. Moreover, the Tunisian government archives are incomplete as they must be supplemented by archival material found in France. In sum, my purpose was to learn the historical lessons (ʿibar) offered by the life of Bourguiba, as they have become part of a people's memory. This series should be complemented by the book La Tunisie et la France: Vingt-cinq ans de lutte pour une cooperation libre credited to Habib Bourguiba and published by the Néo-Destour delegation in France in 1954, basically in defense of the demand for internal autonomy. An earlier book, Le Destour et la France was written by Bourguiba in 1937 in the same vein.

The main tendency of these books is to highlight the role of the Néo-Destour in the struggle for independence, to the exclusion of all other groups and parties. By devoting the two volumes V and VI of the series to Bourguiba himself, Sayah narrowed this historical perspective even further so that all credit for the struggle for independence goes to Bourguiba, to the exclusion of all other leaders. In fact, Sayah may be considered as the depository of the historical dimension of Bourguiba's legitimacy. It is also interesting to note that the collection began to be published following the failure of the socialist experiment of the 1960s and served to shore up the faltering legitimacy of the political order created by Bourguiba.

Over and above the collection itself, Mohamed Sayah has been instrumental in organizing the series of autobiographical lectures given by Bourguiba at the Institut de la Presse et des Sciences de l'Information in 1973. These lectures were published under the title Ḥayâtî, Ârâʾî, Jihâdî [My Life, My Opinions, My Struggle]. The French version, Ma Vie, mes Idées, mon Combat, was published in 1977 by the Tunisian Ministère de l'Information. These lectures may be viewed in the same light as the Histoire du Mouvement National Tunisien series. They constitute a contribution to the reinforcement of Bourguiba's historical legitimacy but, in this case, as a response to the crisis following the elimination from the Party of the liberal tendency represented by Ahmed Mestiri at the second Monastir Congress in 1972. This autobiographical series of lectures supplements the official biography, Habib Bourguiba: Ḥayâtuh,

Jihâduh [Habib Bourguiba: His Life, His Struggle], published by the Tunisian Ministère de l'Information in 1966.

It is also under the aegis of Mohamed Sayah that the Ministère de l'Enseignement Supérieur et de la Recherche Scientifique sponsored a series of conferences on the history of the Tunisian nationalist movement[27] and, here again, the working language at the conference was French. It was rather incongruous to listen to various Tunisian historians, sociologists, economists, give their papers on the Tunisian resistance to French domination, in French. Less incongrous was the participation of a number of French specialists who also delivered their papers in French. French historians, such as Charles-André Julien and Henri de Montety, have actively participated in the construction of the "official" history of the Tunisian nationalist movement.

A particularly glaring example of this genre is Camille Bégué, at the time Sécrétaire général de la Société des écrivains de l'Afrique du Nord, who wrote Le Message de Bourguiba: Une Politique de l'Homme. Published in 1972, Bégué's book has to be viewed as a double apologetic: on the one hand, an apology of the continued French presence in Tunisia even after political independence and, on the other hand, an apology of Bourguiba's rejection of the Socialist experiment of the 1960s before putting an end to the more liberal tendencies of Mestiri. It is obvious from the acknowledgement Bégué presents that the manuscript was read by the Tunisian ambassador to Paris and by Mohamed Sayah, officially the longest-lasting Minister in Tunisia and unofficially the "official" historian of Bourguiba's regime. It is thus obvious that the book was consistent with the "accepted" history of the Tunisian nationalist movement. Bégué's ambiguity towards the exploitative nature of the Protectorate is illustrated by the following quote:

> La présence seule des Européens, leur succès, leur prospérité, leur style de vie êut pu entrainer les indigènes sur le chemin du progrès. Mais qui s'aviserait d'imiter les infidèles?[28]

Without realizing it, Bégué had, in fact, put his finger on the Tunisian mode of resistance - a silent refusal of France and an insistence on Islam as the element most clearly distinguishing the "indigènes" from the "colons". Bégué notes:

> Les rapports de Bourguiba et de l'Islam meritéraient une étude exhaustive à partir de sa formation et des premiers articles écrits en arabe en 1929. Seul, un islamisant averti pourrait composer cette délicate histoire d'une âme qui naît dans une obédience, traverse l'humanisme et débouche sur l'Absolu transcendant et personnalisé.[29]

Some attempt now seems to be under way among younger Tunisian scholars to escape the tentacular hold of the "official" school of history. The main shift would be away from the exclusiveness of the contribution of the Néo-Destour Party and of Bourguiba to the struggle for independence. It is possible that this tendency might reinforce the "legal" or "institutional" dimension of legitimacy in Tunisia which is now so necessary in view of Bourguiba's age and the need to prepare for his succession.

Among the most important of these new contributions is the book by Mohamed-Salah Lejri, Evolution du Mouvement National Tunisien des Origines à la deuxième guerre mondial, published in two volumes in 1974. Although Lejri tries to present a balanced picture of the contributions of different groups to the Tunisian independence struggle, he still identifies the Néo-Destour with Bourguiba. Moreover, he does not distinguish between the two meanings of "nationalist" in terms of nation- or state-building and in terms of struggle for independence. Since he also used the terms "Mouvement National Tunisien", his basic framework of legitimacy is still the Tunisian "personnalité", rather than an Arab and/or Islamic entity. Nonetheless, it is a beginning and his work is all the more valuable because he incorporates many documents.

Another relatively critical work was published in 1979 by Ali Dimassi, Habib Bourguiba: L'Apôtre de la Liberté tunisienne. The book is described as "un livre loyal",[30] but it does not fit into the Party line because it does not refrain from showing Bourguiba as liable to error and subject to reproach.

Ali Mahjoubi has completed a doctoral dissertation on the early phases of the Tunisian nationalist movement which has been published in 1982 under the title, Les Origines du Mouvement

National en Tunisie, 1904-1934. Mahjoubi attempts to explain the origin and the ebbs and flows of the movement by the changes occurring in the economic field.

In general terms, there can be no question that the economic factor is important in considering ideological movements but Mahjoubi depreciates all other factors since he does not distinguish between necessary and sufficient causes nor does he identify limiting conditions. He traces every ebb and flow of the nationalist movement to the economic changes occurring either immediately before or concurrently with developments in the political and ideological sectors; for example, he explains the April 1922 crisis by the expectation of a low harvest and by the general post-War economic crisis as the franc lost value and the terms of exchange between Tunisia and France deteriorated to the detriment of the former. In the same way, he considers that the issue of naturalization and Islam in the early 1930s was caused by the economic crisis which hit both France and Tunisia in that period. Although the economic factors are to be considered fundamental, social changes (existence of lumpen-proletariat), political changes (elections in France in 1932) and ideological changes (crystallization of the issue of Tunisian nationalism through the Islamic dimension of the Tunisian "personnalité"), though perhaps contingent, also operated at the same time to produce an explosion. The work is particularly valuable in that it is based on archival and on original newspaper materials. Again, the frame of reference for Mahjoubi as for Lejri and Dimassi is "Tunisian".

Among the few works written in Arabic on the Tunisian "nationalist" movement is al-Ṭâhir Abû al-Qâsim ʿAbd Allâh, Al-Ḥarakah al-waṭaniyyah al-tûnisiyyah; ruʾyah shaʿbiyyah, qawmiyyah jadîdah, 1830-1956, [The Tunisian Patriotic Movement: A New Populist Nationalist Perspective] which is fundamentally different in several ways from the works mentioned above. The fact that the book was published with no place of publication, publisher or date of publication is indicative of how sensitive the subject is. It deliberately brings in the role played by groups other than the Néo-Destour; e.g. the armed popular revolts, the labor movement, the contributions of Zaytûnah- or Arabic-educated intellectuals. Perhaps more to the point, it offers a different basis for the historical dimension of political legitimacy by the mere fact of being written in Arabic, because it emphasizes the Arab personality of Tunisia.[31]

This different basis of legitimacy is clear in the title itself where the author uses the terms "Tunisian Patriotic Movement" rather than "Tunisian Nationalist Movement" to mark the idea that this movement is not based on either nation-building or on the independence struggle within Tunisia alone but is simply part of the process of liberation on the level of the Arab world. This is made clearer by indicating 1830 as the beginning of the struggle for independence, when the "West" first occupied a part of the Arab world, in Algeria.

In the light of political events in Tunisia since the strike of 26 January 1978 and the continued struggle between the Union Général des Travailleurs Tunisiens and the Socialist Destour Party, works dealing with the history of the labor movement in Tunisia are also important. Among these are the two books by Mustapha Kraiem, Nationalisme et Syndicalisme en Tunisie, 1918-1929, published in 1976, and La Classe Ouvrière Tunisienne et la Lutte de Libération Nationale (1939-1952), published in 1980. The second book, in particular, offers an interesting view of the role of religion as the means to promoting consciousness of the injustices inherent in the colonized situation of Tunisia.

Another type of source for a reconstruction of Bourguiba's thought is an edited collection of his speeches published by the Ministère de l'Information. The collection, up to the present, has 20 volumes, covering the period from 1955 to 1965, under the simple title Khuṭab [Speeches]. Bourguiba's speeches from 1965 to 1982 are still in the form of individual pamphlets. The comprehensive collections should be completed by the following two selective collections: Citations choisies par l'Agence Tunis-Afrique-Presse with a preface by Chedli Klibi, and Khuṭab mawlidiyyah [Speeches made on the Occasion of the Prophet's Birthday].

A partial collection of Bourguiba's speeches had been prepared earlier by Aḥmad al-Râṭînî, covering the period between 8 April 1956 and 20 March 1957, and was published in 1957 under the title Ḥadîth al-jumʿah [Friday Speeches].

This type of source poses a different set of problems. Since the collections do not seem to be used in terms of historical legitimacy, the main problems are technical. In the first place, Bourguiba generally used Tunisian Arabic in his speeches and the collections are written in modern literary Arabic. In fact, I was told that two separate teams worked on these speeches; one team to translate the Tunisian Arabic into French and the other group to "translate" it into literary Arabic. In order to get a flavor of his style, I was offered some records of Bourguiba giving a speech. In the second place, Bourguiba's style does not lend itself to simple analysis as most of his speeches are unstructured. Part of his charisma lay in his capacity to reach the simple "man on the street" by keeping his speeches in the format of conversations. Each speech, therefore, does not have any one main topic but wanders from one subject to the other as Bourguiba intuitively responds to the needs of his audience in a spontaneous fashion.

There does exist a list of these speeches, under the title of Habib Bourguiba: Index Chronologique des Discours, Interviews, Déclarations et Conférences, 1955-1971. Unfortunately, it is not an "index", but a simple list; it does not distinguish between speeches, interviews, declarations and conferences and the researcher is at a loss as to where to find each item. Moreover, it does not have any topical entries which could have helped in identifying the pertinent speeches on any one subject. Finally, it is not clear whether the collection of speeches is complete since not all the entries indicated in the Index are to be found in the collection itself.

As a case study, the choice of Bourguiba follows naturally from my previous work on Michel ʿAflaq.[32] Bourguiba, born around 1903, and ʿAflaq, born around 1910, may be considered to be of the same generation. Bourguiba studied in France in 1924-27, just before ʿAflaq arrived to undertake his university studies in 1928-32. It may, therefore, be assumed that they fell under the influence of very similar European currents of thought. Where ʿAflaq represents the contemporary history of the Eastern half of the Arab world, Bourguiba represents the contemporary history of the Western half. Where ʿAflaq is a Christian, Bourguiba is a Muslim. Both Bourguiba and ʿAflaq, to different degrees, are men of political thought and action. Both participated in the founding of political parties which continue to exist: Bourguiba with the Néo-Destour in 1934 and ʿAflaq with the Arab Baʿth around 1944. Consequently, the political thought of both men has not been expressed in systematic treatises but needs to be reconstructed from speeches and essays produced in the heat of political action over a relatively long period of time. And during the present period of the rise of militant or integralist Islam (i.e. of the option to subject politics to the exigencies of religion), it is particularly relevant to consider those figures - such as Bourguiba and ʿAflaq - who offer alternative solutions to the problems of the relationship of religion and politics in general and of the relationship of Islam to Arab politics in particular.

The first part of the study consists of a narrative biography where historical events are considered in the light of Bourguiba's own life and thought. The second part is a topical analysis of a choice of his speeches and essays in order to reconstruct his views of Islam and politics. The choice of essays and speeches will be limited by that issue which, derived from Bourguiba's own expresssion, best illustrates the problematic of the relationship between religion and politics, namely the search for legitimacy through a clear definition of identity or, in his terminology, of "personnalité".[33] This is complemented, in the conclusion, by considering a number of Tunisian writers from a younger generation who have also struggled with these issues.

The division between the narrative and the topical sections is a result of the history of Tunisia itself. Until autonomy was obtained in 1955, political legitimacy was subsumed under the broader problem of the relationship of Tunisia to France, within the framework of the Protectorate. Once autonomy was achieved in 1955, then the issue of political legitimacy appeared relatively independent of external factors and focused on the proclamation of a Tunisian Republic in 1957, defining the political community, the political authority, and their interrelationships.

Of course, this periodization does not mean the watertight compartmentalization of the narrative and the topical sections for two reasons. The first reason is that the issue of political legitimacy did not arise <u>ex nihilo</u> but had a history previous to the time period during which it crystallized, as the debate about a constitution fundamental to the Destour Party illustrates. The second reason is that at least two of the four key terms identified above, "personnalité" and "action", are best understood in the light of historical narrative. Consequently, the post-independence time period identified in the topical section is itself a symbol of the problem under consideration and strict chronology is partly transcended in order to bring together all the elements concerning the issue at hand.

The main discovery of this study is that Islam did play a role in the history of the Tunisian nationalist movement on two levels. It was considered as a fundamental component in the process of defining the specificity of the Tunisian nation, source of legitimacy of the Tunisian nationalist movement both before and after independence. Moreover, as a fundamental component of the Tunisian "personality", it influenced the mode of communication used by nationalist leaders to mobilize the masses.

The biographical approach served to focus the issue through the prism of one man's life-story, Habib Bourguiba. It revealed that even this most secular of Arab leaders could not shed the Arab-Islamic heritage of Tunisia precisely because Islam, as a fundamental component of the Tunisian "personality" and as the language of the masses, held the key to political legitimacy.

Chapter II

THE FORMATIVE YEARS (1903-1920)

HISTORICAL BACKGROUND (1861-1907)

Bourguiba was born around the beginning of the twentieth century, some twenty years after the establishment of the Protectorate in Tunisia and the beginning of the Tunisian struggle for independence. In several respects, Tunisia presented then and still presents the image of a relatively more homogeneous society than other areas of the Arab world.

Already by the middle of the nineteenth century, the population was overwhelmingly Sunnî Muslim (of the Mâlikî legal school) and Arabic-speaking, so that even the Beylical state apparatus, which had previously used Ottoman Turkish, began to use Arabic.[1] This is not to suggest that there existed absolutely no ethnic or other distinctions among the population. Historians of the Tunisian pre-colonial period describe societal distinctions, not simply in terms of class but also in terms of regional origin, ethnic membership and political power: the mamlûks (freedmen of the Ottoman decision-making administration), ahl al-makhzan (civil servants and, by the nineteenth century, of native Tunisian or of second-generation mamlûk origin), ahl al-ʿilm (savants or people of knowledge, usually academics and jurists; interchangeable with ahl al-makhzan in terms of origin), baladîs (the Tunis bourgeoisie of merchants and artisans, connected with both the ahl al-makhzan and the ahl al-ʿilm), âfâqîs (from the provincial towns, with pejorative connotations of of inferiority to the baladîs), aʾrâb (tribesmen, both nomadic and settled).[2]

Some of these distinctions clearly illustrate the historic inertia of "consciousness" where Arabic-speaking descendants of several Tunisian-born generations still distinguished themselves as of "Arab" or of "Berber" or of "Andalusian" or of "Turkish" ancestry. While these distinctions were mainly inoperative reflections of past objective social formations, the distinction between "Arab" and so-called "Turk" still reflected actual social phenomena in the mid-nineteenth century. The "Turks" (actually Turkish-speaking mamlûks of various ethnic origins) entered the country with the Ottoman conquest of 1574 and were characterized by their adherence to the Ḥanafî legal school and their concentration in government positions. During the latter part of the nineteenth century they were, to all practical purposes, assimilated within Tunisian society. This process is an illustration of social mobility and change; where it had usually been assumed that social change in "traditional" societies was practically inexistent, recent scholarship has put such an assumption into doubt even for the pre-colonial period of the eighteenth and nineteenth centuries.[3]

Slightly trailing behind those of Egypt and of the central Ottoman Empire, Tunisia's "reform" movement began in earnest during the first half of the nineteenth century, more or less following the same pattern as Muḥammad ʿAlî's efforts in Egypt to modernize the primary government instrument, the army. These efforts, as in Egypt, inevitably spilled over into the institutions of élite recruitment: the founding of a military academy staffed by European officers in 1840, an educational charter for the Zaytûnah Mosque-University in 1842, and the creation of the famous Collège Sadiki in 1875 by the foremost Tunisian reformer, Khayr al-Dîn Pasha al-Tûnisî.

In Tunisia, as in Egypt, the "reform" movement may be distinguished into two phases. The early nineteenth century reforms were undertaken by the rulers themselves - Muḥammad ʿAlî in Egypt and Aḥmad Bey in Tunisia - to use modern technology and organization for the purposes of obtaining greater autonomy from the Ottoman Empire and of consolidating their own rule. On the international scene this was marked by the insistence of Aḥmad Bey to be treated by the European states as a full sovereign. He accepted the invitation to visit France because it had been addressed to him directly but refused the invitation of Great Britain because it was presented through the Porte.

> Probably the most important things to remember about this dynasty are that it clarified and defined the political entity of Tunisia and gave her an independence which was more than just paper recognition. This was particularly clear in cases of foreign recognition and the conclusion of treaties. To quote an example of such treaties one may keep in mind that Hamouda Bey (1782-1814) concluded treaties with Denmark, Holland and Sweden, without any reference to Constantinople.[4]

In contrast, another stream of reform appeared during the latter half of the nineteenth century, carried by an alliance between certain factions of the mamlûks, the ahl al-makhzan, and the ahl al-ʿilm led by Khayr al-Dîn. This alliance had the opposite objective, to limit the powers of the rulers and to translate the accumulating wealth of its own factions into political power. Concomitantly, an attempt was made to regain the status of Tunisia as a province of the Ottoman Empire in an effort to buffer pressure from various European states. This effort was refused by most European states, especially France, who insisted on the status of Tunisia as a sovereign state rather than a dependent province of the Ottoman Empire. Of course, this refusal did not go to the extent of annulling the privileges accorded by the Ottoman Empire to European subjects through the Capitulations.

Turning the usual interpretation - that these reforms were a result of pressures imposed by the European powers - upside down, these reforms could be considered to reflect the continuation of developments within Tunisia itself; namely (1) the weakening of the Ottoman hold on the province, perhaps because of the inability to continue recruiting mamlûks with the result that this "class" was seriously diminished in Tunisia, (2) the rise of a Tunis merchant/artisanal bourgeoisie and (3) through the Mâlikî connections (in the fields of education, law, and religious rites) the involvement of the âfâqîs in the camp of Islamic reform. This development continued during the Protectorate period, while the Tunis bourgeoisie gradually weakened to the advantage of the Sahel âfâqîs as is indicated by the prominence attained by such personalities as Bourguiba himself.

A recent critic of dependency theories, Paul Brenner, argues that "the particular, historically developed class structures" through which the processes of capitalist expansion in Third World countries occurred have been largely neglected in the work of such writers as Gunder-Frank and Wallerstein.[5] The view that the "state-building" and "nation-building" phases in some Third World cases preceded colonial occupation and was more a result of "indigenous" forces than of "exogenous" forces contrasts with the view that imperialism was the fundamental mechanism initiating the "nation-building" phase. Even Marxist writers tend to confuse the two processes involved in nationalism in Third World countries and to conclude that both "nation-building" and the "struggle for liberation" phases were a result of colonialism.[6] In any case, the focus on the changing class structure in Tunisia itself would help in explaining the socio-economic development particular to that country within the general framework of world capitalist development in the past century. From this perspective, the penetration of the Arab world by European forces may be viewed, not as the determining factor, but as a dependent variable in the struggle of who gets what when, how and where.[7][4]

The efforts of Tunisian reformers during the second half of the nineteenth century, such as Khayr al-Dîn and Ibn Abî al-Ḍiyâf, to play one European state against another and to involve them in the proposed reforms may then be considered as the means by which they could pressure the Bey. It is this reformist push which culminated with the 1861 Constitution, attempting to check the Bey's absolute powers by the creation of a "legislative" chamber with some say in the budget.[8] Unfortunately, these checks were insufficient to prevent the Bey from contracting a loan at exorbitant rates from European financial firms in 1863; of a nominal loan of 35 million francs, the Bey received only 29 millions for which he had to pay 65 millions in annuities of 4 millions over 15 years working out to the rate of about 12 percent per year. This first loan, guaranteed by the revenue of the majbâ taxes led the Finance Minister to double the taxes, which measure directly induced the 1864 insurrection. The insurrection failed and, in the following years, Tunisia suffered drought and famine with disastrous effects on the economy. This led the Bey to contract further loans, always at exorbitant rates, so that by 1866 the Tunisian government was in the obligation to pay an unbelievable 41 million francs in annuities to cover its debts.[9]

With the revolt of 1864, the Bey suspended the Constitution. Close to bankruptcy, the country was forced under the tutelage of an International Financial Commission (actually France, Britain and Italy) in 1868. The ten years between 1868 and 1878 were marked by the suspense of waiting to see which of these European powers would eventually undertake the full responsibility.

Having established her presence in Algeria, France regarded Tunisia as her "legitimate" sphere of influence but this pretension was disputed by Italy and Britain who were her partners in the International Commission. Finally, at the Berlin Conference of 1878, Bismarck cut the Gordian knot by encouraging France to seek expansion in Tunisia as compensation for the loss of Alsace-Lorraine to Germany. With the balance tipped in the favor of France, Britain quickly acknowledged the interests of France in Tunisia in return for an acknowledgement of its own interests in Cyprus. Italy was left empty-handed. Yet it was only three years later that France found the Protectorate as a formula to validate the occupation of Tunisia, both on the international scene and on her own domestic scene.

Tunisia is perhaps distinctive in the high degree of historical continuity linking the present order, represented by the Socialist Destour (<u>dustûr</u> in Arabic means constitution) Party, to the past, symbolized by the Constitution of 1861, indicating a certain awareness that the fundamental issue at hand is one of nation- or state-building and that the involvement of France was and is simply a complicating factor in that process. In the pre-Protectorate period, the nationalist movement in Tunisia is analogous to the various nationalist movements in Europe between the seventeenth and nineteenth centuries. Generally speaking, these movements were the expression of a rising bourgeoisie's struggle to limit the ruler's power justified in the name of some form of "divine right", by appealing to a legitimacy residing in the "nation".[10] In Third World countries this struggle was interfered with by the domination of the colonial power over the political process which then becomes interwoven with the efforts to achieve political independence. Consequently, this second process should be more properly termed "independence movement" or "liberation struggle" during the period of political domination. In Third World countries, nation-building continues to be interfered with by the domination of the neo-colonial power over the economic sectors, usually inhibiting the ability of the national bourgeosie to take over the state.

In the light of this argument, the historiographical problem of dating the beginnings of the Tunisian "nationalist" movement has not been properly posed. Most historians consider only the second aspect and differ on when the issue of independence became salient; for example, Charles-André Julien and Roger LeTourneau date its beginnings to the French occupation of Tunisia itself in 1881 while others attempt to link it to a wider context, usually taking the French occupation of Algeria in 1830 as the signal for the beginning of European domination of the Maghrib.[11] If the distinction between "nation-building" and "independence" movements is kept clearly in mind - with the first referring to the movement towards building a state based on a legitimacy residing within the nation and the second referring to the movement to be independent, politically in the first instance, of external domination - then the Tunisian nationalist movement began in the second half of the nineteenth century and is symbolized by the Constitution of 1861. Similarly, the Tunisian "independence" movement began in 1881 with the armed resistance made in the South against French occupation but was formulated only in 1907 with the establishment of Le Tunisien and the appearance of the Young Tunisians.[12]

Such a thesis, that "nationalist" movements in the Third World involved the two aspects of establishing a nation-state and of achieving independence and that the first could have preceded the second, is reinforced by new studies which indicate that the Industrial Revolution was a world-wide phenomenon and that a budding bourgeoisie, based on industrial as well as mercantilist capital and ethics existed at least in some Third World countries such as Egypt and Tunisia. Based on these general considerations, we may then proceed to periodize the Tunisian nationalist movement into the three broad phases of pre-Protectorate, Protectorate, and post-Protectorate such that the "state-" and "nation-building" aspects held central stage during the first and third phases and the "independence movement" held the lime-light during the second stage. Our study of Bourguiba will be mainly concerned with the Protectorate and post-Protectorate phases which may, in turn, be divided into the following periods:

1) From 1881, the French occupation, to 1907, when an articulated "independence movement" began with the founding of the newspaper, Le Tunisien, French organ of the Young Tunisians led by Bash Hanba and in reaction to the hesitation of France in applying the politics of "association" and its tendency to keep slipping towards a policy of "assimilation". This meant a reconsideration of the image of France as a partner in the process of bringing the Tunisian bourgeoisie into its own, as the Protectorate failed to help the local landed bourgeoisie transform itself into an industrial bourgeoisie and effectively limited it to subaltern bureaucratic and, later, professional functions. This period represents the historical background which set the scene at the birth of Habib Bourguiba.

2) From 1907 to 1920, when the Destour Party was established on the basis that Tunisia was already "constituted" before the establishment of the Protectorate and that, consequently, the politics of "assimilation" could not be applied. The Destour's main platform was to argue for the re-enactment of the Constitution of 1861. The fact that the first organ of expresseion founded by the Young Tunisians, Le Tunisien, was in French indicates that a measure of "active syncretic acculturation" had already occurred.

3) From 1920 to 1955, the proclamation of the autonomy of Tunisia. In fact, the autonomy accords may be considered as a return to the first spirit of the Protectorate whereby Tunisia and France could be viewed as partners in the process of working towards building Tunisia into a modern nation-state. This period may be divided into two parts, with 1934 marking the relative radicalization of the Tunisian "independence movement" as the Néo-Destour was established.

4) From 1955 to the present; in some ways, a return to the nation-building phase characterized by the problem of defining the political community and establishing a legitimate political authority. The issue of political legitimacy and the role of religion in the process of nation-building represented in the establishment of the Republic of Tunisia and the proclamation of Bourguiba as President for life became central.

The Protectorate had actually begun as a military occupation by French forces in March 1881 claiming that a party of the Kroumir tribesmen of North-Western Tunisia, whose tribal lands straddled the so-called frontier between Tunisia and Algeria, had attacked French settlements across the border. On 14 May 1881 the Bey was compelled to sign the Treaty of Bardo but the occupation of the country was not as easily completed as had been expected - because at least some Tunisians resisted, particularly in the South and "more or less in the same area as the rebellion in 1864 against the majba tax...Sfax, Gabes, and Kairouan".[13]

It took ten days of bombardment and hand-to-hand combat in the streets to subdue Sfax and Gabes after which Kairouan submitted peacefully. Nonetheless, miliary rule was instituted in the South almost for the whole duration of the Protectorate. Despite the fact that the French military occupation of Tunisia encountered armed resistance in the South, such resistance is not considered within the "official" history of the Tunisian nationalist movement, probably because it was not formulated in any coherent ideological program. The same may be said of the 1883 protests and the 1885 urban riots against the municipal taxes imposed on merchants and artisans and the confiscation of certain urban ḥabûs. These "disturbances" were severely repressed by exiling the leaders to the South.[14]

The regime of the Protectorate itself was formally instituted only in a second treaty known as the "Convention de La Marsa" signed on 8 June 1883 by the French representative and the Bey.[15] As far as the Arab world is concerned, the Protectorate is one of several forms of political domination by European powers. The first form of domination was the simple military conquest followed by settlement and the "refoulement" of the "natives" of which Algeria, Libya and, aberrantly, Palestine, are the examples in the Arab world. The second form was the Protectorate of which Tunisia, Egypt and Morocco are the examples. The third form was the system of Mandates instituted following the First World War. In terms of historical evolution, these forms represent different stages in the development of world capitalism[16] and the institutionalization of international law.

The high costs which France had incurred in the fifty years needed to complete the annexation of Algeria created reluctance in the French parliament to approve the funds necessary for the military occupation of Tunisia. Thus the unpopularity, in

France itself, of an expensive "direct administration" precluded the simple annexation of Tunisia. A new formula was devised, the Protectorate, whereby the "native" administration was to be maintained and, under the guidance of French authorities, taught to administer the country in a modern fashion. It was thus imperative that France also have the right "to initiate administrative, judicial and financial reforms which it judged useful."[17] For the reformists whose first priority had been the limitation of the Bey's arbitrary powers, the articles of the treaty appeared to fulfill this primary aim. Bourguiba himself is supposed to have reported that this idea had spread as far as the southern parts of Tunisia.[18]

At the time, therefore, it was not inconceivable to project the possibility of co-operation between the French authorities and those reformists hoping to "modernize" the country by limiting the Bey's powers. Thus, a French commentator could write in the early 1900s, "Aussi, lorsque la France, après 1881, reprit cette oeuvre de réorganisation, les indigènes virent dans ses administrateurs les continuateurs de Kheireddine."[19] And an unidentified member of the Young Tunisians could state when France established the Protectorate, there rose great hopes tha it would put an end to the abuses of the Beylical regime.[20] These hopes were the underlying background of the relative quiet in Tunisia between 1885 and 1910. Egyptian reformists, such as Muḥammad ʿAbduh, following the British occupation of Egypt in 1882, were willing to work with the occupying power in an effort to assimilate European methods and institutions within the framework of their own social and cultural heritage. In other words, having failed in muqâwamah (resistance), there seemed to be no choice for Tunisian reformers as well but to adopt a policy of iṣlâḥ (reform).[21]

In the early stages of the Protectorate these Tunisian reformists were encouraged by French liberals so that this first period 1881-1907 may be characterized as an experiment in the politics of "association" between Tunisian reformists and French liberals. It was during this period of relative amity between French and Tunisian political leaders that Habib Bourguiba was born. He grew up during a period when the experiment was proving itself a mirage as the Protectorate was gradually transformed into a regime of direct administration.[22]

TIME AND THE FAMILY

It is believed that Habib Bourguiba was born on the 3rd of August 1903. Because the process of registering births, marriages and deaths was not precise in Tunisia as the twentieth century began, the 3rd of August was arrived at by cross-checking family histories. The year 1903 was officially accepted mainly because all the identification papers used to register him at school referred to this date. Nonetheless, there has been some doubt about the date, the year 1902 being a strongly possible alternative. Habib is known to have completed primary school, at that time consisting of seven or eight grades, in 1913 and, if 1903 is accepted as the date of his birth, he would have been less than ten at the time, having begun school at the age of barely three. It is much more likely that he began school between the ages of four and six and that he completed primary school when he was between eleven and thirteen years of age, which would indicate 1902, rather than 1903, as the <u>latest</u> possibility.[23]

The sibling order into which he was born is interesting. Habib was the youngest of eight children, only one of whom died in childhood. His being the youngest did not automatically imply behavior characteristic of the Benjamin because the age difference between him and the immediately older sibling, a girl, was seven years.[24] This meant that the children were divided into two sets and that Habib effectively occupied the position of an only child in the second set as well as the position of a Benjamin in the first set. This view is supported by the naming pattern; the older boys (girls did not really count then) were named Mohamed, Ahmed, M'Hamed (the pronunciation of Ṃuhammad in the Tunisian variant of Arabic) and Mahmoud - all based on the root Ḥ-M-D - while our Bourguiba was named Habib, the beloved.

His feeling of being special and separate from his brothers and sisters was probably reinforced by the stories he was told about his birth. While all his brothers and sisters were born in the ancestral home, Habib was born in a modest house his father had rented while their new house was being built. He was also told that his mother bit into a cloth so as not to cry out while laboring to give him birth, because it was rather embarrassing for a couple to have a child at such an advanced age - his father being about 55 and his mother about 40 years old.[25]

The Benjamin position in the family, in itself, also created ambiguity. On the one hand, it meant that he was the most privileged since, according to traditional custom where the younger is the responsibility of the older, he was cared for by all his siblings as well as by his parents. This is symbolically portrayed in the 1911 family picture[26] where, instead of the father being surrounded by his five sons, Habib - the youngest - was surrounded by his father and four older brothers. More pertinently, this meant that several members of the family were required to and actually did support Habib financially. The material advantages of this situation became obvious when Habib, unlike his brothers, was enabled to go beyond Collège Sadiki to the Lycée Carnot and on to university in France precisely because he was funded by his brothers, each in his turn. On the other hand, as Benjamin, he had to defer to his elders. Though nurtured by all his siblings as well as his parents, he suffered the indignity - as bottom man on the family totem pole - of having to address his brothers as well as his father with the title of "sî" (Tunisian for sayyidî, the equivalent of "sir"), to serve and to run errands for all his elders. This hierarchical ordering of the family could easily transform the Benjamin into a rebel because of the "tyranny" of the elder brothers. As the Benjamin becomes older, he reacts in the same way to other strong personalities as he unconsciously lives the "tyranny" of his childhood.[27]

On the psychological level, the two roles, the Benjamin of several children and an only child, were contradictory on several counts. As an only child, and a boy at that, in the second set, and with his brothers away in Tunis for most of the year, Habib grew accustomed to having his mother's, his grandmother's and his sisters' exclusive attention. Whenever his brothers came to visit, young Habib had to cope with five father-figures - his own father and his four much older brothers - sharing his mother's love. They represented five figures of authority, five models to emulate; this multiplicity of models could be part of the explanation for the multiple sides of Bourguiba's personality and for his love of acting, of playing out different roles at different times. Although something is known about each brother, there is not enough in the sources to build a coherent image of each of them, particularly since the main source, Bourguiba himself, seems so bitter about all of them.

Mohammed seems to have been a fun-loving, artistically-inclined fellow who did not succeed in obtaining his due respect as the eldest; Ahmed seems to have been somewhat remote and puritanical, devoted to his work and his family , as he took over the role of eldest son abandoned by Mohamed; M'Hamed, the closest to Bourguiba, remains the most vague; Mahmoud is portrayed as strict and with a fierce temper, despite the fact that he was also a poet.[28] As the youngest, Bourguiba also participated in the household chores of the womenfolk and became famous for his love of cooking among his colleagues later on. This longer contact of more than usual persistence with the female element, combined with his love of acting, perhaps led to his strange capacity to shed ready tears.[29]

During the first of a series of autobiographical lectures Bourguiba gave at the Institut de la Presse et des Sciences de l'Information in Tunis during 1973, he presented an image of his family as poor and deprived. He stated, "I was born in a poor family and knew the full meaning of misery during my childhood."[30] This image needs to be qualified and it can be argued that Bourguiba's family was only subjectively poor. While the official biography published by the Tunisian Ministry of Information in 1966 baldly states that the family was middle-class (mutawassiṭat al-ḥâl), there are other indications that the family was relatively well-off and upwardly mobile. According to Bourguiba himself, his paternal grandfather owned a slave and was considered a notable (min aʿyân al-madînah) of Monastir; his father owned at least 132 olive trees and the family was able to afford their own house. Moreover, his paternal aunt kept her own family name after her marriage, as a symbol of her family pride.[31]

Bourguiba also states that the mayor of Tunis itself (shaykh al-madînah) was a relative on his mother's side of the family - in other words, a baladî, of greater prestige than even his father's father. This relationship between Bourguiba's mother, Faṭṭûmah, and the mayor of Tunis personalizes the connection between the small towns and the capital since the economic dimension of the women's contribution to the shâshiyyah industry - washing, spinning, knitting, sewing and cutting the wool - linked the capital with the small towns as well as with the countryside. Bourguiba states that his mother was involved with several of these phases of the industry and, since most women undertook only one of these typically female operations, it is quite probable that this very capable woman had built up some sort of workshop to combine these activities and that her contribution to the family revenue was critical in its upward mobility. Faṭṭûmah was of the Mzali family through her mother, Khadîjah, while her father was Aḥmad Khafshah.[32]

Because his grandmother had been divorced by her husband, she lived with the Bourguibas and, very unusually, she willingly pooled in her money to buy the new house. Her presence probably helped the family, not only by the actual monetary contributions she made, but by participating in the household chores and thus freeing her daughter who could then give more of her time to the money-making activities of the shâshiyyah industry.[33] In sum, the women's contributions were crucial to the family's improving social conditions.

Bourguiba's mother died in late 1913 when Habib was only a boy. Official sources claim that she died at the age of forty; although this would bear out Bourguiba's contention that women in the early twentieth century Tunisia died young because of too many children - thus justifying the program of family-planning begun in the late 1960s - his mother could not have been so young at her own death. In 1913, Bourguiba was at least 11 years old, with a difference of 22 years between him and the oldest child, who would thus have been at least 33 years old at the death of the mother.[34] Unless she had been married at the age of 6 and had had her first child at the age of 7, she was more probably over forty and approaching fifty when she died.

How her death affected Bourguiba at his young age is difficult to judge since he had already been separated from her, around the age of 5, to go to school in Tunis, at Sadiki. Bourguiba claims that this early separation made him all the more attached to her memory and that he never overcame his yearning for her.[35] It may be conjectured that it was this longing for a mother-figure which later attracted him to an older woman. Mathilde Louvain (born Lefras), his future wife, was born in 1890 which, according to Bourguiba himself, would make her about 14 years older than he was.[36] More concretely, the death of his mother, shortly followed by the death of his grandmother, must have placed financial drawbacks on the family as the revenue from the shâshiyyah activities stopped.

Bourguiba's father, ʿAlî Ibn al-Ḥajj Muḥammad Bourguiba, had been conscripted into the Bey's army following the insurrection of 1864, which thus became part of the family's own political culture. Bourguiba recounts that when the city gave in to General Zarrûq, his grandfather was arrested along with several other town notables and was released only after the family had paid over all the precious treasures it could collect. Consequently, despite spending some seventeen or nineteen years in army service and achieving several promotions, Bourguiba's father - perhaps only in retrospect - resented his conscription and discouraged all his sons from following an army career. He is said to have been a young lad of about 15 years when conscripted, which would make him over 50 years old when Habib was born, a double generation gap. As an element in the process of Bourguiba's political socialization, the family's pro-insurrection position and his father's resentment against army conscription may be viewed as symbolizing Bourguiba's anti-beylical attitude in the late 1950s.[37]

It is not clear what the father's occupation was during the some ten years from the time he was released from the army until 1893, when he was appointed shaykh turâb (a government official position), but it is known that he was also appointed khabîr or amîn filâḥî in 1897, which translates as "Agricultural Expert" and is a technical position within the court system, equivalent to expert witness. Moreover, he held the position of shaykh ḥawmah (representative of a town quarter) of the Tripolitanian section of town, which indicates the Libyan origins of the Bourguiba family. Probably it was in these official capacites that ʿAlî Bourguiba became a member of the Municipal Council (al-majlis al-baladî) of Monastir and came into contact with such officials as the mayor and the school principal, both Frenchmen, as well as with the Qâʾid and the Shaykh of Monastir. Perhaps he was also in contact with the Governor of the Province of Sousse in which Monastir was to be found; Béchir Sfar, who was a key figure in the history of the Tunisian nationalist movement, had been appointed to the position in 1908. It is around this period that ʿAlî Bourguiba was able to send a son to Sadiki; the oldest is not known to have graduated but the second son, Ahmed, completed his primary school in 1899.[38]

The extended family, composed of Bourguiba's father, his two uncles and their respective wives and children had lived in one house until shortly before Bourguiba's birth when the nuclear family moved out, first, to a rented apartment and later into their own newly-built house. Whatever the immediate causes of the move, Bourguiba cites the constant quarrelling between the women of the house as the reason which led the brothers to fight amongst themselves to the extent that Bourguiba's father unsheathed his sword - a memento of his army days - against his own brother. The transition of the family from a "traditional" extended mode to a "modern" nuclear mode is symbolized by the family picture taken in 1922 where the father is dressed in the traditional Tunisian garb while his sons and grandchildren are dressed in the European style, except for a "shâshiyyah" or a "ţarbûsh".[39]

It is thus obvious that the family, as represented by both the father's and the mother's socio-economic positions, was not objectively poor. On the contrary, it was part of the provincial "upper middle" class which had experienced some difficulties following the 1864 insurrection but was on its way up again as the nineteenth century was ending. It is only rising expectations coupled with memories of the family's relatively better situation before 1864 which made Bourguiba subjectively poor.

SPACE AND THE FAMILY

Where he was born is an important factor in situating Habib within the historical developments in Tunisia during his formative years, due to the underlying regionalism characteristic of the country. He was born in Monastir (translation of ribâţ, monastery-fortress), considered as an Islamic holy city (ashhar ribaţât ifrîqiyâ fî şadr al-islâm), a town close to Sousse right in the middle of that region of Tunisia known as the Sahel. Despite the generally low population density in the Tunisia of the late nineteenth century, the Sahel was an exception in that the land was individually owned by farmers or by urban landlords (milk) whereas the semi-arid regions of the center and of the south were held by şûfî orders or by semi-sedentary tribes as hanshîrs or large domains. Closer to the capital, land was generally held by government officials in a type of degenerate iqţâʿ or as ḩabûs controlled by the ʿulamâʾ.[40]

The relationship between population and land, land tenure, has been a neglected field of study although it was crucial in the development of many of the nationalist movements in the Third World in general and in the Arab world in particular. In the case of Tunisia, land tenure was an important factor in the nationalist movement, both in the pre-Protectorate (or nation-building) and in the Protectorate (or independence movement) period and requires elucidation in order to understand the social transformations that resulted.[41]

Land tenure in the various Islamic legal systems varied considerably from place to place and over time. In Tunisia, there existed a form of land tenure very close to the modern form of individual ownership known as milk and found in the more geographically favoured areas and, consequently, of dense population. There also existed more complicated forms of land tenure where ownership was effectively double, shared between the actual cultivators and those who provided security. These last may be categorized into three types: beylical, tribal and maraboutic hanshîrs. In general, these forms of land tenure covered the areas of the more extensive cereal agriculture. In the areas of pastoralism beyond these, a form of collective land tenure and use was practised.

At this point we note the greatest social change of the nineteenth century in Tunisia, and perhaps beyond Tunisia in most of the Arab-Islamic areas; namely, the process by which the hanshîrs were transformed from this system of "double tenure" to private property held, most usually, by an absentee urban bourgeoisie. The end of the nineteenth century saw an evolution towards demographic increase and, therefore, a situation of a mass of small property owners in the milk zones complemented by a tendency towards central control of the "double tenure" lands: either by the state confiscating tribal lands, as happened following the 1864 rebellion, or by ʿulamâʾ-controlled ḥabûs gaining on maraboutic lands. This tendency towards centralized control is demonstrated by the Jamʿiyyat al-Ḥabûs (sometimes also called Jamʿiyyat al-Awqâf) instituted by Khayr al-Dîn and administered by Tunis ʿulamâʾ, which might be a factor in explaining the support given to Khayr al-Dîn by "reformist" ʿulamâʾ.[42]

The gut-issue of land-ownership crystallized very early on during the Protectorate period of the nationalist movement. The occupation of Tunisia may then be viewed as the political and military expression of the need to break resistance to the expansion of French capital, particularly in land investment. The "independence struggle" phase of the Tunisian nationalist movement may be viewed as the result of the contradiction between the requirements of expanding French capital and the "indigenous" process of accumulation of capital. In fact, the first foreign buyers of land in Tunisia were not French settlers but powerful finance companies. From 1881 or 1892, a period of so-called private colonization, 50 companies acquired some 443,000 hectares from mamlûk and makhzanî families. Of these, 16 acquired 93 percent of these lands. After 1892, the French authorities organized the official colonization on the "state domains" that had been previously under the control of the Beylical state. To these lands were added confiscated tribal and ḥabûs lands. These lands were then distributed to colonists with easy financing. Between 1897 and 1922, another 400,000 to 500,000 hectares were colonized, mostly by individual colonists. Nonetheless, colonization in Tunisia was characterized by the concentration of large tracts of land in the hands of a few so that, for example, four companies owned 23 percent of the foreign-owned lands in 1937. These policies of colonization were stopped in 1918 in the military-controlled south and in 1935 in the areas under civil control. But by then, there was no escaping the effects as hundreds of thousands of peasants were thrown off the land, creating a "free" labor pool.[43] The evolution of land tenure in Tunisia following the Protectorate may be divided into four phases: (1) from 1881 to 1920, (2) from 1920 to 1932, (3) from 1932 to 1956, and (4) from 1956 to 1969. During the first period, the colonial experience, as far as land was concerned, meant that large French societies penetrated those areas of weakest tenure; namely the hanshîrs held by the Bey and by government officials (as exemplified by the Enfida affair) or by tribes (as exemplified by the Siala lands around Sfax). The new "owners" realized that the very low prices they were paying were in exchange for titles of "eminent" ownership limited by the traditional rights of the "real" users of the land. Despite this, they laid claim to the type of ownership by then common in Europe, which was simple private ownership, reducing the peasants on the land to hired labour with no rights to the land.[44]

Various measures were instituted by the French authorities to gain control of the land: the Land Law of 1 July 1885 modelled on the Torrens Act of Australia to survey and register land; the inzâl legislation of 1886 whereby ḥabus land could be rented to non-Muslims; the confiscation of the Siala tribe's hanshîr through the fiction that these lands had reverted to the Bey following the 1864 rebellion; the decree of 1898 by which the Jam'iyyat al-Ḥabûs was forced to cede 2,000 hectares annually to the Public Domain of the Bey, effectively to the Protectorate authorities; the request by the Commission de Colonisation to suppress all ḥabûs, both private and public; the use of Tunisian state revenues to finance newly-arrived colonists, followed by a complex series of laws beginning with the decree of 12 April 1913 pushing the Tunisian peasants into "reservations", which process was known as "refoulement" and was very similar to the "politique de cantonnement" pursued in Algeria. Thus, at the end of the First World War, almost one million hectares of the best Tunisian land were in the hands of Europeans and hundreds of thousands of Tunisians had been thrown off the land, without any alternative employment. This phase of colonization exacerbated the problems of what may be termed a process of "native land enclosure" and of the change from subsistence to cash crops by throwing the peasants off the land at precisely the moment of a demographic increase. The second period was characterized by two developments: the encouragement of small-scale settlers and the mechanization of agriculture. At the beginning of the twentieth century, "dry farming" was applied in Tunisia, allowing greater colonial penetration and the institution of an official policy of settler colonization, by the take-over of the grain-growing areas of the centre and the south. This movement was further reinforced by the introduction of mechanized means of agriculture during the late 1920s. The third period was characterized by the impact of world events such as the Great Depression, the Second World War and the Cold War. The fourth period, marked by the independence of Tunisia, was characterized by the socialist experiment undertaken by Ben Salah.[45]

In a situation of dependency, the industrial sector in Tunisia was not in any shape to absorb this free man-power which was simply wasted in misery. This was a fundamental contradiction in the expansion of capital in peripheral areas; it "enclosed" the land and "freed" labor but the dominating powers did not permit the growth of the industrial or tertiary sectors sufficiently to absorb this free man-power and thus widen the internal market. On the contrary, the penetration of cheap goods from the métropole pauperized the artisanal industries and the indigenous commercial sectors[46] and added to the numbers of the disinherited. It is the resultant lumpen- proletariat that served as shock troops for the "populist" nationalist movements of the 1920s and 1930s which undertook mass actions in the struggle for independence.

Following the French model, no sense of corporative organization was permitted to interfere between the state and the individual and, thus, the Protectorate served to atomize society within the confines of the Tunisian state. These measures could not fail to shatter the illusion that the Protectorate, limiting the Bey's power, could be used to build a state representative of the Tunisian "nation". From this perspective, it is perhaps no coincidence that it was Béchir Sfar, head of the Jamʿiyyat al-Ḥabûs, who first sounded the alarm in 1906, in a public speech addressed to the Protectorate authorities. This speech is usually held to mark the beginning of an articulate nationalist movement in Tunisia. The list of demands Sfar presented was, in ascending order of importance: "...enseignement professionnel, commercial et agricole largement donné aux indigènes; formation et protection efficace de la main-d'oeuvre tunisienne; relèvement des industries locales par des mesures douanières et autres; enfin, conservation de la propriété indigène."[47]

The link between the issue of land-tenure and the nationalist movement is dramatically portrayed by the personalized account given by Bourguiba of Béchir Sfar's funeral. His father was in Tunis on that day, whether he had come specifically for the funeral or for other reasons is not clear, and young Bourguiba, a teenager by then, walked with him in the funeral procession. At one point ʿAlî Bourguiba clutched Habib's hand and began to cry profusely. Bourguiba states that he suddenly realized that his father did have nationalist sentiments. This seems to have come as a new revelation since the father had recounted to his son the horrors of the Beylical repression following the 1864 rebellion rather than expressed his discontent with the Protectorate occupation. Bourguiba explains his father's reticence about French domination as the outcome of a preference for the lesser of two evils. In fact, Béchir Sfar is also a link between the land issue and the prominence of the Sahel region in the nationalist movement since he had been promoted - actually removed from Tunis - by the Protectorate authorities from Director of thr Jam'iyyat al-Ḥabûs to Governor of Sousse in 1908, for his efforts to protect ḥabûs land from colonial penetration. He had failed to keep public ḥabûs out of colonial hands but private ḥabûs, probably widespread in the Sahel, remained relatively intact.[48] Even in the second phase of mechanized agriculture and land-grabbing it appears that the Sahel, with its regime of private land-ownership, was relatively spared.[49]

In sum, the Sahel seems to have been one region where the owners of land were able to maintain themselves. As a consequence, the Tunisian nationalist movement was built, directly or indirectly, on this economic and demographic base, when the traditional élites, the mamlûks and the baladîs (including ahl al-makhzan and ahl al-'ilm) had been relatively weakened, the working class had not yet developed sufficiently and the landless peasants formed an inarticulate mass. In fact, it is this base of relative economic wealth which enabled the people of the Sahel to take advantage of the new educational opportunities offered in order to transform the new generation into members of the liberal professions[50] and leaders of the inarticulate masses.

With its own roots in the Sahel, Bourguiba's family represented the small town upper middle class. Based on government employment and landed property (his father) and artisanal industry (his mother), the family was in a position to aspire to wider horizons.

EMIGRATION AND THE SCHOOL

The upward mobility of the family is also exemplified by the emigration of Bourguiba's older brothers. The eldest first worked in the theatre in the capital and then as medical assistant in Le Kef. Ahmed and M'Hamed were appointed as translators; the first was posted in Sûq al-Arbi'â and the second in one of the Ministries in Tunis. It is the latter, M'Hamed, who was charged with the responsibility of young Habib when he was sent to Tunis to begin his studies at the famous Collège Sadiki.[51]

Habib boarded with his newly-married brother, and it is not difficult to guess his bewildered feelings at suddenly losing his place at the centre of his mother's attention and becoming a marginal worry in his brother's life. When his sister-in-law died, he was left to the care of the cleaning woman. Would those feelings of shock explain the strange bitterness he expresses against the life his brother provided him with? He complains that his brother provided him with "miserable" clothes and that his shoes were always worn down with holes.[52]

Habib was not breaking any new ground by entering Collège Sadiki; his fourth brother, Mahmoud, was a boarder at the secondary school of the Sadiki at the same time. Actually, Ahmed had already completed his primary school in 1899, M'Hamed in 1900, Mahmoud in 1908 while Bourguiba was to complete his in 1913. The ability of the Bourguiba family to rise through education is illustrated by the fact that one of Habib's brothers married into the family of Ṣâḥib al-ṭâbiʿ (the Bey's secretary) and, thus, became related by marriage even to the makhzanî class, close to the Bey and high in the "traditional" order.[53] This is a clear indication that the Bourguiba family was sufficiently well-off to be able to sustain the costs of four out of five sons through school away from home and, having taken advantage of the new regulations imposed by the French authorities in 1892 at Sadiki, to climb the social ladder.

Established in 1875 by Khayr al-Dîn, Collège Sadiki was conceived according to an original plan. The idea was to provide a bilingual education, French and Arabic, in order to bridge the two cultures representing the "modern" and the "traditional". Sadiki, as a whole, is unique as the earliest and most continuous effort in the Arab world to combine the Arab-Islamic and the European educational traditions and socio-political values. Before the Protectorate, admission seems to have depended almost exclusively on the traditional élite network for the sons destined to careers in government.

Aware that education was one of the main means of élite recruitment, the French authorities had undertaken some of their first "reforms" in this field. The bureau created by Khayr al-Dîn was quickly re-organized as "la Direction de l'Enseignement Publique" and a French official put at its head. The Protectorate authorities thus effectively gained control of all the educational institutions which had been publicly funded, except for the Zaytûnah and its network of kuttâbs. It should be noted that the Zaytûnah created a different élite which greatly exceeded the Sadiki élite in terms of numbers.

The concern of the Protectorate authorities with education is reflected in the comments of a French "liberal" on the occasion of the establishment of the Khaldûniyyah, founded in 1896 with the support of the Resident General, in order to introduce the modern sciences to Zaytûnah students. The point of the comment was that only when the French are able to form the Tunisian elites will they then be able to influence the masses.[54] In 1892, among other changes, the Protectorate authorities imposed an examination as preliminary to winning the Sadiki scholarships for fees, room, board and clothing. This new regulation automatically weakened the hold of the old élite network, based mainly in Tunis, and favoured new social categories. In fact, the relative advantage gained by the provincials was reinforced by the losses suffered by the "traditional" élite of Tunis.[55]

Some commentators hold that the educational policies instituted by the French aimed at assimilation. In the first place, policies of "assimilation" began to be felt in Tunisia only around the beginning of the twentieth century and, in the second place this is somewhat exaggerated in view of the contradictions internal to the Protectorate situation itself as it evolved into settler colonialism. Actually, the reforms instituted by the French authorities did not imply a very great progress in education in absolute terms for the whole country. The greatest share of the budget of "la Direction de l'Enseignement Publique" was devoted to the schooling of the children of colonists and of the Jewish minority. Only 12 percent of Muslim Tunisian children received primary education while 84 percent of the colonists' children enjoyed that privilege.[56]

Nonetheless, the relatively upward social mobility of certain sectors continued. This mobility had begun as early as the late nineteenth century but the trend became quite clear after World War II. In 1939, the Sahel region supplied over half of the new admissions to Collège Sadiki. These new opportunities created a new class which essentially manifested the successful attempt of the

Sahel small landowners and artisans to transform themselves, or more accurately their sons, into professionals capable of filling the role of "interlocuteurs" - able to work within the French administrative structure and, at the same time, to address their countrymen in their own language. In fact, Bourguiba himself was being trained at Sadiki for that specific position.

> He was translating - from and into French - administrative texts, and letters of the kind being exchanged between the French civil servants who administered the country and the Tunisian Caids who carried out their decisions. It was thought that he would make a good official interpreter...[57]

But there was an inherent contradiction in the situation of "interlocuteurs". On the one hand, they had to satisfy the colonizer's need for professionals capable of understanding his language well enough to translate it to their fellow "natives". On the other hand, the same "interlocuteurs" would be listened to only if they could legitimize their position in the eyes of their fellow "natives" by demonstrating that they could also carry the language of the "natives" back to the colonizers. In other words, the "interlocuteurs" were caught between the need to demonstrate their effectiveness with the colonizer as much as with the "natives".

By the beginning of the twentieth century, the Protectorate had clearly succeeded in limiting the powers of the Bey but only for its own benefit without any intention of "associating" the Tunisian élite, neither <u>mamlûks</u> nor <u>baladîs</u>, let alone newly-arrived <u>âfâqîs</u>, in the exercise of power. In fact, "Though Republican and Democratic at home, France behaved like an Absolute Monarch in Tunisia."[58]

FORMULATION OF TUNISIAN NATIONALISM

The earliest efforts at nationalist organization followed upon these educational reforms: the "Association des anciens du Sadiki" was formed in 1905 and the "<u>Jam'iyyat talâmidhat jâmi' al-zaytûnah</u>" (Association of Zaytunah Mosque Students) was established in 1907. The Khaldûniyyah, presided at the time by Béchir Sfar, served as the site where the two élites met, the bilingual élite of Sadiki and the monolingual Arabic-speaking élite of the Zaytûnah.

In 1906, the Congrès Colonial was held in Marseilles and the policy of association was acclaimed. Ironically, the Tunisian delegates had prepared papers calling for the generalization of the French language and culture as the means to achieve access to scientific progress.[59] Again, the Congrès sur l'Afrique du Nord, held in Paris in 1908, reiterated the validity of a policy of association, of which the Protectorate could be considered as an early prototype. In effect, the tension in French colonial policy between territorial annexation and indirect rule found theoretical expression in the two theories of assimilation and association. Nonetheless, the actual colonial policies of France continued to tend towards direct rule and assimilation.

The first indications of an articulate Tunisian reaction is traced to Béchir Sfar's famous speech in 1906. Béchir Sfar was a key figure in this earliest effort at formulating the theoretical bases of Tunisian nationalism, made in the context of the geography and history lessons he gave at the Khaldûniyyah. Consequently, he became known as "the second father of the reawakening" since Khayr al-Dîn had been the first.[60] This effort at formulating the theoretical bases of Tunisian nationalism continued with the founding of the newspaper Le Tunisien, in French in 1907 and in Arabic in 1909, which expressed the discontent of a fraction of the educated Tunisian élite, better known as the Young Tunisians. It was in this newspaper that the ʿAhd al-amân of 1857 and the Constitution of 1861 were analyzed as turning-points in the constitution of a Tunisian "personnalité". Thus, writing about the later phases of the nationalist movement led by the Destour, one commentator noted:

> ...l'idée d'une Constitution n'avait donc pas germé spontanément dans l'esprit de ces nationalistes en mal d'évolution ou de révolution et c'est ce qui explique qu'elle soit démeurée aussi vivace.[61]

This "idea" overarches the basic sociological continuity in Tunisia since no social upheaval occurred but a gradual evolution as one social class rose to ally itself with at least a fraction of an older social class in order to form a new élite which was yet not completely new. Examples of this continuity are the alliance between the mamlûks and the baladîs during the period of Khayr al-Dîn and, under the Protectorate, those Zaytûnah shaykhs who accepted to teach Arabic and Islamic subjects at Collège Sadiki, such as Shaykh Muḥammad Ibn al-Qâḍî, Shaykh ʿAbd al-ʿAzîz Jaʿîṭ and Shaykh Ḥamîdah al-Nayfar as well as Muḥammad al-Aṣram who represented the makhzanî contribution. An illustration of this continuity is the fact that another Shaykh of the Ja'îṭ family had tried to codify civil law and it is believed that the 1956 Code of Personal Status was inspired by it. This evolutionary rather than revolutionary social mobility has been qualified as "relatively upward" because, aside from absolute terms of improved socio-economic status, there also existed a down mobility.[62] These then provided the channels of continuity to such leading figures of the nationalist movement as Mahmoud Materi and Habib Bourguiba himself.

As the articulate reaction began, inarticulate, violent resistance had continued sporadically and flared up seriously in 1909-1915 in the southern regions suffering under military rule.[63] When the 1910 demonstrations organized by the Zaytûnah students spilled over into public riots in Tunis, violence joined with legalist argumentation to mark a major turning point of the Tunisian nationalist movement. Usually, in the accepted versions of Tunisian history, the Zaytûnah disturbances are simply not mentioned since these would place the beginnings of the articulated "nationalist" movement squarely within an Islamic framework. When the role of the Zaytunah is mentioned, it is usually recognized that it played an important role in preserving the distinctive dimensions of the Tunisian identity; "Pour contrecarrer les projets de l'adminis- tration coloniale élaborés par la Direction de l'Instruction Publique (DIP) elle prit la tête de la lutte nationale en tant que gardienne de l'arabisme, de l'Islamisme et des valeurs de base de la société arabo-musulmane de Tunisie."[64]

Actually, these disturbances were not at first presented as reactions on a national scale but were primarily motivated by the bottle-necks experienced by Zaytûnah students who, lacking French language and culture, were being systematically ousted from their traditional positions in government, law and education. Many Tunisian historians hold that the religious symbolism of the Islamic themes was not, in itself, the cause of the riots but point out that a particularly trying economic conjuncture was brought to the fore by the Young Tunisian efforts to raise the consciousness of their fellow countrymen. Consequently, it is quite valid to consider the wave of disturbances known as the Djellaz riots as marking the conjunction between nationalist concerns and violent action. Bourguiba himself gives witness to this turning-point with the simultaneous awakening of his own consciousness.

> The first time that I was shocked by the Tunisian reality in all its bitterness was in 1911. As usual, I was walking from the steps of Bâb Manarah when, all of a sudden, the Qasbah [governmental center, right across from Collège Sadiki] was filled by Zouaves soldiers with their distinctive headdress - similar to the shâshiyyah but with a long thread on which hung a tassle reaching down to the lower part of the neck. I asked about the matter and was told that something had happened at the Djellaz [cemetery] resulting in great disturbances.[65]

Apparently, the Protectorate authorities had decided to register the land of the Islamic cemetery, the Djellaz, in order to transform it from ḥabûs to municipal land coming under their own direct administration. Whereupon a riot erupted. The ability of Islamic symbols to mobilize public opinion is clear in this instance. When word leaked out of the intentions of the Protectorate authorites, crowds quickly gathered and, on the day the survey was to take place, the situation deteriorated and turned into a melee where many were killed. The French authorities reacted harshly by sentencing one to death, exiling several and imprisoning many. Although Bourguiba himself did not attend the public execution, his young imagination worked the scene up to such a point and he described it in such detail and with such color one would have thought he had in fact been an eyewitness.[66]

Most historians of this period also link the Tunisian events with the Italian invasion of Libya and the French occupation of Morocco, events in other Arab-Islamic lands adding to the Islamic coloring of the riots. In fact, the majority of European settlers in Tunis at the time were Italians who occupied, not the high positions of the modern sector of the economy, but the lower echelon jobs (e.g., tramway conductors) from which Tunisians were excluded. Thus, there is a link between Tunisian nationalism and Islam, at least in terms of a felt need to express nationalist concerns in Islamic symbols.

The Djellaz riots were followed by the tramway boycott which began when an Italian conductor ran over a young Tunisian child and was widened into a protest against the systematic hiring of Italians and the exclusion of Tunisians by the tramway company. The boycott was supported publicly by the Young Tunisians. The French authorities again quickly responded by exiling the Young Tunisian leaders - including Abdelaziz Thaalbi, Hassen Guellaty and Mohamed Nomane, closing down their newspapers and, finally, imposing martial rule over all the country, which remained in effect from 1912 until 1921. A majority of Tunisian historians, including the younger, more critical school, consider these incidents as marking a watershed in the evolution of the "nationalist" movement from a position of accepting policies of "association" to a position of emphasis on the issue of independence.

> L'évolution du réformisme mou et aristocratique - au nationalisme pur et dur - évolution due à la radicalisation de la situation, à l'éveil de la masse et à la perte des dernières illusions jeunes-tunisiennes quant à la possibilité d'un réel rapprochement avec des colons profondément racistes et irrémédiablement fanatiques - est donc nette...[67]

Nonetheless, it should be pointed out that both in case of the Djellaz riots and in case of the tramway boycott, these events were not <u>led</u> by the Young Tunisians. On the contrary, they gave their measured approval only <u>after</u> the violence had occurred.

These first violent and, at the same time, articulated manifestations of the Tunisian nationalist movement were interrupted by the state of siege imposed in 1912 and the Great War of 1914-1918, which effectively stifled all opposition to the Protectorate. As the emergency measures imposed in 1912 continued during the Great War, the Tunisian nationalist movement could be pursued only outside of Tunisia by those of the Young Tunisians leaders who remained in exile. Those leaders who were of Arabic culture tended to be based in Berlin and to undertake their actions on behalf of the "Algero-Tunisians" against their common enemy,

France, in the name of Islamic unity under the banner of the Ottoman Empire. As in most of the Arab areas, the response was not enthusiastic and demonstrated the inability of the Ottoman Empire to mobilize the Arab provinces in its cause. In contrast, those of "French culture" tended to be based in neutral Geneva and to undertake action on behalf of all Maghribis without aspiring to separation from France. From both these perspectives, Islamic "Algero-Tunisian" or Maghribi, the Tunisian specificity is subordinated to some other dimension of identity.

Nevertheless, the second tendency, in view of the defeat of the Ottoman Empire, proved to be the more important as the forerunner of the post-War options open to the Tunisian nationalist movement. Faced with the bankruptcy of the policies of "association", the group held on to a separate identity by calling for a Constitution and, with the proclamation of the Wilsonian doctrine, the Geneva group dared to call for independence. At this point, the two groups had sufficient common grounds to formulate a joint platform presented to the Peace Conference.[68]

The end of the war saw the resurrection of the Tunisian nationalist movement with the establishment of the Free Constitutional Party (Al-Ḥizb al-dustûrî al-ḥurr al-tûnisî) in 1920. Whether mistakenly or deliberately, French commentators translated the name first as Parti Libre Tunisien and, finally, as Parti Libéral Constitutionnel.[69] The very first platform of this Party was radical in rejecting all forms of association with France and in calling for independence in the spirit of the Wilsonian doctrine of self-determination:

> Le Destour apparaît donc comme l'héritier du mouvement Jeune Tunisien. Mais les évènements survenus depuis 1911 - conquête de la Libye, du Maroc, évènement du Djellaz et boycottage de la compagnie des Tramways - ainsi que le long et sanglant conflit mondial avaient introduit une mutation profonde dans le mouvement nationaliste. Alors que le mouvement Jeune Tunisien semblait revendiquer un programme politique destiné à assurer l'égalité entre Français et Tunisiens et pourrait, à la limite, être taxé d'assimilationiste, le mouvement destourien [au moins dans un premier temps] prit rapidement un caractère nationaliste [autrement dit, indépendantiste] et se fixa

> comme objectif, la restauration de la personnalité tunisienne menacée par la politique de francisation poursuivie par le Gouvernement du Protectorat.[70]

The influence of these historical events on the political culture of Bourguiba is admitted by Bourguiba himself. He states: "It is natural that all these events had an effect in shaping my personality..."[71] Thus, the story of the "struggle for independence" phase of the nationalist movement in Tunisia becomes the story of Bourguiba.

Bourguiba gives two different dates for his graduation from primary school. On the one hand, he claims he was still in his last year of primary school when the Great War began in 1914. On the other hand, he claims that he obtained his primary school certificate in 1913, just before the death of his mother. The Sadiki archives confirm that Bourguiba finished the primary level in 1913.[72]

Bourguiba seems to remember many of his teachers, both Tunisian and French, remarkably well. Concerning the Tunisian ʿulamâʾ teaching at Sadiki, he had kind words for Shaykh Jaʿîţ but mocked another Skaykh. As for the French teachers, he was sarcastic about their attempts to teach Arabic grammar using Latin categories but he admired their great ease in writing the French language. He particularly admired one teacher who introduced him to Victor Hugo,[73] representative of the last of the eighteenth century Age of Enlightenment in France and of that spirit of sympathy for the disinherited and the miserable.

But, in the Tunisian capital, school was not the only means for his education. One of his favorite activities was to accompany his brother, Mohamed, who managed the theatrical group Al-Shahâmah al-ʿarabiyyah (Arab Chivalry), to the various shows, from Shakespeare to the Arabic classic Majnûn Laylâ [Laylâ's Fool]. The troupe flourished between 1909-1913, competing with the more aristocratic Al-Âdâb [Culture], but with the repressive measures imposed before the World War, it was forced to disband.[74]

Two weeks after his graduation from primary school, Bourguiba sat for the secondary school scholarship examinations; he passed. This meant that he became a boarder at Sadiki with his tuition, room and board, as well as uniform and bi-weekly bath being paid for by the scholarship. Within three years, he obtained the Brevet Elémentaire Arabe.

But, unlike his brothers who finished their secondary level at Sadiki, circumstances led him to obtain his Baccalauréat from the Lycée Carnot and, thus, he was allowed to go on to university in France itself. Bourguiba claims that the reason for which he left Sadiki was the tubercular primo-infection he contracted during the winter of 1919, his last year at the College. On another occasion, Bourguiba states that during the 1919-1920 school year he was supposed to repeat his class. On yet another occasion, he stated that he left Collège Sadiki without obtaining his degree because of a series of "renvois pour mauvaise conduite, grève, etc...". Actually, the "extrait du registre d'inscription", dated 6 Octobre 1920, notes that he was withdrawn from the College by his family.[75] It is quite likely that <u>all</u> these versions are true; that he was unruly, that he had fallen sick in the winter of 1919-20, and that he had failed his last year at Sadiki. Unfortunately, <u>none</u> of these versions corroborates the other to the extent of allowing the careful historian to reconstruct one coherent image which would throw light on the inner Bourguiba - did this event turn him against the general situation in Tunisia or did it turn him against his brothers?

Bourguiba's rendition of these circumstances illustrates his ability to personalize the socio-political drama of events affecting millions of people. For him, the First World War was the cause of his tuberculosis since the poor living conditions at Sadiki were created by the French authorities who, controlling the College's budget, siphoned money away from the College funds for the War effort. He also believes that these circumstances caused his short stature (165 cm.), a sensitive point with him, because he was deprived of proper nourishment during his growth years. Objectively, 165 centimeters is not short for a man in Tunisia as the average height of a Tunisian is not markedly great. Bourguiba's consciousness of being short is more likely due to the fact that he was the shortest of the Bourguiba brothers.[76] Despite Bourguiba's version of the peculiar medical condition whereby one of his testicles kept retreating into the pelvic cavity until it finally atrophied,[77] it is possible that the tuberculosis also affected his testicles. The ability of Bourguiba to overcome social inhibitions by discussing seemingly very intimate matters publicly serves two purposes; on the one hand, it gives the illusion of someone being perfectly open since he is ready to confide the most private affairs to the public and, on the other hand, it does not necessarily reveal his innermost thoughts.

Historically, it has been shown that the French authorities had pauperized the College much earlier by various means; for example, part of the College budget was used for the establishment of Arabic primary schools but this expense should normally have been underwritten by the Direction de l'Enseignement Publique.[78] Consequently, it is just possible that the resulting poor conditions were behind the tuberculosis Bourguiba contracted. Yet, it is the drama of his personal suffering rather than the more general situation of Tunisia being drained of men and resources for the French war effort that Bourguiba highlights. Again, it is the sense of the dramatic that emerges from the claim that, hidden under the sheets of the hospital bed, Bourguiba read the famous manifesto, La Tunisie Martyre, by Shaykh Thaalbi. Thus, the actual historical events - Béchir Sfar's funeral, the Djellaz riots, the tramway boycott - were complemented by La Tunisie Martyre in the task of awakening the political consciousness ofBourguiba and of a whole generation.

After a few weeks in the hospital, young Bourguiba was sent to the town of Le Kef where his oldest brother had been transferred as medical assistant. Fond of literature, particularly of the theatre, Mohamed influenced young Habib both in his love of acting and literature and in his interest in medical matters.[79] Bourguiba then returned to Tunis and, after a family conclave over his future, it was decided that Mahmoud would pay for Habib's studies at the Lycée Carnot, rather than send him back to Sadiki since he had forfeited his scholarship anyway. Even the idea of placing Habib as an apprentice was discussed but rejected. Somewhere along the line either Bourguiba himself or someone in his family had realized that science and mathematics had been weakened at Sadiki and that, consequently, it was not possible for Sadiki graduates to complete the second part of the French baccalauréat, a requirement for university entrance.[80] Instead of being grateful for his brothers' assistance, Bourguiba is bitter about the fact that they even discussed the possibility of placing him as an apprentice. But it is precisely due to this investment of family resources in his education that Habib became one of the very few

Tunisians who managed to gain entrance to the Lycée Carnot, reserved mainly for the sons of French colonists.

His illness had coincided with the end of the Great War and, in the interlude of his recuperation in Le Kef, historical events had taken place which were to shape the main features of the Tunisian "nationalist" movement, crucial to his own and to Tunisia's future.

Chapter III

BETWEEN TWO CULTURES (1920-1934)

RE-ENACTMENT OF THE FORMULATED REACTION

While Habib Bourguiba's hopes of a career as translator in the Protectorate civil service were coming to an end with his withdrawal from Sadiki, the upheavals ensuing at the end of the Great War demonstrated that, throughout the world, great hopes had been raised and quickly dashed. Several events during the First World War and following shortly upon its conclusion - the revolution in Russia, the proclamation of the Wilsonian doctrine of self-determination, the establishment of the League of Nations - had seemed to herald a new era of freedom and justice. But of all the Middle East and North Africa, only Arabia and Turkey preserved their independence; the first due to its lack of interest for the Great Powers (oil had not yet been discovered) and the second by the force of arms of the Great Ghazi, Mustafa Kemal. Instead of the hoped-for independence for the already dominated areas of the Arab-Islamic world, the Mandates were imposed on the remaining parts of the Ottoman Empire, with tragic consequences whose repercussions are still being felt to this day. Moreover, the destruction of the Ottoman Empire during the War and the elimination of the Caliphate in 1924 put an end to all possibilities of an Ottomanist strategy for political leaders in the Arab and the Islamic areas.

The recognition that the Ottoman Empire had failed is a major turning-point for all nationalist movements in the Arab world since it meant that the legitimate community had failed its primary function to protect its own survival as a unit. The legitimate community which had given the Ottoman

Empire its authority had been defined in terms of allegiance to Islam and, with the end of the Ottoman sultanate and caliphate, the legitimate community fractioned and entered into a profound crisis.[1]

It is at this juncture, between the years 1919 and 1925, that the main political organizations crystallized in Tunisia in the form of three political parties - the Socialist, the Destour, and the Reformist - and a labor union, the Confédération Générale Tunisienne du Travail. Following a lull between the years 1926 and 1929, the next period, 1930-1934, represents the coalescence of ideological options when the Néo-Destour undertook to harness violent action to legalistic argumentation. The basic characteristics of the Tunisian nationalist movement were set during this crucial period; namely, 1) moderation as a symptom of social and ideological continuity and of a realistic assessment of power relations between France and Tunisia; 2) utilization of legalistic argumentation rather than force, in view of the balance of power in favor of France; 3) sensitivity to developments in the West, specifically France, as much as to events in the Islamic East; 4) capacity to adjust by modulating tactics within a broadly defined strategy; 5) the four terms identified as keys to Bourguiba's political thought and action - "réalisme", "dialogue", "personnalité" and "action" - were already tenets of one or the other of the above-mentioned political organizations by the early 1920s; 6) in the early 1930s, religion came to play an important role in at least two of the four terms, "personnalité" and "action".

The first political party to be organized, as such, in Tunisia was not Tunisian but French. The Fédération Socialiste de Tunisie was simply a branch of the French Socialist Party and its membership was composed overwhelmingly of French civil servants (fonctionnaires) rather than colonists. It did have some Tunisian members, both Muslims and Jews, but they were a small minority. Following the Tours Congress in December 1920, the majority of the Fédération voted for the Third International and a split occurred. The majority regrouped in the Section Fédérale Internationale Communiste (S.F.I.C) and took over the party newspaper, L'Avenir Social. The minority became a branch of the Section Française de l'Internationale Ouvrière (S.F.I.O.).[2]

Bourguiba was still a student at Collège Sadiki when the remnants of the Young Tunisians still in Tunisia regrouped in an unofficial party called either "le Parti Tunisien" or "le Parti de la Liberté"[3] in order to prepare for the post-War era. Jewish Tunisians participated in the early meetings but the relatively radical tenor of the discussions worried them and they did not continue to attend. The remaining group decided to delegate Ahmed Sakka as their representative in Paris. When the Peace Conference refused to consider the demands presented, on the grounds that they were internal matters within the relationships established with France, Thaalbi joined Sakka in Paris in order to pursue Tunisian demands amongst political, mainly leftist, circles in France itself.[4]

> Seeing the futility of depending on the Peace Conference, Tunisian leaders must have reached the conclusion that their problem was Tunisian-French in essence, and had to be dealt with along Franco- Tunisian channels.[5]

Following the dismantlement of the Ottoman Empire, the recognition that Tunisian demands for the safeguard of the Tunisian "personnalité" were to be obtained through "dialogue" with France was an indication of the "réalisme" of the leaders of the Tunisian nationalist movement, who had concluded that the balance of force was in favor of France. This basic position was common to all the leaders of the Tunisian nationalist movement and differences between the various streams and tendencies within the movement were only contingent as various conditions shifted; for example, as the government in France changed hands, from the Radical/Liberal (1919-1924) to the Cartel des Gauches (1924-1926) to the several National Union governments (1926-1936) to the Popular Front (1936-1938) and so on.

With the failure of the French left during the elections in 1919, a bitter manifesto was published, La Tunisie Martyre. The pamphlet presented the thesis that, before the Protectorate, Tunisia had been making progress in "education, economic development, constitutional government and administration of justice" and that the Protectorate had frozen this progress, sacrificing Tunisia to capitalist interests.[6] The manifesto demanded the return of, at least, internal sovereignty to Tunisia. Written in French, the style of the book was highly inflammatory and, without directly calling for an end to the Protectorate, insisted on the legal existence of the Tunisian state and called for universal suffrage for Tunisian nationals, within a reformed framework of the ʿAhd al-amân of 1857 and of the 1861 Constitution.[7]

It is obvious that the demand for a Constitution was, in fact, a moderate position compared to the more radical demand for independence. This position, without reverting to a defense of the policies of "association", continued the Young Tunisian demand for a Tunisian state constituted in distinction to the French. In other words, the principal objective was to limit the erosion of the internal sovereignty of Tunisia as the Bey's authority was gradually being overwhelmed by the advancing tide of French direct administration. In fact, this was explicitly stated in the Destour newspaper, Le Libéral of 3 January 1925 where it was argued that the objective of the Destour was to lead the French authorities "de rompre définitivement avec les utopies d'assimilation pour admettre un système d'association fondé sur une constitution qui permet aux Tunisiens de faire leur apprentissage de citoyens et d'accéder ainsi au progrès et à la modernité".[8]

Some of the more important currents of thought about the colonies had been developed within the Socialist stream; three main positions may be distinguished as early as the 1907 Congress. On the extreme right was the imperialist current which viewed colonialism as the means of bringing progress to the underdeveloped areas of the world. The center, "conscient de la spécificité des colonies et de leur infériorité", called for certain reforms in order to soften the penetration of capitalism. The third current denied the progressive character of colonialism which, instead of developing the means and the forces of production in the colonies, simply harnessed them to the needs of the metropole. This third current re-asserted the common character of humanity so that radical democracy and a socialist program could be envisaged in all countries. It became synonymous with the Communists after 1920. A fourth current developed following the Socialist/Communist split, which was a compromise between the second and the third positions; namely, that radical democracy and socialist programs were to be applied in all countries but in a gradual manner in order to respect cultural differences. This is the position of Félicien Challaye, a follower of Jean Jaurès and Charles Péguy and a good friend of Bourguiba. This position flows logically from the concerns of Jaurès as he expressed them in a speech entitled "Tunisie: La civilisation musulmane" given in 1912,

> Si nous voulons, outremer, créer les conditions d'une collaboration qui ne soit pas domination, il ne suffit pas, de ne pas exproprier les hommes, il faut encore exalter en eux les héritiers et les continuateurs d'une culture égale à la nôtre. L'homme ne vit pas seulement de pain.[9]

Although unlikely, it is still within the realm of the possible that Habib Bourguiba was able to obtain a copyof La Tunisie Martyre so fast as to be able to read it "under the sheets" while sick in Sadiki hospital.

> Un ami m'apporta un jour - je n'ai pas oublié la date, elle était remarquable, le 1er janvier 1920 - la brochure du cheikh Taalbi, rédigée en français par Me Sakka, la Tunisie martyre. Je la glissais sous mes couvertures et la lisais, subrepticement, très ému. Ces chiffres, ces morts, cette pauvreté, cette humiliation d'être colonisé.... Je pleurais en cachette...[10]

When the Bloc National achieved power in France in 1919, the Tunisian nationalists quickly adjusted their sails and, on 14 March 1920, the group duly constituted itself under the name Al-Ḥizb al-ḥurr al-dustûrî al-tûnisî which is usually translated as Parti Libéral Constitutionnel Tunisien.[11] Within the political context of Tunisian-French relations in 1920, the word "liberal" indicated an attempt to create an analogy with the French Libéraux and, thus, to create some distance with the socialist left. But in Arabic "al-ḥurr" could be understood to refer to national independence as much as to individual liberties. This new organization may be considered as the first true Tunisian party because it had internal regulations, an organizational plan and a program to be followed. It is noteworthy that membership was explicitly open to Jewish Tunisians.

On the whole, the Destour leadership did not differ substantially from the Young Tunisian leadership except that the mamlûk and makhzanî shares were less important. It was still heavily from Tunis and of the relatively affluent classes "de propriètaires terriens, d'agriculteurs, de commerçants et d'avocats", but the membership represented a cross-section of social classes and geographic regions. In the context of the times, it was important to consider the distinction between the propertied classes, "propriètaires terriens, agriculteurs, commerçants" and the salaried classes including professionals such as lawyers. The best characterization of the Destour Party leadership is that of an alliance between a fraction of the "Vieux Turbans" (representing the propertied classes) anda fraction of the Jeunes Tunisiens (representing professionals, mostly lawyers) "sur la base de la sauvegarde des biens habous".[12] The program of the Destour calling for the promulgation of a Constitution postponed, in effect, the demand for independence.[13] The program may be considered to have remained true to the legacy of the Young Tunisians who had defended the policies of "association" whereby French liberals and Tunisian reformers would work, in partnership, for the progress of the country.

The Destour Party did not question the legitimacy of the Ḥusaynî Bey. On the contrary, the Party attempted to derive some of its legitimacy through an alliance with the Bey, since the basic argument was the defense of the internal sovereignty of the Tunisian state and the Bey embodied that state. The latter was tempted to cooperate since limited powers in the form of a Constitutional Monarchy in alliance with the Destour could be considered better than the purely decorative role he had been reduced to under the Protectorate.[14] Mohamed en-Naceur and especially his son, Moncef, thus supported the nationalist demands at this point in time.

Three issues which also represented continuity with the concerns of the Young Tunisians were land tenure, justice and education. The question of ḥabûs land had arisen again as the French Chambers of Commerce and Agriculture in Tunisia met in May 1920 and set up a committee to study how to open up the private ḥabûs land to colonization. In fact, for some Tunisians, this was the issue that took precedence over the Constitution.

> Aussi, le 6 juin [1920], une délégation présidée par Ahmed Essafi reprit-elle son bâton de pélérin. Destination: Paris. Objectif: Défendre les habous et plaider pour l'octroi d'une Constitution.[15]

As a correction to Thaalbi's mistake in depending exclusively on leftist, mainly Socialist interlocutors, the delegations were mandated to address themselves to all political parties in the French capital. Most of their contacts outside government circles were with the Liberals and the Radicals but they also kept some contacts with the Socialists and, following the Tours Congress, with the Communists.

The first delegation succeeded only in preventing the release of private ḥabûs land to the colonists but failed to obtain any of the points of the Destour program. A second delegation was sent in December 1920 which took an even more moderate tone by recognizing the Protectorate as an inescapable fact of history and demonstrated the characteristic realism of the Tunisian nationalist leaders.

> Nous reconnaissons...le Protectorat français comme un fait historique que nous ne devons pas discuter sachant que si la France n'occupait pas dans ce pays la situation privilégiée que lui confèrent les traités, nous serions tributaires d'une autre nation puissante. La situation géographique de la Tunisie, au carrefour des grandes routes de l'ancien continent fait que ce petit pays occupe une place trop importante dans la géographie militaire et économique du monde pour qu'il puisse vivre autonome, hors de l'influence d'une grande puissance européenne.[16]

Thus, despite relative moderation, the failure of the first delegation to obtain any concessions led the Destour to retreat from an insistence on Tunisian nationality as prerequisite to voting rights and to admit French participation in the election of a Tunisian government or, in other words, a measure of co-sovereignty.

On 29 March 1921, the French authorities put an end to the state of siege and a new Resident General was mandated to institute reforms. Lucien Saint then began to re-organize the Conférence Consultative in order to develop public education, to regularize land tenure and to give greater independence to the judiciary. The Conférence Consultative established in 1896 had only French representation until 1907 when 16 Tunisians were added for a minority representation. While the French community elected its representatives (after 1905) by universal suffrage, the Resident General appointed the Tunisian members. The reformed Grand

Conseil, established in 1922, had two sections - one with 56 French members, the other with 41 Tunisians - which deliberated separately. The Grand Conseil had limited jurisdiction and a Conseil Supérieur, dominated by the Protectorate executive, decided the issue if the French and Tunisian sections disagreed. After World War II, the Grand Conseil was modified to include equal numbers of French and Tunisians. Nonetheless, the Tunisian section was elected by a very restricted suffrage, the jurisdiction of the Conseil was scarcely expanded, and the Protectorate executive was still capable of taking emergency measures without consulting the Conseil.[17] In fact, the actual measures of reform proposed did not come anywhere near the Destour program and, more often than not, seemed to work against Tunisian interests. For example, in creating a Ministry of Justice and effectively withdrawing the judicial powers of the Bey from him, the Protectorate authorities transferred these powers to the jurisdiction of French law in general (except for cases of personal status which remained under the jurisdiction of Sharî'ah courts) so that Tunisian lawyers were forced to obtain French degrees in law in order to practice.

Addressing a petition to the Bey, the Destour argued that:

> Les premières décisions de la commission s'inspirent de vues susceptibles de porter atteinte aux droits des Tunisiens et faire disparaître leur personnalité de sorte que si ces décisions étaient exécutés votre trône n'aurait plus la moindre autorité et votre peuple perdrait toute dignité et toute existence propre. On tend à assigner la proportion du tiers à la repré- sentation indigène dans les assemblées élues. De même la justice tunisienne est menacée: on soustrait votre peuple à votre souveraineté. On attend de vous d'employer toute votre autorité à conserver le prestige de votre trône et à maintenir la personnalité de votre pays.[18]

In contrast, the third political party, the Reformists led by Hassen Guellaty and organized in April 1921, appeared willing to accept Lucien Saint's reforms.

The Reformists may be considered to have had a double origin. Many of the members of the group had been among the Young Tunisians and had belonged also to the pre-1920 Fédération Socialiste de Tunisie. In fact, Hassen Guellaty and Mohamed Nomane had accompanied the Fédération leader, Duran-Angliviel, to the Tours Congress and had voted against the Communist demands. On their return to Tunisia, they found themselves in a minority position and divided along ethnic lines. The Reformist Party, led by Hassen Guellaty, grouped around the Arabic newspaper, Al-Burhân, which began publication in April 1921. The French members had constituted themselves a branch of the S.F.I.O. around the newspaper Tunis-Socialiste which began publication on 1 March 1921.[19] Even the term "Reformist" pointed to the double origins of the group; in French "réformiste" pointed to the position of the minority socialists at the 1920 Tours Congress while in Arabic "işlâḥ" referred to the Arab-Islamic reformist tradition best represented by Muḥammad ʿAbduh.

The Reformists abandoned the demand for a constitution and limited themselves to requesting a Budgetary Assembly with a say in the finances of the country, instead of a Parliament to which the executive would be answerable. Instead of universal suffrage, which would have drowned the French colonist votes, they limited voting rights by property and education.[20] It is with the Reformists that we first find a member of the Bourguiba family, M'Hamed, who is listed as wakîl (advocate). Several sources list Mohamed rather than M'Hamed Bourguiba, but the first was a medical assistant, not an advocate, who was working in Le Kef at the time and Habib Bourguiba was recuperating from tuberculosis under his care. The probable mistake could be due to the easy confusion between the two names in Arabic, since the vowelling would not necessarily always appear. Interestingly enough, it is also from this group that Bourguiba chose a lawyer, Mohamed Nomane, when he was arrested in 1938.[21]

It is with this group that we first find explicitly stated that mode of action which, following the Second World War, was to become the hallmark of Bourguiba, "la politique des étapes". The program of the Reformists published in Al-Burhân, 18 September 1921 states:

> Nous disons que l'objectif que nous visons est de parvenir, par des étapes successives et méthodiques, à conquérir dans l'ordre, le travail et la paix, le droit d'avoir ici, un jour, les institutions des pays libres et

> indépendants - c'est-à-dire un parlement législatif fort, composé de Tunisiens et de Français élus, un pouvoir exécutif désigné par le consentement des gouvernés et responsables devant le parlement - et de réaliser ainsi le self-government franco-tunisien qui fera de cette belle Tunisie un des plus riches dominions de la France.

Guellaty wrote in Tunis-Socialiste (28 août 1921):

> Et effectivement, une dizaine de jours après notre arrivée à Paris, nous étions définitivement fixés sur l'impossibilité d'obtenir la constitution telle que nous l'avions rêvée et sur l'inopportunité d'insister sur le Parlement législatif et la responsibilité du gouvernement. Je suggérais alors aux délégués que, en maintenant les deux premières revendications comme l'expression d'un idéal politique légitimement formulé et poursuivi par la population tunisienne, il était sage et pratique de reconnaître spontanément qu'avant d'atteindre cet idéal, il était indispensable de franchir certaines étapes préparatoires...[22]

Moreover, this is the first group that explicitly justified its positions by reference to a proper evaluation of reality or, as Guellaty called it, "la juste notion des réalités".[23] And in both attitudes they were close to the post-1882 ʿAbduh, who opted for reform rather than revolution when faced with the grim reality of the overwhelming power of the British.

In the attempt to preserve what could be preserved under trying conditions, the early reformers had attempted to distinguish between the eternal principles of Islam - such as the creed of unicity and the ethical requirements of justice and equality - and those precepts dependent upon historical contingencies. The argument deduced from this basic premise, of a distinction between eternal principles and contingent precepts, is that Islam itself takes a gradualist approach so that its precepts are suited to its historic reality and it can thus be effective.

> [Islam] is the religion which holds to the principle of gradualism in legislating its laws according to [limiting] conditions. There is

> nothing which states or indicates that the stage achieved during the Prophet's lifetime was the hoped-for final [stage] after which there would be an end since gradual [evolution] is linked to the difficulties of those issues for which gradual [steps] are to be taken.[24]

One may then understand that the basic concern of the Salafiyyah (return to the salaf or early ancestors) movement, led by ʿAbduh, was an effort to get rid of the multiple accretions of historically contingent precepts by a return to the first and, presumably eternal, principles of Islam.

The sociological differences between the leadership of the Destour and of the Reformists are difficult to pin-point but, as with the differences between the Young Tunisians and the Destour leadership, they seem to have been differences of quantity rather than quality as the alliance of class fractions within the Reformist leadership tended to have a higher percentage of professionals, particularly lawyers, than of land-owners or artisans and merchants. A more serious difference was the inability of the Reformists to attract a wider membership beyond Tunis, the capital. Mahjoubi notes that "le parti réformiste n'a aucune audience populaire et se limite à un cénacle d'intellectuels."[25] The lines of demarcation between the Reformists and the Destour, both heirs to the Young Tunisians, were not as clear-cut as might have been thought precisely because of their shared origins. Guellaty and Nomane as well as Thaalbi had been exiled with Bash Hanba in 1912.[26]

The reason usually given for the divergence between the Destour Party and the Reformists - that the latter believed a more moderate program had better chances of success - should be placed within the context of developments in France; when the Tours Congress in December 1920 accepted the conditions imposed by the Russian Communists, the majority of the French Socialists first went along and only a dissenting minority withdrew. The Fédération Socialiste de Tunisie, of which Guellaty and Nomane were members, held to the minority position. On their way back to Tunisia, Guellaty and Nomane met with the Destour delegation in Paris and, thus, it would appear that, at the very beginning of the Socialist/Communist split, the Destour sympathized with the Socialists; its relations with Guellaty and the book published by Duran-Angliviel, Ce que la Tunisie demande à la

France, in support of the Destour, testify to that. Once the majority of the Fédération in Tunisia voted for the Third International, then the winds appeared to have changed. If the Destour, though close to the liberal center, proposed - as a tactical measure - to work with the majority rather than with the minority, this could explain Guellaty's and Nomane's decision to establish the Reformist Party. When the Bloc National government turned against the Communists, Lucien Saint felt free to dissolve the Fédération Communiste in Tunisia on 17 May 1922 after having jailed its president and suspended its newspaper.[27] The Destour was then to pay heavily for its tactical mistake, when the Communists quickly lost ground. The Socialists and the Protectorate authorities did not easily forget and the accusation of being in alliance with the Communists was continuously held against the Destour.[28]

In the meanwhile, the Tunisian representative in Paris, Farhat Ben Ayed, succeeded in obtaining a jurisprudential opinion in July 1921 which stated that the Tunisian Constitution of 1861 was still valid and was not in contradiction with the Protectorate as defined by the Bardo and the La Marsa treaties. He also succeeded in persuading some members of the French Chambre des Députés to present a bill linking the proposed loan with Tunisian self-government in February 1922. The legal opinion (a <u>responsa</u>, very similar to a <u>fatwâ</u>) was obtained from Joseph Barthélémy and André Weiss, the first deputy and professor of constitutional law at the University of Paris, and the second professor of international public law and Vice-President of the International Court at the Hague. Two fundamental points of the document were that the Constitution of 1861, though suspended, could not be abrogated unilaterally by the Bey and that the Protectorate did not modify the constitutional state in Tunisia. In answer to the question about the re-enforcement of the Constitution, Barthélémy wrote that, since Constitutional reforms were not mentioned in the Marsa treaty, these were beyond the jurisdiction of the Protectorate authorities.[29] On 2 February 1922, a resolution presented by Pierre Taittinger and signed by 26 deputies was deposited for presentation to the French Chambre des Députés. This resolution made constitutional reform a condition in order to permit a loan to the Tunisian authorities.[30]

But these gains were quickly annulled when the Bey threatened to abdicate following the declarations a French newspaper alleged he had made in which he distanced himself from the Destour. Huge demonstrations were organized by the Party in April 1922 in order to express support of the Bey. Finally, the Bey accepted to retract his threat of abdication in hopes of opening discussions on a program of reforms he himself proposed. His hopes came to nothing when, at the end of his visit to Tunisia, the President of France, Alexandre Millerand, declared that "La France est à jamais en Tunisie." And instead of the favorable resolution promised to Ben Ayed, a resolution was passed by the Chambre des Députés asserting the will to "maintenir en toutes circonstances l'autorité et les droits de la France en Tunisie" by encouraging the "petite et moyenne colonisation".[31]

With the coming to power of the Cartel des Gauches in France in May 1924, the nationalist movement in Tunisia took heart. Again, there seemed to be a rapprochement between the Destour and the Socialists but it cooled off somewhat when the Destour decided to address itself directly to the French government. A third delegation was sent in November 1924 to refute the strangely contradictory images alleged of the Destour, of being Communist and fanatically Muslim at the same time. On the one hand, the Destour protested that it could not sympathize with "une doctrine en contradiction flagrante avec l'Islam" and, on the other hand, maintained that it was not conservative but "résolument moderniste". It also distinguished itself from the Communists in that the Destour was against the use of violence and that "son action s'inscrit dans la légalité la plus stricte". Moreover, it had no interest in an alliance with the Communist Party "qui ne compte en Tunisie qu'une vingtaine de membres, qui n'a en France que 26 voix dans la chambre de députés et dont la doctrine et les méthodes d'action effraient les pouvoirs publics."[32] Actually, the Communists offered unsolicited support as part of their general policy - at this point in time - of lending support to nationalist movements in their struggle for independence.

The Destour was liable to lose the good will of the Socialists on another count as well when the S.F.I.O. and the Reformists aligned themselves with the French labor unions, the Confédération Générale du Travail (C.G.T.), against the creation of an independent Tunisian labor union. The Destour had at first tended to favor the new Tunisian labor union as the Party sought to widen its base, beyond its heavily bourgeois and petit bourgeois origins, to the working classes.[33]

As with the Djellaz riots and the tramway boycott, thought had followed action when the Confédération Générale Tunisienne du Travail (C.G.T.T.) took shape not as a result of a concerted thought-out plan but after action had been undertaken spontaneously. On 13 August 1924, the dockers in the port of Tunis had struck and the strike had then spread to Bizerte and to the mine workers in the south. It was only after the mine workers at Metlaoui and Redif had struck that M'Hamed Ali, future founder of the C.G.T.T., went there to support and organize them. At that point in time, the Destour contributed to the financial relief of the dockers' families. In December 1924, M'Hamed Ali al-Hammi founded the C.G.T.T. and and attempted to maintain a structure independent of the Destour Party just as much as of the C.G.T. Though accused of collaboration with the Communists, the C.G.T.T. seems to have been inspired mainly by the Spartacus school of thought in Germany and attempted to defend corporatist rather than nationalist ends.[34]

The C.G.T.T. failed when, on 5 February 1925, the leaders were arrested and exiled. In the meantime, the third Destour delegation to Paris had failed to accomplish anything. Accordingly, the Destour sought to moderate its positions further and, following the example of the Cartel des Gauches in France, sought rapprochement with the Socialists in Tunisia. On 18 February 1925, the Destour joined the Reformist Party, the Tunisian Section of the Grand Conseil, the S.F.I.O. and the C.G.T. in a cartel for joint action but without fusing their programs.[35] Allied to these moderate groups, the Destour was safeguarded from allegations of extremism.

When the Herriot government fell, the Destour undertook more active protests with strikes and demonstrations throughout Tunisia. This "durcissement" of the Destour seems to have also been affected by the revolts in the Rif and in Syria. While the Destour expressed its support for these revolts in fellowship with other Arab-Islamic peoples, the Socialists maintained their anti-nationalist position on the basis that "qu'elle qu'en soit l'issue, un mouvement nationaliste travaille toujours pour la haine, la régression et la servitude."[36] At this point too, action by the

Destour membership base preceded organization and justification by the leadership.

> On assiste alors à une certaine distorsion entre la base et la direction du parti destourien. La première étant toujours disposée à une action radicale, la seconde prèchant la modération pour freiner cet élan révolutionnaire. Dans la nuit du 29 au 30 septembre 1925, de nombreux militants destouriens improvisent, contre la volonté de leurs dirigeants, à l'occasion du Mouled [mawlid al-nabî, en commémoration de la naissance du Prophète Muḥammad] une manifestation à caractère nationaliste.[37]

In effect, the language and the context used by the base were not derived through legalistic argumentation, but were inspired by religious symbols.

As the Cartel des Gauches limped along before finally collapsing in the summer of 1925, drastically repressive measures were taken in Tunisia. What came to be known as the "décrets scélérats", by which political action and the press were to be muzzled, were promulgated on 29 January 1926.[38] A typically Tunisian realistic assessment of the strength of the decrees patched up any differences within the Tunisian Cartel between the Destour and the leftist parties. Under these circumstances, and from 1926 to 1929, the Destour returned to the tactics it had followed during the 1922-1924 crisis; to concentrate on organizational work, on reforms in the economic and educational fields and to avoid all action that might provoke even greater repression.[39]

CULTURAL IMMERSION

Meanwhile, at the end of September 1921, Bourguiba had enrolled at the Lycée Carnot which catered mainly to French and other non-Tunisian students in contrast to the Collège Sadiki, whose students were practically all Tunisian. He obtained his Baccalauréat, première partie, in 1923 and his deuxième partie in 1924.[40] The Lycée Carnot still stands at the cross-roads between the Arab madînah and the new French-built quarter of Tunis. This was a far different world from the fragrant trees and Arab buildings around Sadiki. At one end of the main street which crossed the madînah Cardinal Lavigerie's statue was to stand and at the other end the imposing new cathedral - two symbols of the presence of Christianity in the world of Islam. At Sadiki, Bourguiba had had to respond to the baladî disdain of him as a provincial green-horn, an âfâqî. At Carnot, he had to respond to the French "others" within the framework of the image "they" had created of Tunisians. His blue eyes gave him a "carte d'entrée" by evoking the historical links between the northern and southern shores of the Mediterranean but his dark skin would not allow him carte blanche since it continuously reminded "them" that he was not French but an exotic "other".

The exotic "other" was interchangeably "Tunisian", "Arab" or "Muslim" in the French literature on Tunisia. That no distinction was drawn between these categories may have been due to the inability of most French to distinguish the pertinence of each category to various contexts. The tendency to use "Muslim" may perhaps be explained by the ontological absence of Christian "Arabs" in Tunisia, since all Christians were not Tunisian. Jews were absent from the nationalist movement. Why Jews did not participate in the various nationalist movements in North Africa while Christians in the Middle East did so to an important extent is an interesting question, since it is related to the issue of how religion is to be conceived of in terms of the national personality. In Tunisia, Jewish Tunisians had requested as early as 1908 to be placed under French rather than Tunisian jurisdiction. A proportionately much greater number of Jews than Muslims availed themselves of French citizenship following the naturalization law of 1923. There were a few Jews at various stages of the Tunisian nationalist movement but nowhere near the representation their numbers warranted. On the whole, the participation of Jews within the nationalist movement after the 1930s was practically nil and we only find them in action within communist or socialist circles.[41] Thus, all Tunisians were Muslims and non-Muslims were not considered Tunisians.

On admission to the Lycée Carnot, Habib was placed in the class for the Première Partie du Baccalauréat but the 18 months of inactivity prior to that and the curricular differences between Sadiki and Carnot made it difficult for him to keep up and he was dropped back one class. This, and his more mature years, allowed him to breeze through the year with great ease, giving him a taste of success so that he was ranked first in the Philosophy section of the Baccalauréat for all Tunisia.

During his years at Carnot, a fourth historic event occurred - following the Djellaz riots, the tramway boycott, and Béchir Sfar's funeral - that was to leave its imprint on young man Bourguiba. On 5 April 1922, he claims to have participated in the huge demonstration which protested the Bey's rumoured abdication. Carried along by the massed crowds, he could not fail to be influenced by the intoxication of the group in which the individual achieves power by the loss of all individuality. The magic of mass "action" was to be filed away for future moments. Although some sources claim that he became a member of the Destour Party following the demonstration, Bourguiba claims only that he "considered" himself to be a member of the Destour at this point.[42]

Whether public life had begun to attract him, as he claimed, or whether the reforms in the administrative system had decreased the possibilities for a career in the public service, is difficult to judge. Beyond the immediate personal reasons of Bourguiba, there was also the general contradiction between the aspirations of the Tunisian élite and the interests of the Protectorate executive; in 1913, the Department of Finances had 616 French employees out of a total of 1270 (almost 50 percent); Agriculture had 141 out of 219 (65 percent) and overall, out of 11,500 civil servants, 7000 were Europeans (66 percent). Perhaps the reason for this choice was simply that for the Baccalauréat, philosophy was weighted double the weight of mathematics and of science.[43] In any case, he then chose ethics for concentration in his last year and opted to go to France for his law degree.

Indeed, as soon as he finished his Baccaleauréat, he left Tunisia for France to study law in Paris. The choice of law was almost natural in a family where at least two brothers, M'Hamed and Mahmoud, were working as wakîls or advocates. The reforms instituted by Lucien Saint had widened the jurisdiction of French civil law courts so that only personal status was left to the jurisdiction of the Sharî'ah courts. Within the new system, only by obtaining French university diplomas could young Tunisians hope to function. Bourguiba also took courses in political science, public finance section, and in psychology.[44] Perhaps with hindsight, Bourguiba states,

> Je m'attachais à découvrir les rouages de cette civilisation, le secret de la puissance de ce pays qui réduisait le mien à la condition coloniale afin que, connaissant bien mon vis-à-vis, je sois en mesure, le jour où j'engagerai le combat, d'adopter la tactique appropriée pour le dissuader et l'amener à changer de politique. Bref, il me fallait faire le point des forces antagonistes en France.[45]

Bourguiba arrived in France in November 1924, just after the election of the Cartel des Gauches and almost at the same time as the third Tunisian delegation to Paris which ended in humiliating failure, not having succeeded in even obtaining a meeting with Herriot, the newly-elected President. Bourguiba first had to solve the immediate problems of room and board, given the meager funds which his brother Mahmoud was able to send him. He established himself in the heart of the Latin Quarter, Place Saint Michel, where the Paris he met was the toiling Paris, the Paris of the working classes crowding around the famous market-place, Les Halles. But his situation improved soon enough when the limited funds sent by his brother were quickly supplemented by a scholarship from Collège Sadiki. Though in principle reserved for Sadiki graduates, the scholarship (some 2,000 francs) was nonetheless sent to Bourguiba.[46] Habib's ability to manage money allowed him to indulge in his first passion, the theatre.

> Ainsi j'arrivai à Paris, à l'automne de 1924. Je n'avais pas seulement choisi les études juridiques pour me former en tant qu'homme publique. Je tenais aussi à l'enseignement permanent de cette grande capitale, à cette leçon quotidienne de la vie et du passé. Quelle richesse.... Je sortais, j'allais au bal parfois. J'appris le charleston; comment un jeune homme aurait-il pu vivre, en 1925, sans danser le charleston? ...Ma grande passion pourtant, c'était le théâtre. La Comédie-Française, surtout, et l'Odéon.[47]

But studies and the theatre were not the only occupations of Habib in this Paris of the Gay Twenties, of Josephine Baker and the Charleston. This was also the Paris of the Cartel des Gauches and of the heirs of Jean Jaurès. Watching the procession accompanying the remains of that great man through the streets of Paris to the Panthéon, the burial place of heroes,[48] Bourguiba must have recalled the funeral of Béchir Sfar and wondered if he himself would die a great man too.

Bourguiba's attitude to heroes is intriguing as it indicates the type of personality which he most admired. All heroes of armed resistance come in for sharp criticism except Ataturk; al-Daghbajî, hero of the armed resistance of the south of Tunisia, was "ignominously" hanged; ʿAbd al-Karîm, hero of the Rif rebellion, was a "simple man" and even Jugurtha, hero of the Berber resistance to the Romans, was strangled in prison[49] - all were failures, in his view. Other than Ataturk, only Béchir Sfar, representing the Arab-Islamic culture and Jean Jaurès, representing French-Western culture, are mentioned by Bourguiba with respect and awe. Both were men, not of violent action, but of the spoken - and the written - word.

When exactly did Habib Bourguiba decide to become a successful hero, if it was a conscious decision?. When did he decide to "combat" France? Which historical event triggered his consciousness - the Djellaz riots in 1911, the tramway boycott and the exile of the Young Tunisians in 1912, Béchir Sfar's funeral in 1917, publication of La Tunisie Martyre in 1920 or the mass demonstration in support of the Bey in 1922? Or should we look for deeper psychological causes - did the shock of racial discrimination, against which not even his blue eyes could protect him, trigger his anger? Or did his brothers, particularly M'Hamed, affect him by their example? Or was it simply the love/hate relationship between dominant and dependent?

From 1924 to 1927, Bourguiba was in Paris at a juncture in his life when a young man is most open to that "prise de conscience" which is to mark him indelibly by a France at the apogee of its power, just as the post-War inflation was being brought under control and just before the Crash of 1929.

> Mon premier grand souvenir, c'est celui du transfert au Panthéon des cendres de Jaurès. C'était émouvant, dans le Quartier Latin. C'est ce jour-là que je vis pour la première fois la statue d'Auguste Comte, sur laquelle étaient gravées ces mots: "Vivre pour autrui..." ...je me disais...que tout cela c'était ma formation d'homme, et que je saurais le mettre au service de la Tunisie. Et j'allais assister à des meetings politiques, à

> des réunions communistes notamment, à la Mutualité. J'y voyais des gens de couleur, des hommes venus de bien des horizons, Africains, Indochinois, Antillais. Et j'y voyais aussi des Français qui appuyaient les revendications des peuples colonisés. Tout cela me donnait à réfléchir. Ainsi, ces hommes luttaient pour la liberté de leur patrie, et des Français les comprenaient et les aidaient...nous étions au temps du Cartel des Gauches. On parlait du "mur d'argent". Qu'est-ce que cela signifiait pour la France, et pour mon pays? Je sentais que nous serions toujours dominés et grugés. J'avais entrevu...que la colonisation n'était pas seulement l'humiliation, c'était aussi l'exploitation, un déplacement de richesses; qu'un courant économique était organisé de telle façon par le mécanisme du budget, de la loi, que le colonisé était victime d'une hémorragie financière permanente. Vraiment, je n'ai pas perdu mon temps, rue Saint-Guillaume.[50]

Bourguiba was in France to witness at first hand the success of the Cartel des Gauches in 1924 and their ignominous collapse in the summer of 1926 due to their inability to solve the economic problems created by the needs of reconstruction after the War and an inflation so severe that the franc had declined to 14 percent of its 1914 purchasing power. The Cartel des Gauches was followed by the Union Nationale government where men of the left - Radicals and nearby groups - held the "political" ministries (Interior, Agriculture, Public Education) and men of the Right held the "economic" portfolios (Finance, Public Works, Pensions). This was the government that succeeded in restoring France's finances, at least until the great crisis of 1929.

For Bourguiba, France was forever the France of 1924-1927, the France of national union in the best tradition of Republicanism. This is the France that represented the best in the Third Republic, the last breath of eighteenth century Cartesian rationalism and nineteeth century positivism. Although Bourguiba himself points again and again to the influence of Auguste Comte, it was not Comte's positivism which attracted him as much as the spirit of self-sacrifice. In fact, Bourguiba states that he had been deeply impressed by the inscription found on the pedestal of that famous man's statue, "Vivre pour autrui". Adopting the motto, Bourguiba felt that "It was the expression of the precise purpose of the life I intended to live and of the goals I had set for myself."[51]

I believe that Jean Jaurès and Henri Bergson were the major influences on his intellectual development in France, outside the legal studies he pursued. The teenage literary taste for Victor Hugo, Lamartine and Alfred de Vigny matured into the social concerns treated by Jaurès and Bergson.[52] But in his later years, Bourguiba reverts back to his earlier loves and does not tire of reciting de Vigny's "La Mort du Loup",[53] reflecting his continued obsession with action and with his place in history. The frequency with which he cites this poem calls for a quotation. The wolf, having been shot by the hunter, seems to be saying as he dies:

> Il disait: "Si tu peux, fais que ton âme arrive
> A force de rester studieuse et pensive,
> Jusqu'à ce haut degré de stoique fierté.
> Où, naissant dans les bois, j'ai tout d'abord monté.
>
> Gémir, pleurer, prier est également lâche.
> Fais énergiquement ta longue et lourde tâche
> Dans la voie où le sort a voulu t'appeler,
> Puis, après, comme moi, souffre et meurs sans parler.[54]

France between 1914 and 1927 appeared victorious in all fields, military and economic as much as cultural, before sceptic relativism and absurdist existentialism had appeared and it is therefore no wonder that what Bourguiba said about Khayr al-Dîn would seem to apply to his own case.

> Like all who go to Europe and come back dazzled by what they had seen of that towering civilization, he [meaning Khayr al-Dîn] wished to achieve something by which he would open the eyes of the people, even by just a little, to that civilization.[55]

French culture exerted such a great attraction for Bourguiba that it could be said of him "Cet Arabe est françisé jusqu'au bout des ongles" and "L'Apôtre farouche de la personnalité arabo-musulmane tunisienne est un example vivant d'assimilation parfaite de l'Occident."[56] And yet Bourguiba held on to his Tunisian soul with its Arab and Islamic dimensions. Parallel to Alfred de Vigny, he appreciated al-Mutanabbî, parallel to Lamartine,

Bourguiba liked Aḫmad Shawqî; and parallel to Jaurès, Bourguiba remembered Béchir Sfar.

It is believed that Bourguiba in Paris was frequently in touch with "l'Etoile Nord-Africaine" led by Messali Hadj but presided at one time by the Tunisian Chedly Khairallah. He also attended various leftist party meetings where he is said to have met Mahmoud Materi, future president of the break-away Néo-Destour.[57] At some period in time, he roomed with Tahar Sfar and Bahri Guiga, also future leaders of the Néo-Destour. One of the most lasting friendships that Bourguiba made, probably at these meetings, was with Félicien Challaye with whom both he and his wife corresponded after his return to Tunisia. Félicien Challaye wrote a book on Charles Péguy tracing the influence of both Jean Jaurès and Henri Bergson on Péguy. It is through these contacts with effervescent centre-leftist groups that Bourguiba absorbed "cet humanisme qui caractérisa son action politique."[58]

The satisfaction of obtaining degrees in political science, where he ranked 17th in a student body of 190 in the public finances section,[59] and presumably in law, must have been great. Actually, Habib was not the only one of the Bourguiba family to pursue a law degree. As early as his last year at the Lycée Carnot, he had made it a habit to pass all his notes to his brother, M'Hamed, who then succeeded in obtaining his own "deuxième partie du baccalauréat" and his university degree in law from the Université d'Algers. Despite the age difference, there is a striking physical resemblance between the two brothers which might have reinforced their closeness.

During those three years in France, Bourguiba had met, lived with and married Mathilde Louvain, a French widow quite a few years older than he. His family life seems to have been more of an embarrassment than anything else, a duty and a burden he had to endure as he plunged into his career.

> Au cours de ma troisième année parisienne, au moment où allait s'achever ce cycle parisien, trois mois avant mon départ, une épreuve redoubtable fond sur ma tête: un enfant! Au moment de préparer les examens! J'étais malade, et entre deux soins, la venue du bébé, je préparais mes écrits. Enfin, je passai.[60]

RE-IMMERSION IN TUNISIA

Bourguiba began his law internship as soon as he arrived in Tunis in August 1927 but it was only in late 1928 that he was able to hold down a position, after moving from one law office to another. His instability at work was also reflected in several residential changes. It is not clear if or when he passed his bar examinations since he claims to have lost his internship, because of his political activities, just before opening his own office in 1931.[61]

The years 1929-1930 are points of no return in Bourguiba's life when his political activities began to overtake all else. They represent the transition of Habib Bourguiba from a restless lawyer to a full-time political activist, passing through a stage of political journalism. His first article, "Le Voile", appeared in L'Etendard Tunisien on 11 January 1929 and he became a regular contributor to La Voix du Tunisien in February 1931.[62]

Both L'Etendard Tunisien and La Voix du Tunisien were edited by the same Chedly Khairallah who had been president of the Etoile Nord-Africaine. Interestingly enough, the nationalist press of French expression took a more radical tone than the Arabic-language newspapers. First in this line was the weekly, L'Etendard Tunisien, founded by Chedly Khairallah, which appeared from 4 January 1929 to February 1930. Khairallah stated in the introduction that the newspaper was "une tribune libre, offerte à tous les hommes, sans distinction aucune, qu'intéressent les destinées de ce pays."[63] The second, La Voix du Tunisien, appeared intermittently and in various forms between 26 March 1930 and 27 June 1950 (as a weekly between 26 March 1930 and 15 February 1931, as a daily from 16 February 1931 to 24 November 1932; ceased to appear on that date as it was abandoned by the Destour; reappeared on 28 March 1933 as a weekly then as a bi-weekly; was suspended on 31 May 1933; reappeared as a weekly from 6 April 1933 to 27 June 1950). Following the Eucharistic Congress, a group of Tunisian leaders representing a spectrum of opinions, principally of the Destour Party, decided to support the newspaper as a daily, despite Khairallah's continued insistence on keeping the newspaper independent of any party. Its editorial committee included Mahmoud Materi, Tahar Sfar,

M'Hamed and Habib Bourguiba. The program announced by the newspaper attempted a minimal consensus in order to maintain a minimal cohesion among its financial backers. The third in the series was L'Action Tunisienne which appeared exactly during those periods when La Voix du Tunisien was on the wane; first as a daily from 1 November 1932 until it was suspended on 30 May 1933, then as a weekly from 16 December 1936 until again suspended on 10 April 1938, following the events of 9 April 1938.

The articles published in these newspapers continued to take a more radical tone as they began to attack the Protectorate itself throughout the 1930s. Bourguiba too contributed to this attack; he wrote,

> ...comme un Etat ne peut être à la fois sujet et souverain tout traité de protectorat, en raison même de son objet, porte en lui son propre germe de mort.... Une évolution inévitable y mettra nécessairement un terme.[64]

These early articles reveal the fundamental ideas that were to guide Bourguiba's political thought and action: "l'intangibilité de la personnalité nationale et de la souveraineté politique du peuple tunisien, l'idée d'un nationalisme ayant des racines dans les principes mêmes de la civilisation française...et l'émancipation progressive de la Tunisie."[65] In this conception, the Tunisian "personnalité nationale" is to be recognized in its distinctive social customs and history, both of which had to a large extent been formed by the Islamic religion and the Arabic language.

Three historic events heralding the 1930s served to further highlight the link between religion and the national "personnalité". Two of these, the celebration of the centennial of the occupation of Algeria and the proclamation of the Berber ẓâhir in Morocco, occurred outside Tunisia. But the third, the Eucharistic Congress of the Catholic Church celebrating the revival of the North African bishopric in Carthage, was held in Tunis itself in 1930. The symbolism used, young men parading with Crusader crosses, recalled the religious wars of the Crusades when Louis IX failed to occupy Tunisia. Bourguiba comments:

> This Eucharistic Congress was nothing short of a disaster for our country. The streets of Tunis were invaded by clergymen from every

> corner of the world, so that it was difficult to go out. With the priests were young men dressed in costumes recalling those of the Eighth Crusade led by King Louis IX which was stopped on the plains of Carthage in 1270 when King Louis died of the plague. Wearing the Crusade uniforms, these young men carried banners on which were written "the Ninth Crusade"; in other words, we have indeed entered Tunisia while Louis IX had failed to do so in the reign of al-Mustawfî bi-Allâh. Among the members of the organizing committee in Tunisia, whose chairman was the Pope, were the Bey, the Ministers, the ʿUlamâʾ, the Shaykh al-Islâm and the Bâsh Muftî.[66]

The religious symbolism which the French authorities had evoked during the Eucharistic Congress simply justified the Islamic dimension of the Tunisian "personnalité" as the basis for the nationalist struggle against assimilation. For example, Chams-Eddine Ladjimi made the following conclusions about the effects of the Congress:

> L'enseignement qu'on doit tirer de ce congrès c'est d'être unis derrière notre religion et que celle-ci soit notre moyen d'action. L'instruction qu'on a reçue si elle doit nous libérer des superstitions et des fausses croyances ne doit pas nous faire renier notre religion qui a marqué le progrès de l'humanité et qui a donné naissance à l'une des civilisations les plus brillantes que l'histoire puisse enregistrer. N'oublions pas que notre loi est tout pour nous et que nous n'échapperons aux tentacules de la pieuvre assimilatrice qu'en renforçant nos attaches avec Mahomet. Evoluons, évoluons certes mais dans le cadre de nos coutumes, nos traditions, nos moeurs, religieuses et nationales. Adaptons-nous aux necéssités du siècle, marchons résolument d'un pas sûr dans la voie du progrès, sous la bannière verte du prophète.[67]

In conclusion, the Eucharistic Congress justified the view of Islam as the preserver of the Tunisian "personnalité". Therefore, the defense of Islam became inseparable from the defense of the nation and religious feeling became indistinguishable from the nationalist struggle. It was in the name of Islam that the Destour Party called on the Bey who, since the suppression of the Caliphate by Mustafa Kemal in 1924 was the "spiritual" head of the country, to decline the honor of presiding at the Eucharistic Congress. Thus, in an echo of the Djellaz incident, we find French-educated Tunisians presenting a defense of Islam in the best French. In this manner, Islam served as a de-legitimizing factor vis-à-vis the Protectorate régime while it simultaneously served to legitimize the concept of a Tunisian state. The main text of the letter protests against the religious aspects of the Congress:

> L'esprit que le congrès manifeste outrageusement et qui nous est une cause de regret et de peine nous fait un devoir à nous qui sommes vos loyaux sujets, élévés dans le culte des sentiments islamiques qui sont vôtres, de venir respecteusement vous supplier de vous joindre à votre peuple pour désapprouver le caractère attentataire de ce congrès en déclinant la présidence d'honneur. Il est certain que l'esprit de croisade et l'évocation du programme de Saint-Louis ne sont guère des manifestations empreintes de sagesse et conformes aux lois de l'hospitalité surtout dans un pays qui a déjà plus de treize siècles de fidélité à la foi musulmane. Confiants dans les hautes vertus de Votre Altesse, dans son attachement aux principes de la religion musulmane, dans sa ferveur à défendre sa foi et les croyances de son peuple afin que l'Islam demeure en ce pays la religion intangible, nous avons le ferme espoir que notre prière sera exaucée.[68]

Interestingly enough, there is a year-long gap in the collection of articles written by Bourguiba between 23 February 1930, with an article criticizing the Socialists and published in <u>L'Etendard Tunisien</u>, and 23 February 1931, with an article attacking the Protectorat and published in <u>La Voix du Tunisien</u>. Consequently, we lack any published record of Bourguiba's participation in the Eucharistic Congress controversy.

Towards the end of that eventful year, a rumour spread that the fiftieth anniversary of the 1881 occupation of Tunisia would also be celebrated. As a follow-up of the celebration of the one-hundredth anniversary of the French occupation of Algeria, it seemed to indicate the will of the French authorities to reduce Tunisia, a Protectorate, to the same status as Algeria, an annexed colony. Also, to add injury to insult, the fabulous sum of 300 million francs was allotted, out of the Tunisian state budget, for the celebration at a time of impending economic crisis.[69] On this occasion, the religious symbolism of Christian France dominating Muslim Tunisia was muted and the two legitimizing themes of the Protectorate were: "la mission civilisatrice" and "la pérennité du Protectorat" based on the Bardo and the La Marsa treaties. Similar to the Eucharistic Congress, the celebration of the fiftieth anniversary of the 1881 occupation was viewed by Tunisian nationalist leaders as an affront to the Tunisian "personnalité". Thus, it was decided to defend the Tunisian "personnalité" by transforming La Voix du Tunisien from a weekly into a daily newspaper and Bourguiba was invited to participate.

Exasperated by the newly aggressive tone of the French-language nationalist press, the Protectorate authorites issued, on 12 May 1931, a court injunction against the editorial board of La Voix du Tunisien, of which Bourguiba was a member, accusing the group of "excitation à la haine entre les races". Their case began on 9 June 1931 and, in protest, the sûq shops were closed and a large crowd assembled in front of the court house. Confronted by this popular support, the Resident General then decided to "negotiate" with the newspaper team and the case was postponed to 24 July 1931 to be finally dismissed for lack of evidence.[70]

Rather characteristically, Bourguiba soon split off from the group. He explains himself by displacing events just slightly so that one event is used to explain the other when, in fact, their sequence precludes such a causal link. He claims that Khairallah had been in touch with the Resident General, without advising the newspaper editorial board, in an effort to negotiate the court order against them. In Bourguiba's own words,

> When we left the meeting with the Resident General in La Marsa, I asked Chedly Khairallah if he had met with the Resident General that morning. He answered in the affirmative, claiming that he received his instructions only from the Party. When I asked him about the Party, he identified it as the Destour Party. I retorted that we had grouped ourselves as a

> newspaper team because the people had delegated us to work in their name, not simply within the limits of a Party.[71]

According to Bourguiba, this altercation was the reason for his resignation. Surprisingly, Bourguiba does not admit allegiance to the Destour but considers that he was elected by the Tunisian élite and, consequently, was a representative of the people; "Muntakhab min qibal a'yân al-bilâd alladhîn yumaththilûn al-sha'b" (elected by the notables of the country who represent the people).[72]

But since he wrote at least two more articles in La Voix du Tunisien, "Autour de la crise agricole" (10 October 1931) and "A propos de l'insaisissable Mahjoub" (22 October 1931), it is obvious that he did not resign from the newspaper immediately after the meeting with the Resident General in July. On the contrary, on 2 July 1931, he published an article, "La Voix du Tunisien à la Maison de France", in which he defended the newspaper.[73] Although probably begun by the Resident General incident, it is much more likely that the split actually occurred following the 22 October 1931 article in which Bourguiba criticized Khairallah with biting sarcasm. And within a couple of weeks, in mid-November 1932, most of the editorial board withdrew from the newspaper and founded L'Action Tunisienne, probably with some Destour financial backing. Bourguiba himself states that the new newspaper "s'honore d'avoir vu le jour en plein accord avec le Destour."[74]

Again, there were difficulties keeping the editorial board together. But this time it was not Bourguiba who resigned; first went the Executive Director, Ali Bouhajeb, and then the Editorial Secretary, Bahri Guiga.[75] When M'Hamed Bourguiba published an interview with Mohamed Chenik, member of the Grand Conseil, Ali Bouhajeb wrote an article critical of such an action. Habib Bourguiba was able to intercept the article and to edit out several lines which were particularly harsh on his brother. He followed this with an acerbic article attacking Bouhajeb on a personal level whereupon Bouhajeb resigned along with Bahri Guiga.[75] Despite this setback, the Bourguiba team survived as Habib devoted the greater part of his time to the newspaper. In the meantime, the Executive Commission of the Destour established, in March 1933, a third newspaper, La Voix du Peuple, to transmit its own views. Bourguiba commented:

> Résultat: trois journaux tunisiens se disputant la confiance du peuple en se jetant à la face - ou dans les coins - les pires accusations, essayant de se discréditer les uns les autres pour le plus grand profit d'une prépondérance triomphante.[76]

To some extent, the evolution of these newspapers is an indication of how the relationship between the Destour and the Socialists evolved, and in some ways it parallels the development of relations among the various leftist parties in France itself. Sometime in the late 1920s the Reformists seem to have disbanded, or perhaps a split had occurred as a new generation of young Tunisians began to participate in political forums and held to a more radical line while others re-joined the S.F.I.O. Habib Bourguiba seems to have been in touch with the Socialists through his brother M'Hamed and with the Destour through his professional contacts with Salah Ferhat.[77]

His first article, "Le Voile", though a result of a presentation at the Socialist Club, reflected a break with the internationalist position of the Socialists and an insistence on the Destour thesis of the specificity and legitimacy of the Tunisian "personnalité". This was exactly the time when the S.F.I.O. in France entered into a period of crisis culminating with the split of the "Néo-Socialistes" in 1933.[78] The Neo-Socialist split in November 1933 grouped a strange mix; on one side, old-hand jaurésiens like Renaudel and Ramadier and on the other side real "N!eo-Socialistes" like Déat, Marquet and Montagnon. By November 1934 they had fused in the parliamentary group, the Union Socialiste Républicaine, which included republican socialists of 1905, some of the French socialists of 1919 and some of the members of the Parti Socialiste de France. At its maximum, the group represented some twenty thousand card-carrying members but, with the elections of 1936, they lost many seats and conceded failure. The Néo-Socialiste positions are hereby presented in some detail mainly because they seem rather similar to the positions later held by the Néo-Destour. The fundamental problematic posed by the Néo-Socialistes was not really new; namely, how to adapt socialism in the face of the continuing survival of capitalism? The historical context of the question was new as the economic crisis began to catch up with France. The Néo-Socialistes differed from main-stream French Socialists on six counts: 1)

Instead of viewing property as the source of social injustice, the Néo-Socialistes considered the "control" of the forces of productio as the main issue; 2) The Néo-Socialistes gave great importance to the state and went beyond the reformist position of seeking power through the democratic processes of elections to the revisionist position of seeking mastery over the state by mass action; 3) The Néo-Socialistes held that the socialist order need not be exclusively proletarian but should be an alliance between proletarians and the exploited middle classes; 4) Heirs to Jaurès, the Néo-Socialistes unhesitatingly defended "l'intégrité nationale" in evident contradiction with the principles of the International; 5) The Néo-Socialistes were ready to enter into coalition with a wider spectrum of parties tending towards the right than was the S.F.I.O.; 6) The Néo-Socialiste position may be summarized as more action-oriented; "Nous voulons agir, nous voulons transformer le monde dans lequel nous vivons", Déat was quoted to have said. Finally, Touchard denies the thesis that the Néo-Socialistes were attracted by Fascism.

THE ISSUE OF NATURALIZATION

The issue of naturalization came to the fore when, at the end of December 1931, the *muftî* of Bizerte gave a legal opinion in which he held that a French-naturalized Muslim was not to be buried in the Muslim cemetery.

> ...c'est la *fetwa* ou consultation juridique, donnée à cette occasion à la demande du *caid*, par le *mufti* de Bizerte, le Cheikh Idriss Ech-Chérif, qui est la plus lourde de conséquences. En effet, pour la première fois en Tunisie, une personnalité religieuse affirme publiquement que le naturalisé est un rénégat et qu'il ne peut par conséquent pas, en vertu des prescriptions islamiques, être inhumé dans un cimetière musulman.[79]

Pressured by the authorities, the *shaykh* limited his *fatwâ* to the specific case he had responded to on the grounds that the individual in question was a drinking man. Mass demonstrations took to the streets to protest the burial of any ex-Tunisian Muslim French national in Muslim cemeteries. This issue became so important in the nationalist press, since it symbolized the crux of the Tunisian nationalist movement, that it needs to be explained in some detail.

While the decrees of 1889, 1910 and 1921 and the law of 20 December 1923 had gradually eased the conditions for obtaining French citizenship, they were still restrictive enough that only 710 Muslim Tunisian families had availed themselves of the privilege; only those Tunisians who had volunteered to serve in the French army, who had obtained a secondary school degree, who had married a French national, or who had rendered signal services to France were given French nationality. In fact, it was the French left that agitated for further easing of these restrictions as a means of achieving its ideal of assimilation considered as a requirement for equality between French and Tunisians.[80]

Before 1927, nationality was part of civil law and Muslim Tunisians hesitated to become French nationals as this would mean that they might come under French law in terms of personal status; i.e. marriage, divorce and inheritance. When nationality became part of public law in 1927, the two aspects could not be separated; questions of personal status became questions of state. It is most probable that Jewish Tunisians acceded to French nationality (or citizenship) more readily because their co-religionists in France itself had solved the relationship of personal status to nationality, following emancipation. This issue of naturalization allowed a simplification of the dimensions involved as the Tunisian "personnalité" came to mean exclusively Muslim and, within Tunisia, Muslim meant Tunisian; leaving no room for a non-Muslim religious dimension to the Tunisian "personnalité". The religious authorities in Tunisia itself do not seem to have reacted to the 1923 law but the Arabic nationalist press did not hesitate to ostracize any Tunisian Muslim who dared apply for French nationality.[81] And yet the issue did not gain prominence except some ten years later. Some historians explain this time lag by considering religion as a "trigger" of more fundamental material causes. More than a "trigger", it was the language in which the general socio-economic crisis in Tunisia could be communicated. Once again, Islam was serving as a delegitimizing factor, calling into question the dominant order of the French Protectorate.

Natural calamities - lack of rain in 1930 and 1931, floods and locusts in 1932 - were multiplied by the lack of any defenses against the Great Depression as it hit France, to which the Tunisian economy was tied hand and foot. Tunisian exports to France were left unsold and prices simply collapsed. Although 1933 saw a great improvement in climatic conditions and agricultural production, the world economic crisis affected the external markets for Tunisian agricultural exports while the crises of 1930 and 1931 shrank the internal market. The mining sector was in even worse condition, since it was completely dependent on exports and there was no heavy industry in Tunisia. Finally, the under-valued franc meant that imported goods were that much cheaper than local production and flooded Tunisia. In sum, while the crisis hit everywhere, in dependent countries its effects were much worse as the terms of exchange deteriorated and the prices of primary products declined at a faster rate than the prices of manufactured products.[82]

While the French colonists in Tunisia suffered from this crisis, thousands of Tunisian small landholders saw their land seized as they failed to pay their taxes or their debts. This pauperization became generalized to the artisans and the merchants. Whether in the "traditional" or in the "modern" sector, workers saw their salaries decrease by an average of 20 to 40 percent when they were lucky enough to hold a job. The tragic situation in Tunisia is witnessed to by Camille Bégué when he describes his arrival in Tunis:

> Pour atteindre le fiacre le plus proche, il faut marcher sur les orteils des hommes et sur la tête des enfants qui s'aggrippent au voyageur, saisissent les bagages, hurlent: "Porter, missiou! Porter, missiou!" tandis que les femmes voilées de noir, nourrisson sur le bras, une grappe de bambins morveux accrochés aux jupes, psalmodient la prière de l'aumône. Une odeur âcre et fade de graisse végétale rance dilate les narines et gonfle l'estomac jusqu'à la nausée. Ils sont là par centaines et par centaines, loqueteux, les visages maculés de crasses bariolés, les mains noires s'efforçant d'arracher au navire les deux sous ou la pincée de miettes qui tromperont leur appétit. Ceux qui débarquent pour la première fois à Tunis se laissent attendrir, distribuent quelque monnaie ou quelque relief de repas, vivement reprimandés par les habitués. Quand on connait le pays, comme le connait le facteur

> corse ou un cocher maltais, on sait qu'il faut chasser cette racaille à coup de pied dans l'arrière-train. Des voleurs, des chenapans, des "bon à riens", vous dis-je, tout juste capables d'exploiter le "roumi" qu'ils détestent en attendant de le dévorer. Et qui ne comprennent que la chanson de la trique. Un geste de bonté ils le taxeront de faiblesse et en profiteront aussitôt pour vous manger la soupe sur la tête.[83]

The economic crisis in Tunisia was even further exacerbated by the fact that it had been preceded by a further expansion of colonization as mechanization permitted the exploitation of less favorable lands. Between 1920 and 1930, 3,600 tractors and 1,000 mechanical harvesters were imported so that the European sector of agriculture in Tunisia became one of the most modern in the world.[84] As usual, the Tunisian peasants were simply expelled from the land but in even greater numbers since mechanization reduced the man-power needs of the colonists. This new wave of dispossessed peasants further swelled the ranks of the displaced unemployed. At the same time, Tunisia experienced a demographic boom as the population increased from 1.8 million in 1921 to 2.3 million in 1931. These displaced peasants migrated to the towns to multiply the numbers of the unemployed and the underemployed, the lumpen-proletariat; "...les paysans sans terre étaient...une force sociale passive, mais une force sociale qui a rendu la colonisation totalement incapable de résoudre les problèmes socio-économiques nés de son implantation dans les campagnes.[85] It is this critical demographic mass that triggered the radicalization of the Destour and the split of the Néo-Destour.

But the peasants were not alone to suffer; further up the social scale, a contradiction between the interests of French civil servants and the socialist tenets they had preached became acute. As the economic crisis created an atmosphere of insecurity, French civil servants became all the more reluctant to envisage the possiblity of relinquishing their positions in favor of their Tunisian counterparts. In 1932, French employees outnumbered Tunisians 2 to 1 in the administration which totalled some 11,000. This works out to one French administrator per 2,500 Tunisians, making Tunisia one of the most heavily administered countries. To add insult to injury, French employees were paid one-third more than their Tunisian colleagues doing the same kind of work. For the year 1932, French functionaries cost over half the Tunisian state budget; some 357 million francs out of 602 million.[86] Thus, the economic crisis of the early 1930s reduced the contradictions between the two main factions of French colonists, the settlers and the civil servants. As a consequence, there was a marked reduction in Socialist support of the Tunisian nationalist cause and Bourguiba noted in his article published on 15 April 1933, "Grattez le Français le plus intelligent, le plus libéral, le plus 'à gauche', le prépondérant apparaît."[87] The crisis also reduced the acuity of contradictions among the "indigènes" and led to an alliance between dispossessed peasants and underemployed professionals. Finally, the economic crisis sharpened the antagonism between French and Tunisians.

Bourguiba wrote a series of articles in L'Action Tunisienne, "Le Sahel à l'Agonie", in which he described the difficulties experienced by his own home region. The bitterness of new poverty was made worse by the awareness of the lack of any measures taken to help the "indigènes". He wrote:

> Vous avez jugé que le fellah est une quantité négligeable par rapport au colon; qu'il doit être encore sacrifié parce que vous n'avez rien à craindre de son côté: erreur, encore erreur! C'est avec de pareils calculs qu'on prépare dans l'ombre les grands bouleversements pour le jour où le fellah aura perdu tout espoir dans la sincérité de la France. Vous avez administré la preuve à ce fellah, par votre discrimination scandaleuse, que vous gouvernez le pays en étranger, pour le compte exclusif de vos compatriotes, en vertu du droit de conquête, de la loi du plus fort.
> C'est bien.
> Le fellah s'en souviendra!
> Que vous le vouliez ou non, Monsieur le Ministre, c'est bien le commencement de la fin!.[88]

Having obtained his degree in Public Finance, Bourguiba was particularly interested in the economic dimension of the problems experienced by Tunisia. His essays reflect the influence Socialist doctrine had had on him and, at some points, he attacked the "idealist" school in the name of the "scientific socialism" he had learned in France. He wrote:

> "Vous substituez, a écrit Marx en 1850 pour motiver sa démission de membre du Comité Central de la Ligue Communiste, vous substituer à l'évolution révolutionnaire la phrase révolutionnaire." (Jaurès, Etudes socialistes, p. 36).

and, from the same article,

> Etre socialiste, enfin, c'est se pénétrer de cette autre vérité non moins fondamentale entrevue, il y a plus d'un demi-siècle par Marx lui-même, que le capitalisme porte en lui son propre germe de mort: anti-patriotisme dans la Métropole, nationalisme dans les colonies, ce sont les sous-produits inévitables de la grande machine capitaliste qui finiront tôt ou tard par en encrasser les rouages, par en détraquer le mécanisme.[89]

His interest in the economic effects of the colonial relationship is demonstrated by the impressive number of articles he wrote on the subject; actually, the majority of his articles in the collection, Habib Bourguiba: Articles de Presse (Volume I of Histoire du Mouvement National Tunisien), treat this subject. Bourguiba's views of the economic consequences of colonialism may be considered as an early analysis of the unequal exchange forced upon the weaker partner. In two particularly penetrating articles, Bourguiba demonstrated that the budget, elaborated by the French authorities and rubber-stamped by the Tunisian Grand Conseil, was not a neutral financial necessity but a political instrument which favored the colonists and pauperized the Tunisians; in other words, it served as the mechanism for the transfer of wealth from Tunisian into French hands.

> La domination coloniale, dans ce contexte, était essentiellement conçue comme une vaste entreprise d'exploitation, se traduisant par la pauperisation des autochtones et le transfert des richesses entre les mains des Français.[90]

In these articles, Bourguiba demonstrated his Voltairian style, easy and clear, which passes from serious journalism to structured analysis without break and with touches of sarcastic humor here and there. Dimassi notes that these articles "mettaient Bourguiba dans la place qui lui convenait réellement: dans l'opposition, loin des compromis si compromettants du pouvoir qui use si vite."[31]

Aside from the economics of the situation, Bourguiba interested himself also in the ideological and political implications of the issue of naturalization. According to him, the Protectorate authorities had succeeded in obtaining a fatwâ (responsa) stating that a Muslim could become a French national without losing his "religion" but no other independent source confirms this. According to a study specifically devoted to this issue, the fatwâ in question was in response to the question: Is the repentance of a Muslim, who naturalizes himself as a citizen of a country not conforming to Islamic law, acceptable?[32] The answer, given in the affirmative, only served to confirm that naturalized Muslims were in fact renegades since they would need to repent before they would be buried in Muslim cemeteries. The logic had not escaped Bourguiba, who wrote:

> ...un fait nouveau s'est produit depuis les incidents de Bizerte, qui n'a pas manqué d'ancrer dans les esprits la conviction que les naturalisés ne sauraient être considérés comme des Musulmans tout à fait orthodoxes. On le trouve dans la question même posée aux ulémas. C'est l'obligation pour le naturalisé qui désire rentrer dans le giron de notre religion, de se présenter devant le Cadhi, de réciter la "Chahadah" et de renier toute autre religion que celle de Mahomet. N'est-ce pas là une façon de renouveler sa foi musulmane, et ne peut-on pas en déduire qu'avant cette formalité, le naturalisé n'était pas tout à fait dans la pure orthodoxie?[33]

The nationalists quickly realized the resentment of the Tunisians when on 14 April 1933 there was a spontaneous mass demonstration as the people refused to pray behind those imâms who had been passive towards the issue of naturalization. For the next two months, mass demonstrations took place in Tunis to prevent the burial of a French naturalized Tunisian which ended with several wounded and numerous arrests. Lifted on this human wave, Habib Bourguiba, as chief editor of L'Action Tunisienne, was invited to meet the Bey in order "to express the people's discontent." Protest spread to the other towns as the crowds flocked to the mosques to recite the latîf, a prayer for times of calamity. Islam served not only to express the discontent of the Tunisian masses but also to transmit their protest outside Tunisia; particularly to Egypt where several newspapers accused France of proposing to de-Islamize, de-Arabize and disunite the Maghrib.[94] Bourguiba wrote several articles on this occasion, of which the following quotation is illustrative of his position:

> Il [le peuple] en avait plein le coeur et cherchait une occasion de le dire au Gouvernment, de lui signifier qu'il en avait assez, qu'il n'est plus dupe de ses illusions et qu'il se dresserait de toutes ses forces contre toute atteinte à son existence et à sa personnalité.[95]

Encouraged by the audacity of the masses, the Destour Party held a Congress on 12-13 May 1933 during which the Executive Commission was enlarged to include the radical team of L'Action Tunisienne; that is to say, Mahmoud Materi, M'Hamed and Habib Bourguiba as well as Ali Bouhajeb and Bahri Guiga.

> Depuis quelque temps, et à la suite du vaste mouvement que nous avons créé par notre action au sein de la population tunisienne, l'union de tous les militants, de toutes les énergies, de toutes les forces de résistence nationale était à l'ordre du jour.... Le grand Parti Libéral Constitutionnel, avec son organisation formidable, était la formation tout indiquée qui pouvait unir et unifier toutes les tendances du nationalisme tunisien, à condition qu'il abandonne ses méthodes désuètes et son ancien programme largement dépassé par les évènements et ne répondant plus aux aspirations profondes du peuple.... L'indépendance de la Tunisie, complétée par un traité d'amitié et d'union avec la grande République Française, garantissant à la France ses intérêts légitimes et les intérêts de toute la colonie étrangère, tel sera l'idéal du mouvement nationaliste tunisien, mouvement destiné surtout à faire de la protection française une entente spontanée entre deux peuples libres, sans aucune idée de prépondérance ou de domination, laquelle n'a plus sa raison d'être en présence de la

> solidarité profonde des intérêts vitaux des deux peuples. Au sein d'une Commission Exécutive élargie, Bouhajeb, Guiga et les trois directeurs de l'"Action Tunisienne" ont été reçus à bras ouverts après avoir prêté serment de fidélité au Parti et à la Nation.[96]

This is the first indication that Bourguiba had become officially affiliated with the Destour Party.

A new charter of internal regulations was adopted representing a return to the first ideas of the post First World War position. Independence or external sovereignty was given greater priority than internal sovereignty and the first was considered as the means for achieving the second.

> ...le but qu'il assigne à son action politique, est d'amener la libération du peuple tunisien et de doter le pays d'un statut intangible et stable sous la forme d'une Constitution qui sauvegarde la personnalité tunisienne et consacre la souveraineté du peuple.[97]

Actually, the congress and the new organization and program were undertaken as an expression of defiance in the face of the "decréts super-scélérats" signed 6 May 1933 which limited Tunisian human rights of expression and of assembly. These decrees led to the suspension of the newspaper, <u>L'Action Tunisienne</u> on 27 May 1933, the dissolution of the Destour Party on 31 May 1933, and the appointment of a new Resident General, Peyrouton, known for his toughness. Nonetheless, symbolic gains had been made as the authorities admitted that separate space should be set aside for naturalized Muslim French nationals. Despite this official concession, the tense situation exploded when, on 8 August 1933, a naturalized boy died in Monastir and the local French representative attempted to force his burial in the Muslim cemetery. Public outcry was such that the police had to intervene and shoot into the crowds with one dead and several wounded.

Whereupon a delegation of some seventy persons led by al-Shâdhilî Qallâlah came to Tunis to meet with Bourguiba, who had just used the occasion of his son's circumscision in Monastir to form a party cell. Having defended Chenik only a few months earlier, and with his brother Ahmed married into the Beylical family, Bourguiba had sufficient contacts to take it upon himself to arrange for the delegation to meet the Bey and present their complaint. When he was blamed by the Executive Commission of the Destour Party for the action, taken without consultation with the Commission, Bourguiba defended himself on the grounds that he had acted as a Monastiri lawyer and not as a Party member. Nonetheless, he tendered his resignation on 9 September 1933.[98]

His resignation followed shortly after Peyrouton's arrival in Tunis. Trying to feel the pulse of the nationalist movement, Peyrouton had asked to meet with the Executive Commission of the Destour Party. At the meeting, Peyrouton clearly told the Executive Commission that France had the power and the will to put a stop to any "new disturbances". According to Bourguiba, the Executive Commission had made a vow of secrecy about the meeting but Bahri Guiga informed him of what had transpired and Guiga was asked to resign. Whereupon Tahar Sfar, Mahmoud Materi and M'Hamed Bourguiba also resigned. Although none of the sources indicates what exactly was supposed to be the secret, it is probable that the Commission made the secret tactical decision to keep a low profile as it was calculated that the new Resident General represented too high a risk. It is possible that the younger team of Materi, Sfar, Guiga and the two Bourguibas did not agree, had calculated differently and believed that a stronger demonstration of nationalist protest would yield results justifying the risks.

> Quoi qu'il en soit, malgré l'appui que rencontrent les dirigeants nationalistes auprès des masses tunisiennes et de l'opinion démocratique française, les décrets "super-scélérats" posent le parti destourien devant le dilemme suivant: S'agit-il de braver les autorités du Protectorat et de continuer, en dépit de cette nouvelle législation et des risques de déportation qui en découlent, à ameuter les masses populaires contre le système colonial ou de temporiser en "attendant des jours meilleurs"? Il y donc là deux tactiques contradictoires: profiter de l'appui et de la mobilisation des masses populaires pour aller de l'avant ou observer une pause pour éviter une répression qui risque d'être fatale au parti destourien et à ses dirigeants?[99]

Thus, on the eve of the "première épreuve de force", the Destour Party leadership was of two minds. On the one hand, the members of the original Executive Commission tended towards caution and "se défient généralement des mouvements de masses populaires de peur d'en être débordés et même compromis". On the other hand, the new team recruited during the May 1933 Congress was ready to ride the tidal wave of the masses.[100]

The difference between the radical periods of 1919-1926 and of 1933-38 were double, on the level of the leadership and on the level of the membership. In the first period the leadership had broadened somewhat to represent a relatively wider alliance of classes. During the second period this tendency was emphasized as the young French-educated professionals of provincial origin held a greater share within the alliance. In the first period the membership was recruited along the "traditional" network of social relations of landlords/tenants and merchants/artisans between the capital and the small towns. During the second period the economic crisis and the pauperization of the peasants had combined to create an unemployed pool of sub- or lumpen-proletarians in the cities who had nothing to lose and were ever ready to swell the numbers of any mass demonstrations. The "official" school of the Tunisian nationalist movement protrays the Destour, in contrast to the Néo-Destour, as the party of the reactionary land-holding Zaytûnah-educated bourgeoisie of Arab-Islamic culture. But the newer, more critical school attempts to correct this image by demonstrating that, on the one hand, the Destour leadership included many French-educated professionals and, on the other hand, those of Arab-Islamic culture represented the modernist tendency interested in reconciling Islam to modern conditions. As indicated before, the commonly-held opinion that the "Old" Destour was limited to an intellectual élite of the bourgeoisie of Tunis, the capital, is more true of the Reformists than of the Destour, which had succeeded in establishing almost a hundred cells throughout the country. But to claim that both the "Old" and the "New" Destours were mass parties is also an exaggeration as the critical element of the "lumpen-proletariat" was not included within the "Old" Destour alliance of class-fractions.

Also in an attempt to distinguish the Néo-Destour from the Archéo-Destour, the "official" school portrays the second as an elitist party while the Néo-Destour is characterized as a party of the masses. Again this image needs to be nuanced; it is obvious from the struggle between the two to take over the various cells that the situation was not as clear-cut. In fact, by 1934, the Old Destour had established some 70 to 130 cells throughout Tunisia and had a membership estimated between 30,000 and 100,000, a respectable order of numbers for the population at the time.[101] Hermassi distinguishes several types of nationalist movements in the Maghrib: (1) the "nationalitarian- scripturalist" stream which insists on the "reaffirmation of national, cultural and religious integrity"; (2) the "liberal modernization" stream which held Europe as their model of development and which divided into two types - the liberal constitutionalists and the populists; and (3) the "mobilization élite" which was basically a post-independence alliance between the radical intelligentsia and the workers. Hermassi places Bourguiba and the Néo-Destour within the "populist liberal modernizers" which is basically correct with the amendment that the "populist" aspect led to the insistence on the "reaffirmation of national, cultural and religious integrity".[102] Thus, the difference between the two Destour Parties lay more in the tactics chosen for action rather than in ideological choices or sociological background of the leadership. Thus, the main distinguishing mark between the Archéo-Destour and the Néo-Destour was the latter's willingness, not only to brandish, but actually to use, the weight of the masses.

> Il est même probable que l'aile radicale du mouvement national tunisien pratique alors une politique "d'entrisme" dans tous les rouages du Destour, pour imprimer à ce parti ses propres méthodes d'action. Il s'agit, plus précisément, d'aller chercher les masses là où elles se trouvent et d'utiliser les structures du Destour pour les dégager de l'emprise des vieux dirigeants et combattre ses derniers sur leur propre terrain.[103]

And here is a clue to the role of Islam in the history of the Tunisian nationalist movement. Islam incorporated that system of concepts and symbols with which the common man identified and whose language he understood. Islam was communication between this "new" leadership and the "new" masses. A particularly harsh judgement on such language is that of L.C. Brown who holds that,

> ...the literature of the traditional society was more evocative than rational. It was a language of symbol, syllogism and simile...utterly foreign to Cartesian doubt, Pascalian introspection, Romantic self-expression or Bergsonian evolutionism.... As a corollary of this mentality and this literary style public utterances and writings were more nearly a performance than a serious debate of principles.[104]

But Bourguiba, artisan of the possible, stated:

> Le rôle de l'élite n'est donc pas de forcer son allure au risque de se détacher complètement de la masse qu'elle a la charge de guider. Bien des fois, si cette élite veut faire oeuvre utile et durable - et non pas seulement du tapage et de la réclame dans l'unique intention de paraître à la page - bien des fois dis-je, elle se trouve de rebrousser chemin pour reprendre contact avec cette masse, non pas pour la flatter ou la laisser croupir dans la servitude...mais pour la guider plus sûrement et avec plus de chance de succès dans la voie du progrès.[105]

THE NEO-DESTOUR

Effectively, Sfar and Bourguiba addressed themselves to the Ksar Hellal Destour cell and, not without difficulty, were able to swing it to their view of the situation. Bourguiba presents the decision to address themselves to the Ksar Hellal cell as a spontaneous, implusive gesture that he and Sfar agreed upon in the car on their way from Monastir where Habib's sister lived, to Mahdiya where Sfar had invited Bourguiba to break the fast of Ramaḍân. Perhaps the spontaneity of the gesture is not as incredible as it might seem with hindsight. Schooled in the realism and moderation typical of Tunisian politics, Bourguiba was the man of tactical adjustments and manoeuvres; "C'est au contact des hommes, de la lutte de tous les jours, qu'il trouvera les ressorts de son action."[106] In sum, Bourguiba followed the typical Tunisian political realism; he distinguished between strategy and tactics, between the final objective - never lost sight of - and temporary measures, the famous "étapes". Yet that distinction was so subtle and quick that one must give credit to Bourguiba's political intuition.

> Etudier le réel, en tirer une orientation provisoire, la soumettre à l'expérience, rectifier le tir quand et aussi souvent qu'il faudra, puis, quand on aura débusqué la vérité, formuler la loi, telle est la démarche de l'homme d'état.... Sur le but, il n'a jamais varié: la Tunisie serait indépendante avec, sans, ou, au besoin, contre la France.[107]

But why the Ksar Hellal cell and not the Mahdiya or the Monastir cells? Perhaps Ksar Hellal itself symbolized the bridge that brought together the political and the labor movements in the Tunisian struggle for independence. Ksar Hellal was an old artisanal center of the textile industry.[108] The economic crisis of the early 1930s had begun to pauperize the artisanal classes as well. Did Ksar Hellal presage the future relations between the Union Générale des Travailleurs Tunisiens and the Néo-Destour?

Some 200 to 300 people were assembled when the decision was taken to call the extraordinary Party congress in Ksar Hellal itself in order for the general membership to attempt to reconcile the two views. As might have been expected, the Destour Executive Commission refused to call for an extraordinary congress, citing the Quranic verse (29:6):

> O ye who believe! If a wicked person comes
> To you with any news, Ascertain the truth, lest
> Ye harm people unwittingly, and afterwards
> become
> Full of repentance for what you have done.[109]

The insistence on action at this critical juncture is sharply brought out by the dissident group which then cited the Quranic verse (9:105):

> And say: "Work (righteousness):
> Soon will God observe your work,
> And His Apostle and the Believers:
> Soon Ye will be brought back
> To the Knower of what is
> Hidden and what is open:

Then will He show you
The truth of all that ye did.

The group did not lack Quranic verses about "work" or action (ʿamal); several others could have served just as well since the Qurʾân is full of references to action. The insistence on action is not strange in Islamic doctrine as the many theological controversies on the relative value of faith and action witness to.

The success of the congress, with members of some 60 cells,[110] proved to Bourguiba the value of what he terms "contact direct" as a means, different from the hierarchical organization of the Party, to mobilize the masses.

> When I realized that I possessed a talent for oratory, I felt that it was a turning-point in my life. I had written in the newspaper and here I discovered that I had the ability to communicate directly with the people and that I could deeply affect them and open their eyes.[111]

Bourguiba's early interest in the theatre must have given him the training necessary to become an effective speaker.

> Or, Bourguiba sut trop bien mener cette très difficile tactique du contact direct. Car ce comédien hors pair (le théâtre avait fini par servir à quelque chose) sut toujours bien parler. Sa voix claire, bien timbrée, aux intonations variées, savait être douce et insinuante envers les auditeurs qu'elle voulait - avec quelle énergie - convaincre. D'une douceur infinie, elle était, du reste, toujours harmonieusement accompagnée par de nombreux mouvements de bras et de mains explicatifs, parfois lents, parfois rapides, souvent spontanés, toujours étudiés. Le tout donnant à la personne - qui s'animait d'ailleurs vite en parlant - un charme absolument particulier et une sincérité tout à fait captivante.[112]

The main thrust of Bourguiba's speech at the Ksar Hellal Congress was that the new team had greater credibility among the French authorities. He also made the point that it was precisely the ability of the new team to have the ear of the government in France that led the Executive

Commission of the Destour Party to fear them.

> Ainsi donc, le Résident Général ne trouve comme interlocuteur que M. Ahmed Essafi et ses amis, pendant que les chefs du mouvement qui étaient parvenus à faire entendre leur voix aux Conseils du Gouvernement Français étaient écartés et empêchés de prendre une part, quelque minime qu'elle fut, aux pourparlers.[113]

Finally, he asked for the mandate to pursue their principal objective: "la libération de notre Patrie."

At the end of the day, a resolution was passed dissolving the Executive Commission. Another resolution passed a new charter of internal by-laws which called for a "Bureau Politique" - composed of President (Mahmoud Materi), Secretary-General (Habib Bourguiba), Assistant Secretary-General (Tahar Sfar), Treasurer (M'Hamed Bourguiba) and Assistant Treasurer (Bahri Guiga). A "National Council" was also instituted, composed of the Bureau Politique and thirty members elected from the Party cells. Finally, a Party Congress was to be held annually in order to elect a new Bureau Politique and National Council and to oversee the finances and activities of the Party.

The "new" Destour thought to have solved the problem of political survival by the new organizational plan which was adopted. This new plan called for a double-tiered leadership; the Bureau Politique, which was the effective Executive Commission, and the National Council, which stood ready to replace the Political Bureau with a new team if the Bureau Politique became incapacitated for one reason or another. The support that Bourguiba had lent to M'Hamed Chenik and which had cost him the friendship of Ali Bouhajeb paid off at this time, as Chenik was able to provide financial backing, both directly and through the Agricultural Cooperative, which rallied many small land-owners to the Néo-Destour.[114]

As this historical overview of the split shows, the differences between the "Archéo-" and the "Néo-" Destours was not on the ideological level nor was it between "traditionalists", on the one hand, and "modernists", on the other, since the leaders of the two Destours were basically of the same background. Both were within the modernist stream, heir to the pre-Protectorate reformist tendency of Shaykh Qabâdû and Khayr al-Dîn, of Béchir Sfar, Ali Bash Hanba and

Abdelaziz Thaalbi. Sociologically, the new element to enter into the shifting alliance of class fractions was the lumpen-proletariat; ideologically, the new element was the emphasis on action and on Islam, as the means of communication, necessary for mobilizing mass action. The fundamental difference between the "New" and the "Old" Destour was a matter of tactics, as at a particular moment in history the first called for action while the second bet on quiescence for the sake of survival.

At this critical juncture in the history of the Tunisian nationalist movement, a simple gesture brought out the crucial importance of Islam. The new team was requested to be sworn in on the Qur'ân and it was only after this symbolic gesture that they were accepted as legitimate leaders.[115] Thus began a new era in Tunisian history when the Destour Party was born a second time.

Chapter IV

"L'INTERLOCUTEUR VALABLE" (1934-1955)

LANGUAGE AND RELIGION

During the period of some twenty years between the Ksar Hellal Congress in 1934 and the declaration of autonomy in 1955, Bourguiba spent himself in the struggle for the liberation of Tunisia.

> ...il va s'employer, à présent, à imposer le Néo-Destour, aux vues de la Puissance protectrice, comme l'unique interlocuteur valable, le représentant authentique de la Tunisie tunisienne.[1]

The Ksar Hellal Congress of 1934 did not mark a turning-point in the history of the Tunisian nationalist movement either in terms of program or in terms of the social background of the leadership. The Néo-Destour adopted as its own the Destour program of March 1933. Moreover, the new leadership represented simply a younger generation of the same social alliance of "Young Tunisians" (i.e. mostly French-educated professionals) and the "traditional" bourgeoisie of landowners, artisans and merchants, with perhaps a higher percentage of "âfâqîs" or provincials.[2] Nonetheless, the Ksar Hellal Congress constituted an important milestone marking theentrance of the masses into action and, consequently, the adoption of new tactics for action and the institution of new structures within the Party.

Fundamental lessons had been learned from the 1910-1912 period characterized by the Djellaz riots and from the 1930-1933 anti-naturalization movement. The first lesson was that when the masses took to the streets the Protectorate authorities turned to dialogue with the nationalist leaders. This lesson constituted the essential difference between the Archéo- and the Néo-Destour Parties. The Old Destour did not anticipate the spontaneous action of the masses and only reluctantly attempted to justify or defend mass actions. In contrast, the New Destour was willing not only to use but to encourage and even initiate mass actions. In his testimony against the Néo-Destour following the 9 April 1938 riots, Thaalbi clearly pin-pointed this difference.

> Notre but final est bien celui exposé dans la Charte de 1933, mais nous différons du Néo-Destour dans la façon d'envisager les moyens d'action: Nous faisons appel à la persuasion et à la patience alors que le Néo-Destour fait appel à la violence. Notre travail s'envisage par une action auprès des pouvoirs publics français mais en laissant le peuple de côté et en ne lui faisant pas de promesses.[3]

In contrast, Bourguiba wrote:

> Aucun respect n'est accordé au droit dans la civilisation occidentale moderne, s'il ne s'appuie pas sur une force qui s'impose. Il nous apparaît comme certain que la plus grande force de cohésion du peuple est la solidarité de ses membres. C'est une force morale devant laquelle s'incline tôt ou tard la force matérielle et brutale, à condition de faire preuve de patience, de ténacité et d'esprit de sacrifice.[4]

The idea was to use the power of the masses to bring about dialogue. The realistic assessment of relations between Tunisia and France showed that the balance of power was overwhelmingly in the favour of France. It was obvious that Tunisia would lose any test of strength or "épreuve de force". Consequently, force was to be used not as a direct means to achieve independence but as the means of convincing France of the necessity to negotiate, to dialogue. This interplay of violence and dialogue was the original element in the tactics of the Néo-Destour. Bourguiba, as the leader of the Néo-Destour, became identified with "étapisme" or the politics of stages but, more often than not, his readiness to use violence was ultimately forgotten.

In fact, his final success lay in this readiness to use force whenever "compromise" (compromis) tended towards "compromise" (compromission).

> Il y a compromis et compromission. Le compromis révolutionnaire est acte de courage, de lucidité, pour autant qu'il constitue une étape qui ouvre le chemin et ménage les chances de l'étape suivante. La compromission est abdication, lâcheté, renoncement. Je suis pour le compromis qui permet de progresser vers l'objectif et qui, du reste, n'exclut pas l'épreuve de force, chaque fois qu'elle est inévitable, chaque fois qu'elle nous a paru nécessaire pour déblayer la voie.[5]

In view of these tactics, the period between 1934 and 1955 may be broken down into two main phases. The first phase was between 1934 and 1945 when the Néo-Destour faced a double task: to convince France of the necessity of dialogue and to build the credibility of the Néo-Destour as "interlocuteur valable" by demonstrating that it alone represented and, therefore, controlled the masses or in Bourguiba's terminology "the people". Following the Second World War, this double task was complicated by the appearance of new actors so that neither France nor the Néo-Destour had the monopoly of the scene. It is out of this complicated picture that the compromise of internal autonomy was worked out between Bourguiba and France.

The second lesson was that the masses in Tunisia coalesced and moved only when issues were presented in terms of Islam. Islam seemed to serve as the source of cultural images and modes required to achieve a mass recognition of the injustices inherent in the colonialist situation.

> Il lui était impossible de communiquer son programme, fondé sur les concepts de souveraineté populaire, de neutralité confessionnelle et de séparation des pouvoirs aux masses hors d'état de le penser, sans l'adapter à leur mentalité religieuse et à leurs instincts.[6]

Among the several examples of the evocation of Islam and Islamic themes are the following quotations:

-Au nom de Dieu, le Clément et le Miséricordieux, la guerre sainte a été imposée aux musulmans.

-Au nom de Dieu, le Clément, le Miséricordieux. Dis: faites, Allah verra votre action de même que son apôtre et les croyants.

-Ne croyez pas que Dieu ignore les agissements des oppresseurs.

-Si vous servez la cause de Dieu, Il vous fera triompher et raffermir vos pas.

-Dieu qu'il soit exalté, a dit: "Luttez pour la cause de Dieu, en vous sacrifiant corps et biens. Cela est mieux pour vous si vous êtes sages.

-...la victoire sera en définitive à nous, si nous demeurons convaincus que Dieu est avec nous, car Dieu est du côté de ceux qui tiennent bon.[7]

A link was established between Islam and independence; "l'idéal d'un peuple asservi par la force brutale...persécuté dans ses droits, dans sa personnalité et dans sa religion, est l'indépendance."[8] Moreover, the Néo-Destour leaders did not hesitate to use the mosques as their means for spreading their ideas under the guise of lessons in Islamic history.[9]

Thus, we see Islam acting on two levels: as the cultural mode used to mobilize the people for mass action and, consequently, as a basic ingredient in the definition of the Tunisian "personnalité". Nationalism acted in conjunction with Islam in Tunisia to such an extent that a contemporary commentator noted: "Pour mieux entretenir la germe politique, il est fait appel au ferment mystique."[10]

THE FIRST TEST OF STRENGTH

As Secretary General of the Néo-Destour, it fell to the lot of Bourguiba to devote himself full time to the task of initiating and harnessing the masses to the actions proposed by the Néo-Destour. He travelled from one end of the country to the other, seeking "direct contact" with the people as a means for mass mobilization.

"L'Interlocuteur Valable" (1934-1955)

In his "direct contact" with the people, Bourguiba hit upon an effective language. Putting aside the literary Arabic used by the Old Destour leaders, Bourguiba addressed himself to the people in the Tunisian variant.

> Dès lors, le véhicule magique à communiquer le programme du Néo-Destour - fondé sur des concepts aussi abstraits que la souveraineté populaire ou la séparation des pouvoirs - était opportunément inventé.[11]

Perhaps the political implications of such a choice were not immediately apparent as a reinforcement of the Tunisian specificity whereas the use of the more universal literary Arabic highlighted Tunisia's links with her Arab neighbours. But then the works of William Marçais on the colloquial Arabic in Algeria (Tlemcen) and in Tunisia (Takrouna) were most probably known to the Néo-Destour leaders, particularly the book he had prepared with the help of Abderrahman Guiga, Textes arabes de Takrouna, published in 1925.[12] These works served to make the use of the colloquial variant of Arabic respectable and valorized the provincial culture it vehicled. It is also probable that the "Franco-Arab" education of many of the Néo-Destour leadership, meant to prepare them for the translation of texts, did not prepare them to use literary Arabic orally. This new valorization of the colloquial Arabic variant coincided with their own capacities and served them in their direct contact with the people.

We can imagine Bourguiba walking up to the stage feeling weak in the knees as he struggles to follow up his companions' speeches. Suddenly he lets go his stilted, hesitating literary Arabic and with his arms outstretched reaches out in the language he learned at his mother's knees. The wonder of the communion he establishes is still apparent as he reminisces:

> J'ai souvent réfléchi sur les moyens de sceller l'union du Peuple pour m'en servir comme force de frappe contre la domination coloniale.... La réunion de Ksar Hellal me fit découvrir un autre moyen d'action sur les foules, bien plus efficace, encore qu'il fût harassant. Il s'agit du contact direct avec les masses populaires. L'expérience m'a montré qu'en haranguant les foules, en leur expliquant les évènements et les problèmes, j'agissais

> profondément sur leur esprit et je retournais à ma faveur les situations les plus compromises. Depuis cette date, le contact direct est devenu le crédo de mon action.[13]

It is during this period that Bourguiba achieved recognition as the leader of the Néo-Destour when he held the firmest, compared to the other members of the Bureau Politique.[14] Bourguiba became known as "al-mujâhid al-akbar" (Supreme Combattant). This famous epithet is itself a typical example of how Bourguiba sought inspiration from the two cultures he had imbibed, the Arabic and the French. The Arabic, "al-mujâhid al-akbar", evoked the Arab-Islamic tradition of jihâd or holy war. The French version, "Combattant Suprême", connoted "le bon combat", a cliché found mostly in revolutionary literatures.[15] The richness of these terms was sometimes missed by unaware translators who rendered Bourguiba's epithet differently on various occasions: "Chef Suprême" or "le Grand Lutteur". In fact, the inability of French administrators to fathom the Arabic key terms that opened the flood gates of the masses was felt by that poor police inspector who noted that French-language newspapers were easier to control because French was a less subtle and flexible language than Arabic.[16]

It had been foreseen that the price of a response from the Protectorate authorities was to be prepaid by one or several waves of repression. Consequently, it had been decided to institute a relay of Party leaders by establishing a new Party structure. Three bodies had been instituted: the Congress, composed of all the cell leaders, which was to meet annually; a Bureau Politique which was more or less equivalent to the static Executive Commission of the Old Destour; and, the key innovation, a National Council which was to activate new Bureaux Politiques, previously chosen, whenever the need arose. These new institutions were to provide the flexibility necessary for the Party to survive; between September 1934, when members of the first Bureau Politique were arrested, and May 1936, when they were released, several Bureaux Politiques (ţaqms) had been arrested or incapacitated in one way or another.

Since the beginning of the Protectorate in 1881, the French authorities had seen every protest movement stop whenever its leaders were arrested; at least in the regions under civil administration. In

1885, the protest against the urban taxes was decapitated by the repressive measures of Paul Cambon. In 1912, the exile of the Young Tunisians arrested the nationalist movement. In 1923, the selectively repressive measures led the Destour to compose itself. In 1925, the young labor movement was strangled. The new phenomenon in 1934 was that the arrest of the Néo-Destour Bureau Politique did not stop the waves of violent mass protest. The Second Bureau Politique, headed by Tahar Sfar and Bahri Guiga, attempted to negotiate the release of the first Bureau Politique with Peyrouton, the Resident General, but its members too were arrested on 3 January 1935. A third Bureau Politique, led by Chedly Khairallah, undertook the task but failed to budge Peyrouton. Whereupon Khairallah resigned in March 1935. Clandestine action was then undertaken and repressive measures were instituted in September 1935, November 1935 and in February 1936.

The timing of the 24 February 1936 demonstrations, held simultaneously in Tunis, Moknine, Bourgel, Sfax, Bizerte and other towns, was very effective since Peyrouton was in Paris at the time, reporting that he had destroyed the Néo-Destour. Faced with the obvious fact that the "hard" line of Peyrouton had failed, Paris transferred him to Morocco and named a new Resident General, Armand Guillon. He was mandated to follow a policy of appeasement leading to the release of all the political prisoners held at Borj Le Boeuf and to the revocaton of the "decrets scélérats" instituted by Peyrouton.[17] Peyrouton's methods were not too sensitive to shades of differences between various factions and, by early 1936, Communists as well as leaders of the Old Destour and Zaytûnah students had also been incarcerated.[18]

Some clarification needs to be brought to the 1935 shift to clandestine action. In Bourguiba's version, he was the only one to hold on to the line of continuing mass action while all the other leaders of the Tunisian nationalist movement were for appeasement and a return to the peaceful methods of the Old Destour. In fact, the minutes of the meeting where he expressed his views and which he requested his fellow prisoners to sign do testify to his more intransigent attitude. But he omits to mention that he was relatively more moderate than others at the time as he had defended "l'attitude expectative" against "les partisans de la violence et des positions extrêmes".[19] Moreover, Bourguiba does not mention the fact that the third Bureau

Politique had been the last pre-planned team and that this circumstance left few options open to the prisoners.

Nonetheless, Bourguiba's reservations were to be justified when it became clear that the "soft" tactics of contrite letters had not succeeded with Peyrouton whereas the "hard" tactics of mass action finally led to the removal of Peyrouton. Were these mass actions spontaneous or organized? If organized, by whom, since the third Bureau Politique had resigned? This was the period of so-called clandestine action, and, therefore, it is practically impossible to know for sure but there is some indication that the relay was then in the hands of the Zaytûnah students. According to Bourguiba himself:

> ...notre sympathie à l'égard des étudiants de la Grande Mosquée, où le Néo-Destour puise presque la totalité de ses cadres, nous l'avons montrée en plusieurs circonstances, toutes les fois qu'il s'est agi de défendre leurs intérêts matériels et leur avenir. Celle de la Grande Mosquée à l'égard du Parti a été consacrée dans une circonstance décisive: la manifestation de février 1936 qui fut le véritable coup de grâce à la dictature peyroutienne.[20]

Thus ended what historians of the Tunisian nationalist movement have called "La Première Epreuve de Force". Out of this historic "test", the Néo-Destour leaders gained their most valuable element of legitimacy: they appeared to have been able to bend the Protectorate authorities without seeming to have bent themselves.[21]

THE FIRST DIALOGUE

During the two years between 1936 and 1938, the Néo-Destour Party took great strides. Heavy emphasis was laid upon strengthening and widening the structure of the Party: on 16 December 1936, L'Action Tunisienne was allowed to reappear again after a suspension of over three years; new cells were established so that by the end of 1937, the Party could claim some 400 cells where in 1934 only about 60 cells had attended the Ksar Hellal Congress; youth groups were organized under the name of "Jeunesses Destouriennes"; a Party section was established in Paris in October 1936; a new generation of Party leaders was recruited, most notable of whom was Hédi Nouira; the Party was able to pay regular salaries to its full-time militants; Bourguiba, for example, was paid 3,500 francs a month.[22] There is some indication that Bourguiba was building a group of young recruits who held personal allegiance to him.[23]

Actually, the final release of the Party militants had coincided with the election of the leftist Popular Front government in France, headed by Léon Blum. Towards the middle of June, Bourguiba went to Paris where he hoped greater sympathy would be found for the Tunisian nationalist cause among these progressive political elements. In a letter to Cohen-Hadria, Secretary-General of the Socialists in Tunisia (S.F.I.O.) at the time, Bourguiba wrote:

> Le Néo-Destour est convaincu que les partis de gauche qui forment le Front populaire et qui auront en main le destin de la France auront à coeur d'aborder le problème fondamental des rapports franco-tunisiens, de reviser les méthodes et les doctrines à la lumière des faits, en un mot de concilier les besoins et les aspirations de ce peuple avec les intérêts de la puissance protectrice.[24]

This was not the first time that Tunisian nationalists had sought support among left-of-centre French political circles, as the experience of Sakka and Thaalbi had already set the tone. Tunisian nationalism had made some gains in the period between 1924 and 1936. The election of the Cartel des Gauches in 1924 had inspired the formation of an analogous cartel in Tunisia which was composed of French and Tunisian groups. Similarly, the election of the Popular Front government in 1936 inspired the formation of a similar "rassemblement populaire" but, this time, without any Tunisian groups participating.[25] Despite the 1929 break with the Socialists in Tunisia, Bourguiba had maintained relations with Duran-Angliviel and Félicien Challaye through his wife. It would appear that he also became close to Charles-André Julien, secrétaire-général du Haut Comité Méditerranéen, who acted as advisor to Pierre Viénot, sous-secrétaire d'Etat aux Affaires Etrangères.[26]

The continuity between Bourguiba's views and actions concerning a "dialogue" with the French authorities and the views of the early Tunisian nationalist leaders is remarkable. He considered the

Front Populaire as the heir of the French liberal Republicans with whom the early leaders had hoped to cooperate for the benefit of Tunisia.[27] Effectively, Bourguiba succeeded in meeting with Viénot on 6 July 1935 and with the Resident General in August 1936. In themselves, these were historic meetings since Bourguiba was the first Tunisian nationalist leader to be received at the Quay d'Orsay. In the account Bourguiba gives of his meeting with Viénot, he wrote that he had claimed the right of Tunisia to independence but only as a final aim to be achieved in stages and with the help of France itself.[28]

Actually, as early as 1936, the Parti Frontiste founded by Gaston Bergery and including Félicien Challaye and Pierre Mendès-France had incorporated into its program an article calling for "l'émancipation progressive des peuples d'Outre-Mer, non par une assimilation chimérique, mais dans le cadre d'un ensemble fédéral." Parallel to this political federation the Frontist Party also proposed the application of a North-African economic union in federation with France. Such proposals attempted to avoid the Scylla and Charybdis of "association" and "assimilation" and, of course, allowed Bourguiba to claim independence "in cooperation with France".[29]

As the dialogue continued, Viénot (probably under the infleunce of Julien) progressed from an assertion of the permanent character of the Protectorate, in distinction to the Mandate, to a view closer to Bourguiba's. On 1 March 1937, Bourguiba presented the Tunisian question to an impressive number of representatives of the Rassemblement Populaire. Simultaneously, Viénot made a ground-breaking speech in Tunisia where he distinguished between the "private" interests of the French colonists and the "national" interests of France itself.[30] In fact, what the Popular Front government offered the Néo-Destour in return for social peace was "co-sovereignty". And, at that point in time, Bourguiba tended to accept the bargain.

At the second Néo-Destour Congress, held in Tunis from 30 October to 2 November 1937, Bourguiba pleaded the case of co-sovereignty in the following terms:

> Dire que la Tunisie est un pays de co-souveraineté implique l'existence d'une souveraineté tunisienne distincte, indépendante de la souveraineté française, une souveraineté

> tunisienne qui a son champ d'action formellement reconnu.... A l'heure où la souveraineté tunisienne est devenue un mythe, où publicistes, jurisconsultes et hommes politiques proclament que la Tunisie est terre française et à jamais terre française et demandent qu'on en finissent avec ce mythe devenu inutile et encombrant, il n'était peut-être pas maladroit de se prévaloir du traité de co-souverainté qui contient la reconnaissance formelle de la souverainté tunisienne.

Almost brilliant in his prophetic analysis of possibilities, Bourguiba continued:

> ...Dans un débat de cette importance, il faut regarder la réalité bien en face et envisager toutes les éventualités. On peut concevoir l'indépendance de la Tunisie par une rupture brutale avec la France comme conséquence soit d'une insurrection victorieuse soit d'une guerre étrangère. Je ne parlerai que pour mémoire de l'hypothèse de l'insurrection car en l'état actuel, toute insurrection est vouée à l'échec quasi-certain et ne peut aboutir qu'à d'affreux massacres. Quant à attendre notre indépendance d'une guerre européenne où la France serait vaincue, j'estime que c'est là une vaste blague, car en supposant la chose vraie, il ne faut pas être grand prophète pour prévoir qu'une Tunisie privée de l'appui français ne tarderait pas à tomber dans les griffes d'une puissance de proie et tout serait à recommencer.... En supposant par impossible que la Tunisie devenue brusquement indépendante par l'un des deux moyens cités ci-haut, soit entourée de toutes parts de puissances non seulement pacifiques mais philanthropiques, oui, en supposant, un instant cette chose extraordinaire, croyez-vous qu'elle serait en mesure de se gouverner par elle-même sans danger? ...C'est que l'exercice du pouvoir, dans les sociétés modernes, surtout dans les sociétés démocratiques, ne relève ni de l'empirisme ni de la science infuse. Il suppose non seulement une maturité politique et une organisation économique que nous sommes loin de posséder encore mais surtout une technique gouvernementale que l'élite tunisienne, éloignée systématiquement du

> gouvernement depuis un demi-siècle, a perdue. Est-ce à dire qu'il faille pour cela abandonner tout espoir dans l'avenir et se résigner à une servitude perpétuelle? Pas le moins du monde, car alors nous aurons sacrifié la première donnée, la donnée essentielle du problème: l'aspiration du peuple vers la liberté.... La vraie solution du problème, celle qui tient compte de toutes les données, ne peut-être qu'un compromis entre les différents intérêts en présence.... C'est l'émancipation pacifique et par étapes, grâce à une collaboration sincère et confiante entre la France et le peuple tunisien.[31]

THE SECOND TEST OF STRENGTH

Unfortunately, neither of the two parties was able to fulfill its end of the unconcluded bargain. The first Popular Front government fell on 22 June 1937 while the Néo-Destour monopoly of the role of "interlocuteur valable" was challenged on two fronts: by the "Old Destour" and by the new C.G.T.T. The Old Destour considered the acceptance of "co-sovereignty" as a deviation from the March 1933 program and a return to the positions of the Reformist Party. Bourguiba defended the Néo-Destour position by stating that "Notre stratégie exige que nous nous saisissons du pouvoir en vue de réaliser les revendications tunisiennes."[32] The issue of "co-sovereignty" became clouded by the issue of leadership when Thaalbi, the first leader of the Destour, returned from self-exile on 8 July 1937. Finally, the Néo-Destour succeeded in blocking him and proved that it alone could command the masses.[33]

The second challenge came from an unexpected quarter. As early as November 1936, Bourguiba had known of the plans to set up a Tunisian labor federation independent of the C.G.T. but, in view of the numerical weakness of the Tunisian working class, Bourguiba's main concern remained populist rather than syndicalist. As with M'Hamed Ali's C.G.T.T., the new C.G.T.T. proposed to follow corporatist goals independent of any political party. And, at first, the Néo-Destour was in full support.[34]

But with Viénot gone, Bourguiba needed to re-establish the credibility of the Néo-Destour once more by calling the masses out into the streets.

Having supported the C.G.T.T. in June, he expected the labor federation to support the populist action of the Party. Unfortunately, the labor leader Gnaoui refused to call for a general strike on 20 November 1937 in accordance with the decision taken by the Néo-Destour. The general strike was meant as a concrete expression of the withdrawal by the Party of its "préjugé favorable" towards the second Popular Front government. The refusal of the C.G.T.T. to cooperate led to the failure of the strike. Moreover, the C.G.T.T. became threatening to the Party as it began to organize workers within the traditional sectors of the economy, such as the "arabatiers", who were the conveyer belts to the masses in the bidonvilles -- the base for mass action. Consequently, Hédi Nouira was charged with the task of taking over the C.G.T.T. by tactics similar to those used in taking over the Destour.

When the National Council of the Néo-Destour Party held an extraordinary session on 13 March 1938, the decision to undertake mass actions was re-confirmed. The withdrawal of the "préjugé favorable" had been in reaction to the loss of the position of "interlocuteur valable" and to the need to re-establish the credibility of the Néo-Destour once more through another "test of strength". In the pursuit of this goal, no sacrifice was to be spared; even to the extent of martyrdom; "On développa la psychose du martyre en lisant, dans les réunions publiques, les versets du Koran faisant l'apologie de ceux qui périssent pour leur foi."[35] At this point, Mahmoud Materi resigned as President of the Party since he was reluctant to undertake another "test of strength". He was later to claim that Bourguiba had personnally taken the decision to call for a strike in his own absence.[36]

In the meantime, the situation had deteriorated on all levels. On the international level, world war became more and more likely and, in France, the Popular Front government elected in the face of the rising wave of Fascism seemed incapable of remaining in office. Tension rose high in Tunisia. Events quickly accelerated: within a couple of weeks, the Néo-Destour was accused of entertaining relations with Mussolini and the accusation implicated Ali Belhaouane and Habib Bourguiba.[37] On 3 April 1938, one of the four Néo-Destour teams sent on propaganda tours was arrested and simultaneous demonstrations broke out in Sfax, Monastir, Tunis, Jerba, Kalaa-Kbira, Le Kef, Fahs, Gafsa. Materi undertook an orderly demonstration on 8 April in which women also participated[38] and Bourguiba called for another demonstration on the 10th. But Ali Belhaoune jumped the gun and on 9 April led a demonstration in Tunis which ended in bloodshed. Bourguiba denied all Party responsibility for the events of 9 April 1938.[39] Yet, this was to be the beginning of the second "épreuve de force" between the Néo-Destour and the Protectorate authorities.

As expected, a state of siege was declared, curfews imposed and numerous arrests made (between 2,000 and 3,000). Despite the fact that Bourguiba had not actually participated in the demonstrations, he was arrested the following day and, on 12 April, the Néo-Destour Party was officially dissolved. With 12 other Néo-Destour leaders, Bourguiba was taken to the military prison during the period of interrogation. A reading of the interrogations following the arrests of the Néo-Destour leaders leads one to conclude that it was not the individuals who were on trial, but the proposition of Tunisian independence.[40] With the members of the fourth Political Bureau in prison, a fifth Bureau Politique was formed headed by Bahi Ladgham, Hédi Saidi and Slaheddine Bouchoucha.

In view of the "hard" tactics being pursued by the French authorities which limited the options for protest and raised the price to be paid for political action, it was the turn of Tunisian women to manifest themselves. On the occasion of the arrival in Tunis of the new Resident General, Eric Labonne, a group of Tunisian women took to the streets shouting for the release of the prisoners, particularly Bourguiba. For the first time, Tunisian women - including two of Bourguiba's nieces - were arrested for political reasons. They were soon released for lack of evidence. The women again took to the streets on the occasion of President Daladier's visit to Tunisia on 2 January 1939 and, this time, were sentenced to various prison terms. At their release from prison, they were honored by another demonstration at which the following declaration was made, "Hommes, femmes, enfants, nous servirons tous la cause d'une patrie unique, d'une seule religion et d'une seule langue".[41] Also in reaction to the failure of the French authorities to respond to the Néo-Destour overtures, a guerrilla movement had been organized by the Comité de Résistance, basically composed of Jerba people led by Zarg Layoun.[42] With the spring of 1939, a string of sabotage acts whose targets were the main means of communication, the telegraph and the railways, kept the security forces on the alert.

In the meanwhile, the fifth Political Bureau, in constant touch with Bourguiba through his lawyer Mohamed Nomane, was able to reconstitute many of the dissolved provincial Party cells before being arrested on 15 January 1940. On 14 February 1940 even the Comité de Résistance was also arrested. But there was no stopping the Néo-Destour; for the sixth time in the same number of years, a new Bureau Politique was constituted under the leadership of Habib Thameur in order to pursue the same tactics: tracts and posters, mass demonstrations and sabotage by a new separate organization of <u>fallâqah</u> -- the Black Hand.[43]

THE WAR INTERREGNUM

In the meanwhile, the French authorities removed Bourguiba and 18 other Néo-Destour leaders on 27 May 1940 to the Saint Nicholas fortress prison, near Marseille. Following the humiliating defeat of France at the hands of Hitler's army, the Tunisian prisoners seemed to be the last priority on anybody's list. Finally, on 16 December 1942, they were released by the Germans and sent to Rome.

Having been roundly defeated by the Germans, France found itself in the unenviable position of having failed to "protect" itself, let alone the Protectorates. Under these circumstances, it was relatively easy for Tunisians to sympathize with the Axis powers as in the famous proverb: "The enemy of my enemy is my friend". Despite a note of ambiguity, Bourguiba preserved his options open because he was painfully aware of the danger, in the case of an Axis victory, of falling under Italian domination.[44] Given a choice between Italy and France, he preferred the known evil. Following Germany's failure to invade Britain, Bourguiba seems to have placed his bets on the Allies. A few months before the Allies landed in Tunisia, Bourguiba put his option on record in a letter to Habib Thameur where he instructed him to give support to the Free French. Bourguiba himself claims to have been practically the only Néo-Destour leader who backed the Allies while all the others climbed on the Axis band-wagon between 1940-42.[45] There is also the testimony of Roger Casemajor, Police Commissioner of Tunis, who defended Bourguiba as basically loyal to the Allies.[46]

Bourguiba's resistance to the temptations of taking a pro-Axis position is particularly praiseworthy in view of the fact that many of the French leftists who had been his "interlocuteurs" during the Popular Front government opted for the Vichy régime, such as Gaston Bergery and Félicien Challaye as well as many of the "Néo-Socialistes", such as Marcel Déat and Adrien Marquet.[47] When pressed by the Italians to declare himself for the Axis, Bourguiba insisted on their recognition of Tunisia's independence before committing himself. Bourguiba also declined the role of only spokesman for Tunisia and insisted that any negotiations should be undertaken with the Bey. Actually, Moncef Bey had acceded to the throne on 19 June 1942 and, on 2 August 1942, had presented to the Resident General a wide program of reforms which came to be known as "la charte du moncefisme". The most important point in the "charte" was his acknowledgement of popular sovereignty. This was the same Moncef who had encouraged an alliance between the Destour and the Bey in 1922. Consequently, many nationalists were willing to co-operate with such a progressive Bey who then decided to form a government without consulting the Resident General. The new government included some of Bourguiba's early companions and allies such as Chenik, Materi and Guiga. At the same time, the Bey declared the neutrality of Tunisia.[48]

Soon enough, Bourguiba was returned to Tunisia on 8 April 1943, almost five years to the day since his arrest, and only a month before the Allies were to drive through Tunisia and to enter Tunis on 7 May 1943. In contrast to the Sixth Bureau Politique leaders, Bourguiba decided to remain in Tunisia but, fearing some misunderstanding about his relations with the Axis powers, went into hiding. He then undertook to explain his position through multiple contacts, particularly through Hooker Doolittle, the United States consul. Having sensed the new winds blowing from beyond the Atlantic, Bourguiba had adjusted his sails. The first contact between Bourguiba and Doolittle took place on 17 May 1943.[49] The high level of emotions running through the country during the months before the Allies arrived in Tunis coursed through Bourguiba and were amplified even further as he confesses to falling in love at that time. Only a few days after his return to Tunisia, he met Wassila Ben Ammar. Something about her attracted him and, despite the fact that she was already married, it would seem that she reciprocated his feelings. But it was only 19 years later to the day that they were married.[50]

In any case, the first concrete result of Bourguiba's contacts with the Americans was the regularization of his status; not only did he obtain a "laissez-passer" but all charges against him resulting from the 9 April 1938 incidents were dropped. Actually, Bourguiba had made some conciliatory gestures in the direction of France, but these had not been recognized as such and it took some time for the French authorities to realize that a world of difference "sépare le Bourguiba déchainé de 1938 et le Bourguiba qui offrait ainsi sa collaboration."[51] Thus ended the second test of strength between Bourguiba, leader of the Néo-Destour, and France.

But Moncef Bey was not as lucky and was summarily deposed by the French military authorities who replaced him with Lamine Bey. According to Julien, the Bey was deposed on the allegation of having collaborated with the Axis but, in reality, he was deposed for having asserted himself by naming a nationalist government in 1942 which included representation from the Destour.[52] Julien seems to regret the haste with which the French forced the abdication of Moncef Bey since the prestige he had acquired as a nationalist Bey could have provided the basis of legitimacy for the "reforms" which the French authorities proposed.

> Le général Mast n'eut plus devant lui d'interlocuteur qualifié. Les réformes, qui eussent pu être valablement délibérées avec le bey Moncef, apparurent octroyées par la puissance protectrice et, partant, furent frappées d'une suspicion d'origine qui leur enleva toute valeur.... Ainsi la décision inconsidérée du général Giraud, exécutée hâtivement mais sans conviction par le général Juin, rendit impossible tout rapprochement franco-tunisien et fournit de solides assises à l'opposition destourienne.[53]

During the remaining two years of the war, the Néo-Destour concentrated on the difficult task of rebuilding the Party cells which had been decimated in the aftermath of 9 April 1938. Following the well-tried practice of the pre-War years, several tours of the interior were organized in which Bourguiba participated to re-establish "direct contact" with the people.[54] When the French authorities realized that Bourguiba was trying to rebuild the Néo-Destour, he was placed under town arrest in Tunis.

History seemed to be repeating itself; as the end of the War approached, it was clear that the colonial empires had been drastically weakened. With the proclamation of the United Nations Charter in San Francisco in 1944, the United States emerged as the champion of freedom and justice, once again. On the internal scene in Tunisia, and in view of the expected end of the War, a national front which included the Néo-Destour, the Archéo-Destour, Reformists, members of the Grand Conseil, Zaytûnah representatives as well as a member of the Tunisian Jewish community met as a "Comité des soixante". They put forth a "manifeste du Front tunisien" in February 1945 calling for the complete independence of Tunisia.[55]

Whereupon the French authorities arrested some fifty persons including M'Hamed Chenik, previous Prime Minister, and Mahmoud Materi, previous Minister of the Interior.[56] Thus, at the end of the Second World War, the Néo-Destour found itself cut off from direct contact with the people. It had lost its friends at the Beylical court as well as many of its "interlocuteurs" on the French political scene. It was therefore decided to pursue new tactics, seeking international support, since France was perceived to be vulnerable to international pressure. This could have represented a fundamental change because, since the end of the Ottoman Empire, the Tunisian nationalist leaders had acted upon the belief that independence was to be obtained only through a dialectic with France. As it turned out, the issue did not resolve itself into a new partner in the dialogue, but simply in obtaining support for the Tunisian side of the continuing dialogue with France. This gain appeared as a function of relations between France and the United States as the latter promoted the Marshall Plan and N.A.T.O., and finally decided upon a policy of non-intervention in the dominions of its allies.

Bourguiba was charged with the task of creating international pressure on France. But before embarking on an account of his efforts during the following ten years, it is necessary to trace the socio-economic developments that had occurred in Tunisia during the Second World War and that were to become the basis for the rise of at least two new political formations with which the Néo-Destour had to work.

CRISS-CROSSING DIALOGUES

The war situation had led to a rise in demand for mineral ores, invigorating the mining and transportation industries in the Gafsa-Gabes-Sfax triangle. Moreover, the rise in demand for manufactured goods and the inability of French goods to reach Tunisia led to the establishment of small "modern" industries, particularly in the Sfax region, and to the invigoration of the traditional bazaar economy, both artisans and merchants. Consequently, a new Tunisian labor federation, the Union Général des Travailleurs Tunisiens (U.G.T.T.), based in the Sfax area, was established by Ferhat Hached. Also to be noted is the rise in importance of the Zaytûnah student associations backed by the traditional system of exchange based in the suqs.[56]

Around February 1944, two Zaytûnah organizations were established, Maktabat al-tilmîdh al-zaytûnî (the Zaytûnah Student Library) and Al-Ikhwân al-zaytûniyyûn (the Zaytûnah Brethren) as well as a newspaper, Sawṭ al-ṭâlib (Voice of the Student). Even more important, in February 1945, al-Ṭâhir Ibn ʿAshûr was returned to the presidency of the Zaytûnah. The importance of these associations may be measured by the impressive numbers of Zaytûnah Mosque-University students, some 10,000, most of whom came from the countryside. At first, the Néo-Destour willingly allied itself to both these groups and the outcome of this alliance was the historic meeting held on laylat al-qadr (Night of Power) of 27 Ramaḍân 1365 (22 August 1946).[57]

It is at this meeting that the common program calling for the complete independence of Tunisia and for its membership in the League of Arab States and in the United Nations was adopted. Actually, this was the beginning of a view of "personnalité" totally different from the one which had been vehicled by the dominant tradition within the Tunisian nationalist movement, beginning with Ahmed Bey and culminating with the March 1933 program. This new view questioned the legitimacy of a "Tunisian" specificity and posited the alternative of an Arab-Islamic shakhṣiyyah (personality) as the basis of legitimacy. During the 1950s, an adaptation of Islamic unity was elaborated which accepted the legitimacy of culturally-defined "nations" within the larger Islamic unity and the idea of one Arab nation as the basis of legitimacy gained ground.

In contrast to the previous two Tunisian labor federations (of the 1920s and 1930s), the U.G.T.T. was from the very beginning quite strong as it was based on an important increase during the Second World War in the numbers of Tunisian industrial workers, particularly in the Gafsa-Gabes-Sfax region. It was also not averse to accepting the membership of Tunisian civil servants and teachers; thus, it grouped both white-collar and blue-collar salaried workers. In fact, the role played by the U.G.T.T. following the end of the Second World War was crucial on several counts. First, it provided the Néo-Destour with the pressure tactics necessary to maintain its credibility at a time when the Zaytûnah associations threatened to take over the populist base through a clearer claim to the Islamic cultural tradition. These disciplined actions are illustrated by the famous strike led by Habib Achour against the Compagnie Sfax-Gafsa on 5 August 1947, which ended with several dead and many wounded, and the Enfidaville strike by agricultural workers on 17 November 1950 which also ended in bloodshed. Since the Néo-Destour had come out of the 1938 experience weakened, it was the U.G.T.T. which undertook the pressure tactics but, instead of mass demonstrations fueled by the lumpen-proletariat, it was in the form of strikes by blue-collar workers.[58]

Secondly, the U.G.T.T., particularly in the person of its leader, Ferhat Hached, was crucial in building bridges with the United States when the U.G.T.T. decided to switch from the Communist dominated Fédération des Syndicats Mondiale (F.S.M.) and joined the American dominated Confédération Internationale des Syndicats Libres (C.I.S.L). It was through the connection between the American Unions, the American Federation of Labor (A.F.L.) and the Congress of Industrial Organizations (C.I.O), and the U.G.T.T. that Bourguiba was able to visit the United States and present the Tunisian case to key American political figures.[59] Thus, the old alliance between fragments of the "Young Tunisian" French-educated professionals and the traditional bourgeoisie of land-owners, artisans and merchants which had provided the leadership of the two Destour parties was widened through an alliance with industrial and agricultural workers, taking into consideration that these last maintained their autonomy through the separate organization of the U.G.T.T.. This separate organization always held some possibility of a time limit to the alliance and of future differences between the Party and the

Labor Union.

By the end of 1947, the main actors that would play the scene of Tunisia's autonomy were positioned. On the internal level, in Tunisia itself, several new characters had appeared including the U.G.T.T. and the Zaytûnah associations. On the international level, the "tête-à-tête" dialogue with France had to be broadened, as others became interested in listening and putting in their word. On an intermediate level, the Arab League, as a first step towards the institutionalization of an Arab political system, further complicated the give and take. In sum, the post-war years saw the playing-out of complex sets of relationships constantly shifting in the fluid situation resulting from the Second World War. Tunisia was to live through a third "test of strength" with France before winning internal autonomy in 1955.[60]

QUEST IN THE EAST

As news of the project for some form of unity among the Arab countries of the Mashriq reached Tunisia, hope appeared to arise in the East. Six days after the signing of the charter establishing the League of Arab States, Bourguiba left Tunisia to head for Egypt.

> Les espoirs des musulmans tunisiens se tournaient vers la Ligue arabe. Depuis que le protocole d'Alexandrie, signé par l'Egypt, l'Irak, le Liban, la Syrie et la Transjordanie avait dressé le projet d'une ligue des Etats arabes, l'Islam maghrébin suivait avec passion les efforts pour donner au panarabisme une base concrète.... Le 22 mars, la nouvelle de la signature du pacte parvenait à Tunis; quelques jours plus tard...Me Habib Bourguiba faisait voile vers...la ville où battait le coeur de l'Islam [le Caire].[61]

In a true James Bond fashion, Bourguiba gave the slip to his police followers and fled by boat on 26 March 1945. He travelled south to the Kerkennah islands and a lûd (traditional sailing boat) for the Libyan shores. He then crossed the desert in the company of only one companion; for a city denizen, the month taken to accomplish that trip was sheer torture. They arrived at al-Amîriyyah, close to Alexandria in Egypt, dirty and exhausted, indistinguishable from desert bedouins. Bourguiba was shocked to find out that the frontier officer had never heard of him; without papers or passport, he tried to explain,

> Je suis maître Habib Bourguiba, avocat à Tunis, président du Néo-Destour. Je suis venu rejoindre la Ligue arabe. La France a dressé entre nous une muraille de fer pour empêcher toute initiative de ce genre. Je me suis donc vu obligé de quitter clandestinement mon pays, pour venir en Egypte pays frère dont la sollicitude me permettra de défendre la cause tunisienne....cet officiel apparement si orgueilleux - un petit pharoan, pensez-donc, ne connaissait même pas le nom de Bourguiba; il n'en avait jamais entendu parler....[62]

Bourguiba and his companion were charged with illegal entry while a full report was sent to Cairo, as the bureaucratic procedures required.

In the meantime, Bourguiba was permitted to send telegrams to ʿAzzâm Pasha, Secretary General of the Arab League, and to Lakhdar Ben Hassein, a Tunisian from the Djerid resident in Cairo, President of the "Association de défense des pays nord-Africains" and future rector of the Azhar.[63] Finally, instructions arrived from Cairo to bring the two prisoners to the capital. Once in the city, it became clear that, government offices being closed on Thursday afternoons, there were no specific instructions about their reception. Bourguiba then decided to contact an old friend, Mounier Pillet who had been his link to Mathilde Louvain. Ironically, therefore, it was a Frenchman and not an Arab who was the first to welcome Bourguiba to Egypt. Bourguiba claims that otherwise he found himself isolated and neglected, with his funds dwindling fast. Desperate for support, Bourguiba states that he had to resort to American aid which he obtained from Hooker Doolittle, previously consul in Tunis and, at the time, consul of the United States in Alexandria.

Bourguiba spent over four years in Cairo yet his overall judgement of the Mashriq is rather negative. Several problems blocked his efforts to make known the Tunisian cause in the Arab countries of the East: (1) the ignorance which prevailed among Arabs of the Mashriq about conditions in the

Maghrib; (2) the Palestinian problem so preoccupied the Arab countries of the East that they had little time, energy or funds to devote to the Maghrib; (3) since the Mashriq had not experienced French settler colonialism and since France had pulled its troops out of Lebanon and Syria, the on-going dialogue of the Mashriq was with Britain and the United States rather than with France.[64]

Such a judgement is not very fair since the Arab League did provide him with funds and, even more important, with the opportunities for wider contacts beyond the Arab world. In fact, within a week, Bourguiba was contacted and, within a few months, he was doing so well that he was able to help Chedli Mekki, representative of the Parti Populaire Algérien, in regularizing his papers and in obtaining lodging. Moreover, he was able to offer refuge to Habib Thameur, Taieb Slim, Rachid Driss, Hédi Saidi and Hassine Triki who had been left high and dry at the end of the Second World War when they were condemned for collaboration with the Axis powers. He provided them with passports (courtesy of Iraq), free airline tickets and a monthly stipend of 50 Egyptian pounds. He was also able to rent a large villa, half of which was to serve as headquarters for the Néo-Destour office in exile while the other half was to serve as living quarters for all of them. Thus, the Néo-Destour was the first liberation movement in Africa to establish representation in an Arab country of the East. Building on this base, Bourguiba was also able to participate in 1947 in the creation of the "Arab Maghrib Office", grouping the Néo-Destour and the Archéo-Destour of Tunisia, the Parti Populaire of Algeria, the Istiqlâl of Morocco and the Işlâh of Spanish-zone Morocco.[65]

Bourguiba's concern was to make known the Tunisian cause to various audiences in the East, including the Muslim Brethren of Ḩasan al-Bannâ, the Muslim Young Men Association of Şalâḩ Ḩarb Pasha, the Young Egypt Association of Aḩmad Ḩusayn, the Arab Unity Association of Ibrâhîm ʿAbd al-Hâdî, the Wafd Party of Naḩḩâs Pasha. In the same manner, Bourguiba decided to have direct contact with key Arab governments. First on the list was Saudi Arabia, which he visited in 1945. Then his second trip took him to Syria and Palestine in 1946, where he was quick to note the similarities between the colonialism experienced by the Maghrib countries and that being prepared for Palestine; a settler colonialism "inculquant aux jeunes israelites une mentalité de colonisateurs faite d'arrogance, de mépris de l'indigène et d'orgueil racial."[66] On 4 March 1946, the Arab Maghrib Office presented a memorandum to the Anglo-American Commission proposing, as solution to the Palestine problem, a process of "de-zionization". This effort at sharing the Mashriq's concern did not result in an immediate reciprocal gesture as the Arab League delayed in registering the Maghrib's problems on its agenda. The third trip Bourguiba undertook in the Arab world was to travel to Jordan in order to thank King ʿAbd Allâh for having publicly refused the invitation of Franco, because of the occupation of part of Morocco by Spain.

It is possible that the refusal of the League of Arab States to inscribe the problems of the Maghrib on its agenda led Bourguiba to turn towards the West once more. He was able to obtain a visa to the United States, having already managed to obtain a passport delivered by the French embassy in Cairo. Nonetheless, it was the Arab League Information Office in New York, presided by Cecil Hourani, which paid his bills and it was at a banquet given by Prince Fayşal of Saudi Arabia on 15 January 1947 that Bourguiba was photographed in the company of Dean Acheson, American Under-Secretary of State. Seemingly based on this cocktail conversation, Bourguiba was able to state that he had obtained "l'assurance de M. Acheson que le gouvernement américain serait prêt à appuyer une demande d'indépendance de la Tunisie présentée à l'Assemblée de l'O.N.U."[67] The incident created a great effect in France as the United States had pledged a policy of non-interference in the dominions of its Allies.

Soon after, Bourguiba was asked to resign from his position as Secretary-General of the Arab Maghrib Office under the pressure of rumours alleging that he had pocketed the contributions given by the countries he had visited. It was only when the heads of government of these countries had publicly acknowledged that no money had been given Bourguiba that the rumours died down, but he was not offered his position again. His resignation was a hard blow, not only for his reputation, finally cleared, but for his finances since the Arab League did not channel its contributions directly to each of the representative movements but to the Arab Maghrib Office as a whole.[68] It is more probable that Bourguiba was asked to resign because he was considered to have infringed the agreement among the members of the Arab Maghrib Office not to undertake separate dialogues or negotiations.

A RENEWED DIALOGUE

While Bourguiba was seeking international support, he did not abandon the time-honored "dialogue" with France. In fact, his multiple contacts at the French embassy in Cairo led some of his compatriots to doubt him. More specifically, he was in contact with Michel Soulié, counselor at the embassy, who was of the Radical Party. As in his discussion with Viénot, Bourguiba defended, on the one hand, the sovereignty of Tunisia, but on the other hand, realistically admitted an inevitable dependency on France; "à savoir l'octroi à la Tunisie du statut d'un pays souverain et indépendant, lié à la France par un traité librement négocié, garantissant à la France ses intérêts stratégiques, économiques et culturels."[69] At that point in time, Bourguiba was not in principle against the Union Française promoted by the Fourth Republic on condition that the measure of independence given to Tunisia was credible. He claimed that the membership of Tunisia in the Union Française would not be in contradiction with membership in the Arab League.[70] The difficulties of reconciling a double affiliation to the Arab-Islamic world and to the West have political and economic consequences, beyond the psychological and the cultural,[71] which persist to this day. As the socio-economic structure of Tunisia gradually changed, the various class-fraction alliances attempted to use one or the other option in order to strengthen their own position.

Bourguiba had also kept up his contacts with Tunisian students in Paris through the Néo-Destour section. Between the crucial years of 1948 and 1954, the Néo-Destour section in France was led by the young and brilliant Mohamed Masmoudi who, in fact, became Bourguiba's door to influential liberals in the political and journalistic circles of France.[72] Bourguiba was personally close to Masmoudi so that it is believed he was being groomed as Bourguiba's successor until the Tunisia-Libya debacle of 1974.

At the same time, discussions had been opened between Ben Youssef, as Secretary General of the Néo-Destour, and the French authorities. Of course, if these had succeeded, the result risked to leave Bourguiba out in the cold. He practically <u>had</u> to return to demonstrate that <u>he</u> was the leader whom the Tunisian people trusted and, consequently, the necessary "interlocuteur valable". Bourguiba's suspicions were raised higher when both Ben Yousef and his contacts at the French embassy in Cairo advised him not to return to Tunisia. Consequently, he decided to return and, in fact, the monstrous crowds which appeared at the airport to welcome him amply demonstrated his popularity.[73]

According to Bourguiba, as early as 1948 Ben Youssef had been out to get him. It was at that time that Ben Youssef became Secretary General and Bourguiba was "promoted" to President of the Néo-Destour Party. Bourguiba blames Ben Youssef for organizing the third Party Congress on 16-17 October 1948 at which the decision was taken to relieve Bourguiba of all financial responsibilities. If this Congress was in fact so much to the distaste of Bourguiba, why did it take him almost a full year to react? The question is important, given the future conflict between Bourguiba and Ben Youssef. Did Bourguiba suspect that, after having sacrificed himself so much (seven years of prison and four years of exile), he was being eased out of the more central "dialogue" with France and that he was simply being used to strengthen Ben Youssef's hand in the game of give-and-take? The question is open since the public documents simply indicate a motion of the Congress stating that: "Le Congrès confirme sa confiance dans ses leaders demeurant à l'étranger".[74]

Actually, the 4 August 1949 meeting of the Party National Council was closer in time to Bourguiba's decision to return to Tunisia. But the only indication we have of the transactions of the Council is the cryptic statement:

> Le Conseil National, après avoir approuvé la ligne de conduite suivie par le Bureau Politique, tient à assurer ce dernier de son entière confiance dans la poursuite de la lutte pour la réalisation des revendications nationales par les moyens les plus appropriés.[75]

What was the "ligne de conduite" which the National Council approved of? Was it to continue efforts at opening a new dialogue with France? What about the role of Bourguiba?

In any case, Bourguiba moved quickly to reassert his leadership position by his old methods of "tournées" around the country and of "contact direct" with the people. He succeeded so well that he had no trouble in excluding Slimane Ben Slimane who represented the tendency of rapprochement with the French Communists and the Soviet Bloc. He then dissolved the strong Bizerte Party cell. There is also some indication that the question of armed guerrillas was also at stake -- whether the Néo-Destour should support them or not. It is not at all clear whether there was a centralized command of these fallâqah or, if such a centralized command existed, who was behind it. Bourguiba claims to have organized the Black Eleven, in which Zarg Layoun was involved.[76] The question, at that point in time, was whether to continue with "dialogue" or to prepare for another "test of strength". Although fully aware of the risks, in view of the historic experience of 1936-37 when "dialogue" had ended with the 9 April 1938 disaster -- the decision was taken to continue the dialogue with France. Simultaneously, we note the attempt to follow a policy of "présence" by the Néo-Destour; in other words, of encouraging any and all sectors of society to organize and of being present in all these organizations. Among these organizations were the following: the U.G.T.T., U.T.A.C. (Union Tunisienne de l'Artisanat et du Commerce), the U.G.A.T. (Union Générale des Agriculteurs Tunisiens); Union des Femmes Musulmanes; Association des Anciens Combattants Tunisiens, Jeunesses Tunisiennes.[77]

While the French Communist Party declared itself in favor of the Union Française in December 1949, it had become clear to Bourguiba that he would not be able to obtain popular support in Tunisia for membership in the Union Française. Effectively, a broad front was implicitly formed against the Union Française option. Given this situation, and having demonstrated that his leadership was acknowledged by the Tunisian "people" as a whole, Bourguiba attempted to open a new dialogue with France in the form of an alternative seven-point program. Bourguiba expressed the options he was offering as follows:

> La question n'est pas de choisir entre l'indépendance tunisienne et l'administration coloniale. Le choix se situe entre une indépendance patronnée et guidée par la France, qui laissera subsister une coopération libre et préservera les intérêts fondamentaux de la France et du monde libre, chose encore possible et encore souhaitée par l'immense majorité de

> Tunisiens et une indépendance conquise de haute lutte dans le sang et la haine, avec l'appui de l'étranger, et qui rejetterait la Tunisie vers d'autres blocs à bases confessionnelles ou raciales moins favorable à la France.[78]

Once more, as in his discussions with Pierre Viénot in 1936-37, Bourguiba seemed to be on the point of achieving his objectives. The difference was that he had moved from a qualified acceptance of co-sovereignty to an acceptance of "interdépendance". This was a position not very far off from that proposed by the old Frontist Party of Gaston Bergery and Pierre Mendès-France.

On 11 June 1950, Robert Schuman made a historic statement; referring to the appointment of a new Resident General, Schuman said:

> M. Périller, dans ses nouvelles fonctions, aura pour mission de comprendre et de conduire la Tunisie vers le plein épanouissement de ses richesses et de l'amener vers l'indépendance qui est l'objecif final pour tous les territoires au sein de l'Union française.[79]

As with Viénot, Schuman had to qualify his statement the very next day in order not to antagonize the French colonists, the "prépondérants". Nonetheless, for the first time in the history of the protectorate, a French official was on record as having publicly recognized the time limits of the Protectorate and the possibility, even remote, of Tunisian independence. Moreover, in qualifying his statement, Schuman did call for an end to the "régime d'administration directe" and for the "autonomie interne" of Tunisia. Hopes were raised so high that the Néo-Destour accepted to participate in the second Chenik government of 17 August 1950 which was formed to negotiate the promised internal autonomy, with Salah Ben Youssef as Minister of Justice.[80]

But the dialogue dragged on and on without leading to any important breakthrough. Finally, the U.G.T.T. undertook to shake this lethargic state of affairs. On 25 October 1950, Ferhat Hached called a general strike of agricultural workers in the Société franco-africaine at Enfidaville. Once again, the strike ended in arrests, blood and death. Bourguiba took a nuanced position; on the one hand, he defended the workers' action,[81] and, on the other hand, he did not break off with the French authorities.

Then the Zaytûnah students struck, provoking demonstrations in many of the cities and towns of Tunisia. Such disturbances could mean only one of two things; either that the Néo-Destour could not control all of the activist sectors of Tunisian society and thus its credibility as "interlocuteur valable" was being undermined or it was signaling the return to a policy of "test of strength". Bourguiba had carefully kept his own position open since it was not he who was officially responsible for the negotiations, but the Chenik team. He noted, at the time,

> ...nous voulons bien accepter un tout petit acompte de deux sous quand nous réclamons une créance de mille francs; encore faut-t-il que la pièce de deux sous qu'on nous offre ne soit pas fausse. Or, les "réformes" actuelles represéntent un acompte illusoire sur notre créance officiellement reconnue de l'autonomie interne.[82]

The situation became tense one more time as the French attempted to force their reforms down the throats of the gagging Tunisians, presaging the beginning of the third "test of strength". In preparation, Bourguiba decided to go on a second world tour to drum up international support for the Tunisian cause, leaving on 2 February 1951 for Karachi. But this time his fame well preceded him and he was welcomed with honor whenever he travelled -- after Pakistan, he went to India, Indonesia, Egypt, Britain, Italy, the United States, Spain, Morocco and Turkey. This world tour took the better part of 1951 to complete and, ending in Turkey, gave Bourguiba the opportunity to judge for himself the Kemalist experiment. His assessment was equivocal as he believed that similar results could be obtained by less drastic methods which take into account "l'âme du peuple".[83]

While Bourguiba was on his world tour, Chenik, as representative of the Bey and with the collaboration of the Néo-Destour in the person of Salah Ben Youssef, travelled to Paris on 16 October 1951 to negotiate the terms of the hoped-for internal autonomy. They were shunted from one official to another until, finally, Bourguiba offered to come to Paris to help in unblocking the negotiations. He arrived on the same day that the French authorities finally answered the Chenik delegation in a letter which, without specifiying the terms, offered a mild form of co-sovereignty. But time had passed and, whereas in 1937, the Néo-Destour could choose co-sovereignty as a lesser evil than assimilation, in 1951 assimilation was completely out of the question and co-sovereignty was a greater evil than internal autonomy and, thus, unacceptable. Actually, in 1937 the Néo-Destour was the most radical organized group in Tunisia but, in 1951, it had been overtaken by the more radical U.G.T.T., the Zaytûnah organizations and the fallâqah who were liable to gain greater legitimacy as France had refused dialogue.[84]

THE THIRD TEST OF STRENGTH

A general strike was called by the U.G.T.T., the U.G.A.T. and the U.T.A.C. on 21, 22 and 23 December 1951. On 15 January 1952, the Chenik government resigned and Bourguiba returned to renew his famous touring campaigns to re-establish direct contact with the people. On 18 January 1952, Bourguiba was arrested for the third time -- and despite the interdiction, the Congress of the Néo-Destour Party was held on the same day. The news of the arrest provoked a wave of disturbances culminating in hundreds of dead and wounded so that Bourguiba's credibility as a leader was reinforced rather than weakened and he was able to state in an interview given to Paris-Presse on 22 January: "Il n'y a que moi qui puisse faire accepter aux Tunisiens un compromis avec la France."[85] A week later a military operation, "ratissage", was undertaken in the Cap Bon region and atrocities were committed by the French army.

In France, the new government of Edgar Faure tried to withdraw from the December 1951 position and to return to Robert Schuman's policies while, at the same time, a state of siege was declared in Tunisia and the military were practically given a free hand. But the Faure government quickly fell on 29 February 1952. In Tunisia, this led to a quick series of strikes, repression, followed by more strikes, more repression, until the French authorities lost their cool and decided to arrest the out-going Tunisian Prime-Minister, Mohamed Chenik, along with the Tunisian ministers Materi, Ben Youssef, Badra and Ben Salem as well as Bourguiba. Ben Youssef and Badra had been in France when the order of arrest was given and were able to escape to Egypt just at the time when Nasser was emerging as leader of the Egyptian revolution.[86]

With the Néo-Destour leaders out of the way, the French authorities searched for new "interlocuteurs valables". The Bey undertook to gain credibility by refusing to sign the so-called "reforms" proposed by the Resident General. He also took the initiative of inviting forty Tunisian personalities, representative of the major groupings of Tunisian society, and asked them to work on a counter-proposal of reforms. The French did make some gesture of responding but the mysterious assassination of Ferhat Hached on 5 December 1952 ruined these possibilities, and a new wave of strikes and repressive measures began. Mahmoud Messadi, successor of Ferhat Hached as leader of the U.G.T.T., was arrested. Bourguiba was removed from his prison-exile in the south to the island of Galite.

But a thin ray of hope appeared when the United Nations Assembly passed a resolution asking the two parties in the Franco-Tunisian conflict to continue discussions. At least there was general acknowledgement that the problem lay between two parties and was not an internal matter as France had attempted to argue. Unfortunately, the Bey finally buckled and signed the reforms on 20 December 1952 and municipal elections were called for the spring of 1953. Under the pressure of the Vietnamese revolution, the French government was pressed to find a solution to the Tunisian problem. In September 1953, the new Resident General formed a government led by Mohamed-Salah Mzali from which the Néo-Destour was completely absent. <u>Fallâqah</u> actions began again and escalated tremendously so that insecurity reigned throughout the land to reach even beyond Mzali himself to the Beylical court where the heir apparent was assassinated on 1 July 1953. The incident forced the Mzali government to resign on 17 June 1954[87] and signalled the failure of the French authorities to set up their own choice of "interlocuteurs valables". There remained only two clear choices. The first choice was to use force in order to impose their own conception of what the relationship with Tunisia should be. The second choice was to recognize the Néo-Destour as an "interlocuteur valable", offering to negotiate a political solution in stages. Bourguiba is quoted as stating: "Après nous, si nous, néo-destouriens nous échouons, il n'y aura plus de place que pour le fanatisme, soit le fanatisme religieux, soit le fanatisme politique."[88] At this juncture, Pierre Mendès-France came to power.

FRUITFUL DIALOGUE

In one of his first declarations, Mendès-France took a courageous position by promising some form of autonomy for those countries dominated by France.[89] Bourguiba was transferred from his island prison to the Château d'Amilly in order to be more accessible for the forthcoming discussions with the French government. On his first day, he received the visit of Alain Savary, special envoy of Mendès-France, and offered his seven-point program of 1950 as the basis of discussion. Immediately, Mendès-France accepted the principle of Tunisian self-government and, on 30 July 1954, the Ministerial Council followed suit. In order to demonstrate the seriousness of this decision, both to the Tunisian nationalists (particularly those who threatened to overbid Bourguiba) and to the extremist colonists, Mendès-France flew to Tunisia itself where he announced:

> L'Autonomie interne de l'Etat tunisien est reconnue et proclamée sans arrière-pensée par le gouvernement français.... Le degré d'évolution auquel est parvenu le peuple tunisien, la valeur remarquable de ses élites justifient que ce peuple soit appelé à gérer lui-même ses propres affaires.[90]

Obviously, this was the greatest victory of Bourguiba since _he_ was the Néo-Destour "interlocuteur" who had finally succeeded in convincing France to acknowledge Tunisian self-rule as a pre-condition to negotiating a treaty. A new Tunisian government was formed, led by Taher Ben Ammar, in which four of the ten portfolios were held by the Néo-Destour. As the negotiations began on 14 November 1954, a fortnight after the Algerian Toussaint, the Tunisian _fallâqah_ had not stopped their actions. To demonstrate that he was "valable" as an "interlocuteur", Bourguiba was asked by Mendès-France to put an end to the _fallâqah_ actions. By January 1955, the Néo-Destour had succeeded in collecting the arms of some 3,000 guerrillas. Unfortunately, on 5 February 1955, the Mendès-France government fell. The danger then was a repetition of the experience with the Blum government in 1937[91] and the loss of Bourguiba's French "interlocuteur". But Edgar Faure, who succeeded Mendès-France, was ready to continue and on 22 April 1955, decided to invite Bourguiba to the Presidential palace for discussions around the remaining four points: the southern parts of Tunisia which the French military authorities wished to keep under their control; the representation of French residents on the municipal level; the creation of a mixed economic council; and the status of the French language in Tunisia. The result of this meeting was an agreement to agree between two "interlocuteurs valables". A week later, on 1 May 1955, a huge rally was held at the Belvedère stadium where various organizations were represented as well as the Beylical Court. At the rally, the most important of these collectivities, the U.G.T.T., expressed its support of Bourguiba's efforts and for the agreement reached. But from Bandung, Ben Youssef published a communiqué condemning the accords.[92]

This Bourguiba, the defender of incomplete independence, of what may be viewed as "compromising compromise", is the image generally held of Bourguiba while the image of the Bourguiba "déchainé de 1938" has been forgotten. Yet even this "étapiste" Bourguiba did not forget his ultimate goal -- the independence of Tunisia:

> La dernière étape serait l'abolition de la convention de la Marsa, qui n'aurait plus de raison d'être dès lors que les réformes, que les parties contractantes, s'engageraient à promouvoir, auraient été mises en place. Il ne subsisterait plus que le traité du Bardo, dans le cadre duquel on pourrait fort bien admettre que s'inscriraient les futures relations des deux pays. Il s'agit en somme de faire en sens inverse le chemin parcouru depuis la signature du traité du Bardo.[93]

Although Bourguiba had clearly demonstrated that he, and he alone, was considered by the French government as "interlocuteur valable", he still had to demonstrate that he, and he alone, was the most representative of the Tunisian people. Quickly, preparations were made to transport him to Tunisia and he arrived at dawn on 1 June 1955 where a human tidal wave voted with their feet for Bourguiba by giving him a tremendous welcome. It is believed that almost half a million Tunisians took to the streets to cheer their leader.

> Soudain, une minute de vive émotion dans ce cadre déjà plus qu'émouvant: ce fut lorsque les veuves de Ferhat Hached (accompagnée de son fils) et de Hédi Chaker (avec sa fille) se trouvèrent face au libérateur; elles se jetèrent dans ses bras les larmes aux yeux et le coeur battant. La foule s'était prise d'une frénésie incroyable: elle hurlait, gesticulait, criait, trépignait, agitait drapeaux, mouchoirs ou coiffeurs. Les femmes, en signe d'allégresse, poussaient des you-you stridents. Tous entonnèrent bientôt, spontanément, l'hymne révolutionnaire. Une fôret de mains se tendaient vers les cieux. Même les membres du service d'ordre, oubliant un instant leur rôle, étouffèrent littéralement l'idole pour l'embrasser.'[4]

Ben Youssef was also to return soon. The question was: Would Bourguiba be able to face his challenge?

**INVALID PARAMETER IN FOLLOWING CARD...
.eb /   X/
**ERROR FOUND NEAR LINE 00003 OF BOOK.C5

Chapter V

ANATOMY OF LEGITIMACY

Salah Ben Youssef posed a serious threat beyond his opposition to the internal autonomy accords. Ben Youssef had been Minister of Justice in the Chenik government formed in August 1950 to negotiate a program of reforms much less ambitious than the 1955 accords and, therefore, his opposition to the internal autonomy accords could have been considered as a tactical difference. But, in fact, Ben Youssef threatened the future since he presented his opposition to the accords in terms of a strategically different conception of the Tunisian state and of its legitimacy. The social fission and the civil war in Tunisia which the Ben Youssef "sedition" led to represented the struggle between different class-fraction alliances rallied around antagonistic conceptions of the consensual basis of the future Tunisian state.[1]

The legitimacy of the Tunisian state implicit in the positions of Bourguiba is multi-dimensional: legal, historical,[2] and charismatic. The importance of the legal dimension was literally discovered in the process of analyzing the key term, "personnalité", in Bourguiba's earliest article, "Le Voile". The historical dimension was first noticed in the unusual attention paid by Bourguiba and by the Socialist Destour Party to the writing of the history of the Tunisian nationalist movement. Finally, the charisma of Bourguiba himself is linked to the populism of the Néo-Destour Party and to the de facto option of a one-Party system.

Actually, the key term of "personnalité" underlies the three constituent dimensions of the legitimacy of the Tunisian state. The study of the historical background of the term uncovered the fundamental role of Islam in Tunisian nationalism, in the definitions of the political community and of the state as well as of the relationship between these definitions in Bourguiba's conception.

THE LEGAL DIMENSION

The first newspaper article Bourguiba wrote, "Le Voile", was published in January 1929 and dealt with the situation of women in Tunisia. This article marked his first foray into the public forum. He had taken the place of his brother M'Hamed, who had been invited to participate in a debate organized by "l'Essor", a cultural club linked to the Socialist Party, on "the problem of the veil for Tunisian women".[3] When Bourguiba took the floor, it was expected that this young lawyer, educated in Paris and married to a French woman, would surely make a strong statement against the veil. Not so. Bourguiba, ignoring the minor details of the convenience or inconvenience of the veil, went straight to the heart of the matter; the veil as part of the distinctive social customs formed by Islam was a symbol of the Tunisian "personnalité".

> ...j'ai posé en termes nets et précis le grand problème social qui a toujours été à l'ordre du jour de nos discussions: avons-nous intérêt à hâter, sans ménager les transitions, la disparition de nos moeurs, de nos coutumes, bonnes ou mauvaises, et de tous ces petits riens qui forment par leur ensemble, quoi qu'on dise, notre personnalité? Ma réponse, étant donné les circonstances toutes spéciales dans lesquelles nous vivons, fut catégorique: Non! [4]

The issue of women had, therefore, been shifted or at least linked to the national question; in other words, to the legitimacy of the political order. Durel, leader of the Socialists in Tunisia at the time, responded by stating that "l'individualité tunisienne n'existe pas parce qu'elle n'a jamais existé".[5] And Bourguiba then responded in an article entitled, "Le 'Durellisme' ou le Socialisme boiteux" published by L'Etendard Tunisien in two parts on 1 February and 23 February 1929. In this article, he attacked the Socialists for accepting the fundamental discrimination instituted by the Protectorate, between Tunisians and French nationals, in order to protect French interests.

> Et il est vraiment piteux de voir au prix de quels expédients, de quels tours de passe-passe, la Section Française de l'Internationale Ouvrière en arrive à réaliser ce monument de contradictions et de mauvaise foi: en Tunisie; soutenir ouvertement les intérêts du capitalisme au nom des intérêts "supérieurs" de la patrie; en France, livrer contre ce même capitalisme, ce qu'elle appelle le "bon combat" au nom de principes collectivistes et révolutionnaires.[6]

Essentially, Bourguiba is refusing the internationalist thesis since this had effectively meant the continued exploitation of Tunisia, and he insists on the specificity of a Tunisian entity as a prerequisite to establishing social justice.

> Ainsi l'unité de territoire, la communauté de croyance, de langue, de coutumes, de passé, les joies éprouvées en commun, les revers et les humiliations subis de même, tout cela ne contribue à créer, pour M. Durel, entre les enfants de ce pays, aucun lien, aucun sentiment de solidarité, aucune idée de patrie. En bon internationaliste utopiste, M. Durel n'aime pas les différences qui distinguent les hommes. Alors c'est bien simple: il affirme tout bonnement qu'elles n'existent pas. Très original![7]

Bourguiba here is not very far from Michel ʿAflaq, philosopher of Arab nationalism. While ʿAflaq considers Islam as a product of the Arab genius, Bourguiba considers Islam - "la communauté des croyances" - as a basic component of the Tunisian "personnalité"; in both cases, Islam is a dependent variable, contingent upon the national entity propounded as the source of political legitimacy.

In viewing religion as a necessary component of the national "personnalité", Bourguiba was not an exception although, perhaps, he was the most insistent in the Tunisian context. Tahar Sfar, son of Béchir Sfar and another leader of the Néo-Destour, declared in July 1931 during a speech on the occasion of the celebration of the Prophet's birth, the <u>mawlid</u>; that religion and patriotism were one and the same thing.[8] Bourguiba's position, affirming the need to maintain religion and its cultural consequences as the means to preserve the

Tunisian "personnalité", does not reflect rigidity and a fanatic refusal of change. On the contrary, he wrote:

> L'évolution doit se faire, sinon c'est la mort. Elle se fera, mais sans cassure, sans rupture, de façon à maintenir dans le perpétuel devenir de notre personnalité une unité à travers le temps susceptible d'être perçue à chaque moment par notre conscience.[9]

The term "personnalité" is usually translated into Arabic as shakhṣiyyah. As far as may be discovered, shakhṣiyyah does not have a resonating authentic field in the semantics of classical Arabic literature. In effect, the origins of the term, at least as far as its influence on Bourguiba himself is concerned, seem to lie entirely within the French intellectual tradition. Consequently, a history of the concept of "personnalité" as it evolved in France, with particular attention to the period when Bourguiba was studying there, would provide a framework for the use he made of the term and for its transmutation into the political discourse within the Tunisian nationalist movement.

Etymologically, the roots of the term in French are traced to the Latin persona which referred to the mask, worn to "carry the voice per-sonare",[10] of the theatrical character being acted out on the stage. Only those actors who carried out effective action in the drama were considered as persona;

> ...si l'on se reporte à l'étymologie [persona, masque, rôle de théâtre], la personnalité pourrait se définir "ce qui rend un être capable de jouer un rôle dans le drame de la vie universelle, ce qui lui confère une physionomie propre et une action distincte dans l'ensemble des êtres auxquels il est mêlé". Les décors, les figurants, les comparses, n'ont pas de rôle, n'ont pas de personnalité théâtrale: ne sont des personnes au sens étymologique du mot, que les acteurs engagés dans l'action dramatique dont ils suivent et déterminent, chacun pour sa part, les vicissitudes.[11]

The etymological definition is then followed, in French dictionaries, by definitions specific to the fields of law and of psychology. In law,

> La personnalité juridique, capacité de participer à la vie juridique, appartient, depuis la suppression de l'esclavage, à tous les êtres humains. Mais on a été amené à admettre que certaines institutions, certains groupements résultant du fait de la vie sociale des hommes, devaient, pour répondre aux nécessités qui avaient présidé à leur création, posséder, eux aussi, cette capacité de devenir sujets de droit.[12]

French legal thinking refused to conceive of this "capacité de participer à la vie juridique" as a quality floating around by itself but had to attach it to a legal actor known in French legal literature as "personne juridique" or, more currently, "personne morale". Actually, "personnalité" and "personne" were often used interchangeably so that "personnalité juridique" and "personnalité morale" were found as frequently as "personne morale", at least in the early part of the history of the term when there was still a possibility of attaching "personnalité" to a purpose rather than to an entity. The discussion of the term in the legal sense is then followed by its definition in the field of psychology,

> La personnalité est le complexe unifié, intégré et hiérarchisé de tous les apports biologiques, psychologiques, culturels et sociaux qui font qu'un individu se distingue effectivement de tous les autres et a conscience de son originalité.[13]

As narrated above, Bourguiba spent three years between 1924 and 1927 studying law in France. He also obtained a degree in political science and dabbled in psychology. In this context, another formative factor should be recalled; namely, the influence of Mohamed, Bourguiba's oldest brother, who was active in various theatrical groups. Thus, the concept of "personnalité" united the three intellectual interests of Bourguiba: theatre, psychology and law as they bore on political "praxis".

It was during the period of Bourguiba's studies in France that the debate on "personnalité" was reaching an apogee, under the influence of sociology. Since then, the debate has subsided in the field of law but continues in the field of psychology and psycho-sociology and the literature in these latter fields has become extensive indeed.[14] Consequently, Arab writers presently using the term <u>shakhṣiyyah</u> have dealt with it only from the perspectives offered by the literature in these latter fields. They have missed the juridical implications inherent in the history of the term in its original French,[15] which could not but have influenced Bourguiba's own concept.

Since Bourguiba trained in law, it is imperative that a thorough clarification of the juridical dimension of the term "personnalité" be undertaken in order to understand how it operated in the development of his political thinking. Moreover, Bourguiba was not alone in falling under the influence of contemporary legal thought in France since the majority of the leaders of the Tunisian nationalist movement were lawyers who had trained in France, including Tahar Sfar and Salah Ben Youssef.[16]

The legal discussion of "personnalité" in France had its origins during the latter part of the nineteenth century,[17] as industrial capitalism developed and the need arose to form investment groups and at the same time to limit the liabilities of individual investors. Within the context of the new conditions of an expanding capitalism, the discussion of "personnalité" in the field of law led to a distinction between "association" as a simple sum of individual rights and responsibilities, and "société" (corporation in the contemporary sense) in which an entity, beyond the sum of the individuals themselves, possesses legal rights and responsibilities or, in other words, possesses legal capacity.

> L'association ne constitue qu'un groupement de forces, un faisceau d'individualités réelles poursuivant un même objet, la personne morale [ou société] forme un être nouveau conçu par l'effort de raisonnement et sanctionné par la loi, abstraction pour nos sens, mais ayant, au point de vue du droit, une existence distincte de celle des individus, dont il représente certains intérêts collectifs, et une capacité constituée à l'imitation de celle attribuée à l'homme.[18]

On the whole, there was tremendous resistance to the possibility of recognizing the juridical capacity of entities beyond physical individuals due to the historical legacy of the French revolution of

1789 and the struggle of the new state against the Church, "personne morale par excellence".

> Il ne faut pas perdre de vue que les corporations ont une origine religieuse et que la mainmorte abolie par la révolution française, était une mainmorte ecclésiastique qui menaçait d'envahir tout le sol, en dépouillant les familles et en mettant l'Etat dans la dépendance de l'Eglise, que la Révolution a supprimé toutes les corporations...[19]

Thus, the right of trade guilds (precursors of trade unions) to own property, as much as the right of the Church, was viewed as threatening to establish intermediary institutions between the individual and the state.

> Il existe, à côté des personnes physiques [autrement dit, les hommes], qui sont sujets de droits et d'obligations, des personnes dites morales ou juridiques, qui sont également considérées comme étant susceptibles d'avoir des droits et d'assumer des obligations. Ces personnes ont une puissance patrimoniale qui dépasse souvent de beaucoup celle des personnes physiques. Elles inquiètent le législateur par cette puissance qui ne cesse de croître, car leurs biens ne se transmettent pas et ne se divisent pas au décès, d'où des précautions prises contre le danger de cette perpétuité dite <u>mainmorte</u>.[20]

The capacity of the Church to lay claim to "personnalité" and to constitute itself a "personne morale" based on its ownership of ever-increasing tax-exempt domains posed a fundamental threat to the State which also laid claim to juridical capacity, to "personnalité". In the light of this background, it follows that the French authorities viewed the problem of <u>ḫabus</u>[21] in Tunisia within the framework of their own history, as a threat to the State. Consequently, anyone who was considering a defense of <u>ḫabus</u> from the perspective of French law would be led to consider the "personnalité" of the State. In fact, only a few years before Bourguiba set out to study law in France, the Destour Party had sent delegations to Paris with the specific task of defending this type of land tenure.

The juridical discussion of the concept of "personnalité" had evolved in France around three problems: (1) "personnalité" as a solution to the need for limiting the liabilities of individuals within a capitalist "société" by defining a legal subject to which rights and responsibilities are attached (particularly the right to own property or "patrimoine"), beyond the sum of the individuals concerned; (2) the problem of defining the existence or nature of such a subject; and (3) the problem of the legal capacity of such a subject in the face of the hostility engendered by the French revolution against all corporations and intermediary bodies between the State and its citizens.

The British had pragmatically posited a fictitious person as depository of the sum of individual rights and responsibilities. The German school, beginning with Pufendorf in the seventeenth century and gaining momentum in the nineteenth century with Heise, Brinz, Savigny, von Ihering, and Bluntschli reacted against this position which was considered philosophically weak. In general, the German school tended to consider the "société" as a real person; in other words, as an entity greater than the sum of its individual parts.[22] Savigny was particularly important in the debate as he proposed to demonstrate that history proved the reality of such societies. Moreover, he "rejected the idea of a universal source of law and justice and a universal sanction for laws - in other words natural law - and claimed the national spirit and the unique national history to be the source of all laws, and of the idea of justice prevailing in any nation."[23] Ironically, an added justification of this position - that society was a real person - was achieved under the influence of a British philosopher. Spencer, inspired by biological theories, argued that society is an organism much like the individual human being and, as a consequence, possesses the necessary characteristics which permit it to be considered as a legal subject. The view of society as an integrated organism, "douée d'une conscience, d'une intelligence et d'une volonté propres pour la servir",[24] was also held by Bergson who was a major influence in French intellectual circles during the early part of the twentieth century and whose ideas are reflected in Bourguiba's views.

The main protagonists in the debate about the nature of "personnalité" as legal subject in France were Laurent, as an early precursor, Vareilles-Sommières, Saleilles and Michoud, writing during the 1920s.[25] Vareilles-Sommières accepted the British position of fictitious "personnalité" but Saleilles and Michoud differed by accepting much of the contribution of the German school. The principal originality of the French school was to move the discussion beyond the static conceptions of the German school which tended to view "sociétés" as eternal entities, by bringing in the ideas of the positive sociology of Auguste Comte and Emile Durkheim. Positive sociology maintained the idea that a society is a reality "qui a même valeur d'être que la réalité individuelle, un réel en soi."[26] The main issue was not whether this "réalité" is considered to be a "natural" result of history as it operated to create a culturally-defined community or to be a resultant of concrete interests;[27] the main issue became the question of how effective that "society" was in adapting to changing conditions. Thus, to the actual existence of a distinct society and to the existence of a directing purpose was added a third element, a common will to pursue that purpose.

Consequently, the historical weight created by the legacy of the French revolution against any entities intermediate between the individual and the state was alleviated by the solution first indicated by Hauriou and Renard and systematically presented by Clemens. They finally separated the question of the existence or juridical ontology of "intermediary bodies" and the question of their legal capacity. In the view of Clemens, a collective entity may exist, ontologically, but it acquires legal capacity only through permission or by delegation of authority from the State. But then the State is itself a "personnalité"; how does it acquire, itself, legal capacity? Clemens answers the question in the following way,

> Il y a état, quand il y a dans le groupe conscience de certains buts sociaux naturels et quand la poursuite collectif de ces buts est effectivement voulue et réalisée.[28]

In this definition, it is not enough that the three constituent elements - a material element, meaning the individuals and/or the property concerned; a speculative element which is the purpose directing the action of the entity in question and an element of will which establishes cohesion - exist but there needs to be consciousness of these elements and effective action. In analogy with the individual, consciousness permits the body social to recognize its limits and, thus, identify itself.

> ...la personnalité est l'achèvement de l'individualité, sa forme la plus parfaite, à ce niveau supérieur de l'être, l'individu s'appartient à lui-même de façon pleine et autonome grâce à la conscience claire qu'il prend de lui-même.[29]

And in order to exert its will, the "personne morale" has to act and it acts through physical persons. In the general legal literature on "personnalité" during the inter-War period, these individual persons are not separate legal entities but, as the organs of the "personnalité", are integral parts of the collective body.

> La personne morale ne peut exprimer sa volonté que par les personnes physiques qui agissent en son nom. Ces personnes physiques sont les organes de la puissance morale et non pas seulement ses mandataires ou préposés.[30]

Following the First World War and with the establishment of the League of Nations, the State was formally recognized as "personne internationale" possessing the rights and responsibilities conferred by international law.[31] Consequently, the concept of "personnalité" was a link between civil law, public law and international law.[32] And, of course, any consideration of the "personnalité" of the Tunisian state could only be achieved through the study of the conditions imposed by the Protectorate system.[33]

Translated into international law, the two different options of "association" and "société" had a bearing on the relationship between France and Tunisia. The earlier phase of the Protectorate, as a prototype for policies of "association" implied that France and Tunisia were separate "individualités" or "personnalités" with separate rights and responsibilities pursuing - at least theoretically - the common goal of progress. The indirect administration implicit in the Protectorate formula, whereby the Tunisian government handled internal matters while the French authorities handled external matters, went against the practical experience of the French colonial officials and was in constant tension with their tendency towards direct administration and policies of assimilation.[34] The second phase, roughly marked by the Colonial Congress of 1906 held in Marseilles was characterized by the explicit discussion of the tension between policies of association, which the Tunisian delegates defended, and policies of assimilation which were gradually being implemented and which menaced the separate "personnalité" of Tunisia, in the legal sense. In other words, "assimilation" was equivalent to creating a new "société" threatening to eliminate any need for a Tunisian state as an autonomous partner. It also threatened to place all questions of land tenure under the direct jurisdiction of the State, threatening ḫabus.

As a juridical actor, the State has two roles to play: in relation to the society it governs and in relation to other states. By signing the Treaty of Bardo (12 May 1881), the Bey who embodied in his person the Tunisian state yielded this second role or the external sovereignty of Tunisia to France. But, and this is the point argued by the legalistic defense of the Tunisian nationalist movement, the Treaty of Bardo did not annihilate the Tunisian "personnalité".

> ...the modification in the international personality of the protectorate does not mean extinction. Since the de facto substratum of personality granted by international law subsists, that personality will continue in spite of the change to which the protectorate is subject.... This point seems to require emphasis, that in an international sense, a protectorate, regardless of the degree or kind of civilization prevailing in the country over which it is exercised, contemplates the retention by that country of a personality recognizable as such by international law.[35]

While the Treaty of Bardo may be considered within the purview of international law, the Treaty of La Marsa (8 June 1883) may be considered within the framework of public law. The latter treaty effectively curtailed the internal sovereignty of the Bey as it placed him, the embodiment of the Tunisian state, under the obligation to promulgate any "reforms" which the French government deemed necessary. When the Destour Party first placed the promulgation of a Constitution on its program, it was trying to argue that the 1861 Constitution meant that the sovereignty of the Tunisian state, in the legal sense, was not limited to the Bey but was shared by the Tunisian people. It thus hoped to check the erosion of the Tunisian "personnalité" by re-instituting the limitations placed on the Bey who seemed to be yielding internal sovereignty to France; in other words, to check the erosion of the Tunisian "personnalité", at least in public law, as the means to achieve international independence. In contrast, the 1933 program considered the Constitution as an aim rather than as a means and viewed independence, in the sense of international sovereignty, as the means to achieve popular sovereignty.

In contrast to the concept of "personnalité", whose origins lie entirely within the Western intellectual tradition,[36] the concept of "action" (in Arabic, âmal) creates reverberations in the Arab-Islamic tradition as much as in the French-Western tradition. The title of the newspaper established by Bourguiba was L'Action Tunisienne and its Arabic version was Al-ʿAmal. The Arabic term, ʿamal, and its related derivatives are profuse in the Qurʾân and references to Quranic verses were used extensively by the Néo-Destour Party. The controversy about the relative value of faith and action in gaining merit was one of the fundamental issues in Islamic theology, beginning with the Muʿtazilah during the early part of the ninth century. This controversy centred on the slogan "al-amr bi-al-maʿrûf wa-al-nahy ʿan al-munkar" (whose non-literal translation is to act for the good and against evil but, literally, to order what is known and to forbid what is denied.).

Islam is a commitment to al-amr bî-al-maʿrûf wa-al-nahy ʿan al-munkar. This is a loaded phrase since it means that there is no faith without commitment and no islâm without action and that good intentions are not enough. Among the Prophetic traditions (ḥadîth) which are quoted in support of this idea, that faith alone is not really enough, are the following:

1) Man raʾâ minkum munkar fa-l-yughayirhu bi-yadih fa-in lam yastaṭiʿ fa-bi-lisanih fa-in lam yastaṭiʿ fa-bi-qalbih wa-huwa aḍʿaf al-îmân (whoever of you sees an evil then he should change it with his hand and if he is unable to then with his tongue and if he is unable to then in his heart and that is the weakest form of faith).

2) Al-Qalb lâ yakfî wa-al-îmân al-ḥaqq huwa

> al-îmân al-fa‘‘âl (The heart is not enough and true faith is effectively active faith).[37]

Finally, it is the concept which links Bourguiba to Afghânî and to so many other Muslim militants whose driving slogan reflected their concern for revolutionary effectiveness. Bourguiba himself links the Tunisian nationalist movement to Afghânî rather than to the reformist ‘Abduh; "It began with Jamâl al-Dîn al-Afghânî then Khayr al-Dîn Pasha then Ali Bash Hanba then Ahmad Essafi and Abdelaziz Thaalbi then Habib Bourguiba."[38] Nonetheless, the proponents of the "official" school of the history of the Tunisian nationalist movement attempt to link Bourguiba to ‘Abduh, the representative of the Islamic reform movement who held moderate political positions in the sense that he gave higher priority to internal reform than to revolution against external domination.[39]

Bourguiba's emphasis on "action" is, at the same time, a logical development of his defense of the Tunisian "personnalité". It was not sufficient to assert the existence of the Tunisian "personnalité", only by action would this Tunisian "personnalité" be brought forth and acknowledged. Nonetheless, a "personnalité" had to be embodied in a real entity which, according to Hauriou, is "antérieurement développée". Here is the link with the second, the historical, dimension of legitimacy since it was through historical action that a "personnalité" is created and "l'histoire crée des réalités et non des fictions."[40]

In sum, therefore, "personnalité" as the locus of rights and responsibilities was viewed as a necessary quality of the State. Within its own territory, only the State had juridical capacity which it may then confer upon or withdraw from other entities. The State - as the organ of the nation - is defined "par la nature et l'histoire du peuple de cet état".[41] In other words, the legal "personnalité" of the State is defined by the psycho-social "personnalité" of the nation as it comes into being (être) through history and as it actualizes its future (devenir) through action. Consequently, Bourguiba is able to sum up the situation of Tunisia during the Protectorate in the following evolutionary terms:

> ...tout traité de protectorat porte en lui son germe de mort en raison même de son objet, un Etat ne pouvant être à la fois sujet et

> souverain. Une évolution inévitable susceptible de se manifester sous deux formes opposées y mettra nécessairement un terme. S'agit-il d'un pays sans vitalité, d'un peuple dégénéré qui décline, réduit à n'être plus qu'une "poussière d'individus", qu'un "ramassis de peuples", c'est la déchéance qui l'attend, c'est l'absorption progressive, l'assimilation, en un mot, la disparition totale et inéluctable. S'agit-il, au contraire, d'un peuple sain, vigoureux que les compétitions internationales ou une crise momentanée ont forcé à accepter la tutelle d'un Etat fort, la situation nécessairement inférieure qui lui est faite, le contact d'une civilisation plus avancée déterminent en lui une réaction salutaire: sous l'aiguillon de la nécessité qui se confond en l'espèce avec l'instinct de conservation, il entre résolument dans la voie du progrès, il brûle les étapes; une véritable régénération se produit en lui; et grâce à une judicieuse assimilation des principes et des méthodes de cette civilisation, il arrivera fatalement à réaliser par étapes son émancipation définitive.[42]

THE HISTORICAL DIMENSION

The historical dimension of legitimacy in Bourguiba's conception is intimately linked with the psycho-social aspect of "personnalité". This linkage illustrates the interaction between sociology and legal thought in France during the inter-War period. Thus, we find Bergson asking the same questions as the legists,

> Est-ce que seuls, les êtres humains, les individus, sont des personnes, et les sociétés qu'ils constituent, par leur rassemblement, ne sont-elles pas ou ne peuvent-elles pas accéder au rang de véritables personnes, arrivées à un certain degré de maturité? Pour ma part, je n'hésite pas à l'affirmer. Lorsqu'une société a grandi et mûri, lorsqu'elle est arrivée au point de prendre totalement conscience de soi-même elle est une personne. Lorsqu'une société a des traditions, des lois, des institutions que synthéthisent son passé et y jouent le même rôle que joue la mémoire dans

> chaque individu, elle est une personne. Une société qui se modifie, se déforme, se reforme, s'améliore, créant en soi-même une sorte de nouveau caractère est une personne. Une société qui développe ce caractère dans un certain sens privilégié, et qui, de cette manière, joue dans le monde un rôle spécial, et accomplit une mission parfaitement définie, est une personne.
> La nation peut être grande ou petite, peu importe. Un individu cesse-t-il d'être une personne parce qu'il est de petite taille? Une nation peut être petite et, dans certains cas, cela n'empêche pas que son âme soit grande; de même que dans un petit corps particulier peut résider une grande âme, de même dans un corps social réduit. La société est une personne et elle a, comme toute personne, des droits inviolables. Telle est, je pense, la conclusion à laquelle on arriverait...en considérant la société consciente d'elle-même, la société avec ses traditions.[43]

In the philosophical sense, "personnalité" is that which distinguishes human beings from animals and things, generally, and from other human beings, differentially. Human beings differ from animals and things by two principal characteristics: (1) consciousness and (2) freedom. The emphasis on consciousness and freedom inherent in the concept of "personnalité" resists the tendency to reduce human beings to <u>objects</u> of study.[44] The premise that human beings are <u>objects</u> of forces beyond them implies an ethics beyond law; an ethics without "obligation ni sanction, ...une morale auxquelles les idées de liberté et de responsabilité seront étrangers."[45] The lawyer in Bourguiba could not fail to recognize the anarchic implications of such a position, which undermines the basis of law and the raison d'être of lawyers. Only by holding that human beings possess consciousness and freedom of action could they be considered to be responsible.

This renewed emphasis on the value of the human being in French thought following World War I led to the personalism of Renouvier and of Emmanuel Mounier. Charles Renouvier (1815-1903) is the author of <u>Le Personnalisme</u> (1902) where he emphasizes the juridical aspects, considering the person as a juridical subject with rights and responsibilities. Emmanuel Mounier (1905-1950), of Bourguiba's generation, was influenced by Jaurès and by Bergson through Charles Péguy, as well as by Renouvier, of course. He wrote Révolution personnaliste et communautaire (1935), Manifeste au service du personnalisme (1936) and Le Personnalisme (1949). Mounier distinguished between personality and individuality. Rejecting the Freudian emphasis on the individual, Mounier asserted that only by sacrificing his/her ego-centric individuality could the human being achieve true personality or, in other words, the "nous" must become immanent in the "moi". Mounier adjusted the legalist concerns of Renouvier towards a more mystical sense of love and self-sacrifice, as the basis of certainty. From this "classical" personalism, an existential stream (with Nicolas Berdiaev, Paul-Louis Landsberg, Paul Ricoeur) and a Marxist stream (with Jean Lacroix) evolved. From the metaphysical point of view, "personnalité" is the highest form of being, "être". It is that by which being knows it is; it is that by which the "I" is necessarily different and separate from the "non-I", from the "you". Theologically, God may be considered as the most perfect "personnalité" but the problem would then be how to conceive of God, the one and only, in terms of a "non-God".

Consciousness as reason is, of course, a famous Descartean precept but, at the turn of the century, this precept was mitigated by Bergson, heir to Spinoza and Leibniz, who emphasized intuition as the most important component of consciousness. In his speech in Paris on 29 June 1972, Bourguiba made the link between Bergson and the Arab-Islamic intellectual heritage. He stated, "If our demands borrow from Descartes and Pascal, they draw as well on the Arab-Islamic culture, on the oriental soul and on treasures of imagination and intuition which Bergson himself would not disown".[46]

At either extreme of reason or intuition, consciousness was viewed as a necessary pre-condition of freedom. Freedom is considered as the characteristic which allows a person to exist as such, to be the cause of his/her own actions and, through these actions, of his/her own being (être) Thus, freedom implies the capacity to determine the future (devenir).[47]

Freedom is the necessary element for a dynamic view of "personnalité" since it is through the freedom to act that the transformation and the maintenance of juridical capacity, "personnalité", is achieved. Moreover, this "personnalité" is a coherent whole and indivisible, precisely because it is in a continuous state of change.[48] But the experieence of change and movement is in tension with the need to maintain the internal coherence and unity of this "personnalité".

> En communication avec un monde de situations et de personnes continuellement changeantes, soumise dans son comportement à des expériences de succès et d'échec, la personnalité a souvent quelque peine à maintenir son identité psychique ainsi que sa conception de soi.[49]

These experiences are conditioned by the cultural superstructure which informs the perception of the individuals and shapes their reactions.[50]

On the one hand, each culture tends to produce a specific type of personality. On the other hand, this specific personality may also influence the cultural superstructure as it acts to modify religious beliefs, ideas and behavior. Where these two processes are articulated is considered as the locus of the basic personality of that culture.[51] The interaction between the individual "personnalité" and the cultural superstructure, part of the social "personnalité", has been studied by historical behaviorists and cultural anthropologists. The latter, especially, have worked on demonstrating the influence of early socialization processes and education on forming the basic personality.

> ...la personnalité de base dépend des coutumes "primaires" d'une culture (surtout les pratiques de socialisation des jeunes ou méthodes d'éducation) ...elle sous-tend surtout l'ensemble des attitudes affectives et les systèmes de valeurs dans la configuration d'une person- nalité.[52]

Although elements had been presented by historians and sociologists, the systematic elaboration of the link between the basic personality and the individual was systematized by Abram Kardiner and Ralph Linton in their major work, The Individual and His Society written in 1939. Their work extended the theoretical framework of Margaret Mead, Coming of Age in Samoa (1928) and of Ruth Benedict, Patterns of Culture (1935). Both the fact that they were written in English, a language not readily accessible to Bourguiba, and the fact that they were written much later than his formative period of the late 1920s, suggest that these books were not major influences on Bourguiba. Nonetheless, and as mentioned previously, these theories of personality in the field of psychology form the framework for what later Arab thinkers believed was involved in the term "personnalité".[53]

For Bourguiba, the cultural superstructure which defines the political community and which lends historical legitimacy to his regime is Tunisian. It is this <u>Tunisian</u> cultural superstructure which becomes the source of symbols needed to maintain the consent necessary to transform might into right. But, Islam is a fundamental component of the Tunisian cultural superstructure.

Islam is the bedrock from which a variety of subterranean streams of historical consciousness sprang in Tunisia. These streams of historical consciousness are expressed in "symbol spheres" which set the structure of the exchange or communication networks and lend meaning to the mundane exchange of capital, labor and products. "Symbol spheres" tend to be versatile and elastic as they are functions of a metaphorical mode of cognition and, therefore, are slow to achieve transformation beyond variations in interpretation. It is precisely this metaphorical nature which permits a great measure of change without essential transformation and could create situations where "symbol spheres" are out of phase with the material conditions of society.

> In summary, symbol spheres may be monopolized by one set of legitimating symbols which are so deeply internalized they do not need to be defended. If they are questioned, persons become articulate about them and jump to their defense as absolutes. The existence of such symbol spheres is conditioned by institutional harmony within and between various orders, by a slow rate of institutional change and by a monopoly of the channels of communication and persuasion. When the reverse of these three conditions exists, the chances for countersymbols of legitimacy to emerge are increased.... It is during such periods of transition...that mass movements and collective forms of behavior are likely to appear.[54]

For Bourguiba, the Tunisian cultural superstructure goes beyond the formative influences of Islam as he traces it back to the Berber substratum. He insists on the study of the pre-Islamic history of Tunisia in order to demonstrate the existence of a specifically Tunisian "personnalité" before the coming of Islam and to demonstrate the ability of that "personnalité" to adapt to each historical period while lending each period its own specific flavor. Thus, the interaction between the native Berbers and the Phoenician settlers created the Punic culture, a specifically Tunisian variant of the Phoenician civilization. Similarly, the interaction with the Arabs who came to Tunisia in the name of Islam was expressed in various movements, from open rebellion under the Kâhina to dissident movements under the banner of Islam, first in support of Kharijism then in support of the Fatimids and finally, in an autonomous State, the Hafsids.[55]

In sum, history, for Bourguiba, demonstrates that a specifically Tunisian "personnalité" exists and that it conditions Islam to the same extent that Islam conditions it. Even more to the point, history demonstrates that it was through the action undertaken by the Néo-Destour or rather by Bourguiba himself, as the organ of the Tunisian entity, that the latter achieved "personnalité".

THE CHARISMATIC DIMENSION

The above account of the early period of the Néo-Destour Party leaves no doubt as to the popularity of Bourguiba among the masses of the people, which continued even after the establishment of the Republic of Tunisia.[56] His charisma also operates on a person-to-person level, as his penetrating blue eyes bore into his "interlocuteur". He has presence or, in other words, a strong "personnalité" so that when he comes into a room, it is immediately felt.

The charismatic facet of the concept of "personnalité" is linked to its juridical and historical dimensions, at least according to Bergson. Analogous to the human being, society needs to change in order to survive, to maintain its unity and its identity through time. How is this task to be achieved? Only a hero could accomplish such a promethean task.

> Le principe unificateur de la société...c'est l'élan vital.... La société ne le capte pas, seule une personne en est capable.... Pour y accéder, il faut l'héroisme.[57]

Ben Youssef challenged Bourguiba in terms of all three dimensions of legitimacy: He proposed himself as the heroic "principe unificateur", he proposed the Arab-Islamic rather than the Tunisian "personnalité" as the basis for the historical legitimacy of the State and, consequently, he appeared to favor a unitary state, Maghribi if not Arab, rather than a Tunisian state.

THE CONSTRUCTION OF A LEGITIMATE STATE: FROM PROTECTORATE TO SOVEREIGNTY

Ben Youssef, Secretary General of the Néo-Destour Party, had expressed his opposition to the internal autonomy accords as early as the Bandung Conference, in April 1955. Despite this, or perhaps because of it, Bourguiba, President of the Party, did not wait in Paris for the official signing of the accords on 3 June 1955. The fantastically enthusiastic welcome Bourguiba received on his return to Tunis on 1 June 1955 seemed to indicate that he had the people behind him and that he could swing the support necessary for the implementation of the accords.

But this was not to be as simple as it appeared during those few weeks of euphoria. Even before the return of Ben Youssef, opposition to the accords was being expressed.[58] Since the Ben Youssef "sedition" is one of the most sensitive periods in the history of the Tunisian nationalist movement, the sources available are not sufficiently explicit about the social bases of support offered to Ben Youssef or about the ideological differences he had with Bourguiba. Only indirect references allow us to reconstruct an approximate image of the situation between 1955 and 1961 when Ben Youssef was assassinated.

The primary task facing Bourguiba on his return was to demonstrate, one more time, that <u>he</u> was the acknowledged leader of the Tunisian people. In order to accomplish that task, he had to repair or eliminate any dissensions within the Néo-Destour Party which Ben Youssef's opposition could provoke. As usual, Bourguiba undertook to establish direct contact with the Tunisian people. He travelled through the Sahel and held meetings at the headquarters of national organizations such as the U.G.A.T., the U.T.A.C. and the U.G.T.T.

Bourguiba worked hard to build up support for the accords, mostly among working-class sectors of the population in Tunis and the populist elements in the Sahel region. He had not yet toured the South when the formation of a government was announced for 17 September 1955, in which five of the eleven portfolios were to be held by the Néo-Destour and three more were to be held by independent sympathizers of the Party. But Bourguiba himself did not participate, giving as reason the fact that the government was not a result of popular elections. His position was justified on the ideological order, since the Néo-Destour had always insisted that Tunisian sovereignty resided within the people so that the Bey was reduced to the status of symbol of Tunisian sovereignty rather than the actual embodiment of that sovereignty. It is also possible that, at that point in time, he was not acceptable to the French authorities. Bourguiba then devoted himself to the re-organization of the Néo-Destour Party.[59]

In the meantime, Ben Youssef had announced his return to Tunisia on 3 September 1955 but without indicating any softening in his opposition to the accords. Nonetheless, it would seem that Bourguiba made some efforts at conciliating Ben Youssef, to no avail.[60]

The question of whether or not to unite forces with the Algerians and the Moroccans in the struggle for liberation from French domination was at issue since the establishment of the Arab Maghrib Office in Cairo, under the aegis of the League of Arab States. One could pose the hypothesis that, if a united Maghribi front had actually and effectively been formed, the price which Algeria finally had to pay alone, might have been reduced to a considerable extent. On the other hand, if the territorial bases which independent Tunisia was able to provide for the Front de Libération Nationale had not been available, would Algeria have achieved independence? But this is one of the "if" questions which history cannot answer.

In any case, it would have been extremely difficult if not practically impossible to change the habits formed during some thirty years by the premise that Tunisian independence was to be obtained through "dialogue" between Tunisia, on the one hand, and France, on the other hand. Any other "interlocuteurs" were viewed as incidental.[61]

When he did return, Ben Youssef was received with almost as great popular enthusiasm as Bourguiba.[62] The same masses that had so enthusiastically welcomed Bourguiba were only too ready to give a similar welcome to his rival, Ben Youssef. It took Ben Youssef some three weeks to calculate that he had sufficient support to attempt challenging Bourguiba. On 7 October 1955, he declared his opposition openly when he was given the podium for the Friday sermon at the Zaytûnah mosque. His basic position was the rejection of the internal autonomy accords and a demand for complete independence. Of course, the implications of choosing the Zaytûnah as forum were not lost.

> Pour faire sa rentrée politique, Salah Ben Youssef ne pouvait pas procéder à un meilleur choix: une assistance nombreuse et surtout un jour et endroit qui l'aideraient à se poser non seulement en partisan de l'indépendance totale mais aussi en fervent défenseur de la religion. Salah Ben Youssef, en critiquant les protocoles, se présente cette fois-ci comme le défenseur de l'arabisme et de l'Islam contre le laicisme prôné par le Néo-Destour.[63]

Ben Youssef declared that the internal autonomy accords had implicitly placed Tunisia within the Union Française. Such an affiliation was in absolute contradiction with the fundamentals of the Arab-Islamic "personnalité", basis of the legal and historical legitimacy of the nationalist movement in Tunisia, according to him.[64]

Immediately following this historic "sermon", Bourguiba acted. He called a meeting of the Bureau Politique on 8 October 1955 where Ben Youssef was removed from his office of Secretary General and excluded from the Party. In order to give greater weight to the decision made by the Bureau Politique, a Party Congress was called for 15 November 1955. But the decision was not publicized for four days during which period attempts were made to soften Bourguiba, indicating that Ben Youssef had not yet lost all his friends in the rush for power.[65]

The conflict between Bourguiba and Ben Youssef had multiple levels to it: (1) competition for the effective leadership of the Néo-Destour Party; (2) conflict between different class-fraction alliances expressed in different ideological positions; and (3) conflict between different international alignments. It is difficult to accept that personal competition for leadership of the Party, alone, could have led to the civil strife which Tunisia was to experience during the period. Deeper causes lay with the social alliances that were being worked out in preparation for eminent independence and the take-over of power.

Ben Youssef seemed to have attracted the Zaytûnah-based organizations which were fed by the "traditional" economic sectors of the towns and by the network of zâwiyahs in the rural areas. Both the U.G.A.T. and the U.T.A.C. at first reserved their options but the U.G.A.T. finally opted for Ben Youssef. Soon enough a rival organization, the U.N.A.T. (Union Nationale des Agriculteurs Tunisiens) was established with the encouragement of the Néo-Destour and it succeeded in eliminating the U.G.A.T.[66] In terms of regions, Ben Youssef's origins in Jerba gave him popularity in the South which was a particularly sensitive region as it served as conduit for the Algerian revolution.

In contrast, Bourguiba had good relations with the landed "grande bourgeoisie" of Tunis represented by Chenik and Ben Ammar. But the key alliance he made was with the U.G.T.T., led by the young Ahmed Ben Salah. In terms of regions, Bourguiba could rely on the Sahel and, perhaps, on the Cap Bon through Messadi.

The important point to be noted is that these alliances were not as clear-cut as might be thought at first. Thus, Bourguiba's populist charisma could reach the sûqs and the bidon-villes around Tunis. Moreover, his alliance with the U.G.T.T. gave him access to crucially important sectors in the south, particularly in the Sfax-Gabes-Gafsa triangle.

> Sérieusement menacé pendant plusieurs semaines par la démagogie de son rival que soutiennent...les traditionalistes, certains tenants du Protectorat, Bourguiba l'emporte graĉe à son prestige, mais aussi grâce à l'aide décisive que lui apportent l'U.G.T.T. et son chef, Ahmed Ben Salah.[67]

The social alignments supporting Ben Youssef and Bourguiba had their respective extrapolations on the international scene. Ben Youssef drew support from the Arab East, particularly from Nasser, who was emerging as the leader of the Arab world, and from the hopes of the non-aligned bloc. In contrast, Bourguiba continued in the tradition of the Tunisian nationalist movement by drawing strength from the ability to influence the French authorities.[68]

Interestingly enough, Bourguiba had obtained the support of the Socialists in Tunisia. Elie Cohen-Hadria stated: "Il nous reste à souhaiter...que, au Parti néo-destourien d'abord, dans l'opinion publique ensuite, les thèses de Bourguiba l'emportent sur celles de Ben Youssef."[69] Moreover, a member of the Jewish Tunisian community, Me Albert Bessis, accepted to participate in the transition government formed in September 1955. Since the U.T.A.C. was also presided by a member of the Jewish Tunisian community, Bourguiba received the support of that organization as well.[70]

During the three months between June and September when Ben Youssef had not yet returned to Tunisia, the speeches of Bourguiba were free of any Islamic themes or references.[71] On the day the new government was formed and only a few days after Ben Youssef's return, Bourguiba was in Sfax where he gave a speech calling for national unity. He ended by quoting from the Qur)ân(3:103):

> And hold fast,
> All together, by the Rope
> Which God (stretches out
> for you), and be not divided
> Among yourselves.

Just as Bourguiba was touring the country in order to establish "direct contact", Ben Youssef was doing exactly the same thing but following a different circuit. Whereas Bourguiba seemed to be avoiding Islamic themes in his speeches, Ben Youssef seemed to accentuate them.[72]

The theme of "national unity" became Bourguiba's "mot d'ordre" as well as the concomittant corollary of refusing any alliances with the Arab East and, consequently, with the Islamist element in Tunisian society. Even when he went to Kairouan, the holy city of Tunisia, Bourguiba avoided the mosque, but he could not resist the temptation of quoting the Quranic verse (13:17):

> For the scum disappears
> Like Froth cast out;
> While that which is for the good
> Of mankind remains
> On the earth.

On 15 November 1955, the fifth Party Congress was held in Sfax. The fact that the Congress was held in Sfax, the "home-town" of the U.G.T.T., is an indication of the organizational alliance between the Néo-Destour of Bourguiba and the U.G.T.T. of Ahmed Ben Salah. Actually, Ben Salah had accepted the national unity "mot d'ordre" and had renounced class struggle. Of course, in return for the U.G.T.T. adherence to Bourguiba's mot d'ordre, Ben Salah believed himself to be positioning the U.G.T.T. to play a central role in the new political game that was shaping up.[73] An implicit entente seems to have been reached between the Néo-Destour and the U.G.T.T. On the one hand, a more equitable economic situation was promised and, on the other hand, it was left to the future Tunisian state to provide the mechanisms for such economic equity.[74] Thus, Bourguiba was demonstrating that he could override Ben Youssef despite the fact that, as a native of Jerba, Ben Youssef had commanded widespread allegiance in the south. The Sfax Congress was considered so important that it was termed the Congress of Resurrection (<u>al-ba'th</u>) some 1,000 delegates were present as well as representatives of several national organizations. In his two-hour long opening speech, Bourguiba insisted on the Arab and Islamic dimensions of the Tunisian "personnalité" but pointed out that, by its geography and as part of the Maghrib, Tunisia was Western. He concluded that, therefore, the role of Tunisia was to serve as a bridge between "two great civilizations of which all humanity would be proud."[75] In sum, the main issue before the Congress was a ratification of the internal autonomy accords and the rejection of Ben Youssef's position. Despite the fact that Ben Youssef had not been invited to the Congress, a closed door session of the Congress decided to invite him. This last minute invitation again indicates that Ben Youssef continued to enjoy at least some support from some elements of the Party. Nonetheless, he believed that the Congress was stacked against him and requested that some time be allowed in order to invite those Party cells which were sympathetic to his position. The request was refused and the Congress continued without Ben Youssef.

A comparison between the motion presented by Bourguiba for voting and the final resolution adopted by the Congress indicates that Ben Youssef was not alone in doubting the value of the accords. Whereas Bourguiba asked that the Congress "<u>Approuve</u>

sans réserves la politique menée par le Bureau politique", the final resolution stated that the Congress "Enregistre que le Bureau politique a conduit le mouvement nationaliste à l'intérieur du pays et à l'extérieur dans la bonne voie". The Congress agreed that the accords were a positive step (while Ben Youssef had stated that they were a step backwards because they lent popular legitimacy to the Bardo Treaty) and that "l'indépendance totale demeure le but final". Whereas Bourguiba asked for a mandate for the Political Bureau and for himself as President of the Party to pursue "émancipation" (in view of the "trial" of the concepts of "indépendance", "émancipation", "tutelle" in 1938 Bourguiba was signalling to France his willingness to have an intermediate step between internal autonomy and full independence), the Congress addressed itself to the Ben Ammar government and requested it to work towards total independence. Whereas the accords had kept the police forces within Tunisia under French authority, the Congress called for the creation of a supplementary force which would become the core of a future national army.[76]

The Congress called for general elections and for an Assembly to work on establishing a Constitution within the framework of a constitutional monarchy. The Congress also risked the displeasure of France by voting for a resolution which called on France to end the war in Algeria and to recognize the legitimate aspirations of the Algerian people. In view of the U.G.T.T. role in support of the Party and of the accords, the Congress also undertook to vote for a series of economic resolutions.

Finally, the Congress voted for an enlarged Bureau Politique composed of eleven members and for Bourguiba as President of the Party. Ben Youssef was, therefore, definitely ousted from the Bureau Politique.[77] The situation appeared ironic; as Ben Youssef adopted Bourguiba's populist tactics, Bourguiba began to rely on organized institutions such as the U.N.A.T., the U.T.A.C., and the U.G.T.T. While the Congress was being held in Sfax, Ben Youssef organized a popular rally of some 20,000 people on 18 November 1955 at the Géo André stadium in Tunis. Concomittantly, Islamic connotations appeared at the rally as the crowds called for jihâd. The possibility of Tunisians fighting at the side of France against fellow-Muslims (the war in Algeria was raging) was evoked and served to mobilize the masses.

At the rally, Ben Youssef went beyond his first platform of opposition to the internal autonomy accords to a second issue. He called for Tunisia to affirm its Arab-Islamic "personnalité" in the name of total independence.

> La Tunisie...est une partie indivisible du monde arabe....Elle fait partie de la collectivité arabe, rien ne doit l'en séparer, contrairement à ce que dit Bourguiba ....Bourguiba! ...nous ne pouvons avoir un autre destin qu'un destin arabe...[78]

Actually, the Egyptian representatives at the rally encouraged him to establish a new Party in order to carry out his platform. Even the Néo-Destour faithful to Bourguiba wished that Ben Youssef would establish another Party but it appears that Ben Youssef hoped to accomplish what the 1934 Ksar Hellal Congress had accomplished in effectively taking over the machinery and the legitimacy of <u>the</u> nationalist Party. Nonetheless, he established an autonomous entity, the "Secrétariat Général", on 30 October 1955[79] and thus attempted to base the legitimacy of his opposition on his position of Secretary General of the Destour Party.

Following the Sfax Congress, the struggle between Bourguiba and Ben Youssef shifted to the rural areas in the south-west. The logistics of the Algerian war enabled these areas to obtain arms. The nascent violence of the <u>fallâqah</u> that had marked the last years of the struggle for independence threatened to be transformed into a major Youssefist attempt to regain power.[80]

Beginning in late October 1955, the guerrilla actions gradually amplified to almost the proportions of a civil war but were successfully contained. Finally, on 28 January 1956, the police raided Ben Youssef's home but he had somehow got wind of the impending raid and had fled to Cairo.[81] At the same time, a general sweep of the pro-Ben Youssef activists was made and a total of some 60 to 70 were arrested. In view of the suspected Youssefist sentiments within the Courts, a special Criminal Court was instituted with wide powers to judge the prisoners. These measures provoked a multiplication of violence as the issue of contention became clearly who should be the "constructeurs d'un nouveau régime".[82]

In the meanwhile, France had accorded independence to Morocco and knew quite well that nothing less would permit the "moderate" elements in Tunisia to maintain their credibility.[83] As early as November 1955, Edgar Faure had courageously made a speech in the National Assembly, which he did not later retract, where he projected "l'indépendance dans l'interdépendance" for Tunisia.[84] The fact that he had used the term "indépendance", even though qualified, was considered a great step forward by Bourguiba. But as the Faure government soon fell, it was left to the socialist Guy Mollet to actually carry out the negotiations with Bourguiba. A long debate was first undertaken whereby the Bardo Treaty became the issue in terms of the legalistic framework of essentially very similar positions. The French authorities were ready to concede a Tunisian army and Tunisian diplomatic representation, the main symbols of international sovereignty, as amendments to the June 1955 accords preserving the Bardo Treaty. In contrast, Bourguiba was ready to accept a Tunisian army and Tunisian diplomatic representation but in terms of a new treaty, thus abrogating the Bardo Treaty just as much as the June 1955 accords.

Despite the fact that the National Assembly of France had voted to give the government special powers of undertake the repression of the Algerian war, the Tunisian delegation led by Bahi Ladgham continued to negotiate. On 20 March 1956, a protocole of negotiations was finally agreed upon proposing independence and the abrogation of the Bardo Treaty. Since Bourguiba had no official position within the Tunisian government, he was not present at the ceremonial signature of the protocole.

> C'est évidemment l'opinion intérieure de son pays qui le préoccupe. A quelques semaines des élections à l'Assemblée constituante tunisienne, il s'applique à enlever leurs arguments à ses adversaires [les Youssefists] et à montrer qu'en approuvant les conventions franco-tunisiennes [de juin 1955], il ne s'est pas laissé enfermer dans un univers clos.[85]

In October 1956, Ben Youssef proposed a "sacred union" with Bourguiba but it was too late; Bourguiba had won "indépendance" following the agreement of March 1956 with France and was in a position to give vent to the bitterness of betrayal that Ben

Youssef's sedition had engendered. On 24 January 1957, Salah Ben Youssef and six of his followers were condemned to death for treason in absentia. Despite this, Bourguiba met with Ben Youssef in 1961 in Zurich, Switzerland, but Ben Youssef continued to resist Bourguiba's charisma and no reconciliation was achieved. On 14 August 1961, Ben Youssef was assassinated in Wiesbaden, Germany.[86]

Since the police was still under French authority, the Néo-Destour undertook to organize its own armed bands, specifically in the south-west areas. Moreover, a few concessions were made by the French authorities who transferred certain Tunisian troops, known as Oudjak and Maghzen, remnants of the pre-Protectorate state apparatus, to the Tunisian government. This provoked a reaction among the colonists who increased their support for the clandestine terrorist organization known as "La Main Rouge".[87]

The abrogation of the Bardo Treaty also meant that the French would not protect the Bey, in his role as the embodiment of Tunisian sovereignty within the sphere of public law.[88] The Bey fully understood the implications. In theory, the exact constitutional nature of the Tunisian state was to be determined by a Constituent Assembly and, as the Sfax Congress had voted, within the framework of a constitutional monarchy. On 29 December 1955, the Bey had issued a decree by which the National Constituent Assembly was to be elected by direct and secret universal suffrage. Bourguiba's growing concern for maintaining the integrity of "national unity" led the Néo-Destour to establish a national front which included candidates representing the U.G.T.T., the U.N.A.T. and the U.T.A.C., the Jewish community, the Socialists and the independents. This close relationship between the labor unions and the party assured the Néo-Destour complete control of the Assembly; "Total unity through total organization was the goal."[89]

When on 25 July 1957 Prime Minister Bourguiba presented the Assembly with a proposal for the establishment of a Tunisian republic, the motion was voted in unanimously. Moreover, the Assembly designated Bourguiba head of the Tunisian state while holding the office of Prime Minister as well. At first examination, the deposition of the Bey might seem to have flouted the element of continuity in Tunisian history which is such an essential feature of the concept of "personnalité".

Bourguiba for his part was sensitive to the continuity of Tunisian history and the importance of monarchy; his first action on returning to Tunis, both in 1943 and in 1949, was to seek audience with the Bey. But it was a continuity of which he saw himself as the embodiment and a succession of which he regarded himself as the heir.[90]

Measured in terms of the ultimate test of legitimacy, the ability to succeed, the Néo-Destour Party as an institution and Bourguiba as its organ had proved themselves able to achieve that goal which had eluded Tunisia for so long, independence. Bourguiba had demonstrated courage in the long struggle for political independence and he had been successful. These were "qualities which commend at least as much respect in Tunisia as anywhere else."[91] In effect, Bourguiba had pitted the active historical legitimacy of the Destour Party, which he embodied, against the static historical legitimacy of the Bey. Bourguiba won.

The challenge thrown down by Ben Youssef had contested Bourguiba's position as the real leader of the country. The change in the constitutional program which Bourguiba initiated may be seen as part of his response to this challenge. By becoming the constitutional leader of Tunisia, Bourguiba added to the credibility of his position as the real, effective leader - so long as he continued to achieve success.

Beyond the priority given to the task of state-building over nation-building, international problems had continued to plague Tunisia throughout the 1950s and until the end of the Algerian War. In the first place, regional considerations complicated relations with France. In the second place, the United States alternated between willingness to intervene in the previous dominions of its Allies and a hands-off policy.

Relations with France passed through several crises. The first occurred at the end of October 1956, following the kidnapping of Ahmed Ben Bella and his companions who were on their way to meet Bourguiba and Mohamed V in Tunis. Almost at the same time, the French participation in the combined British-Israeli-French attack against Egypt also exacerbated relations. The two crises allowed Bourguiba to pressure France in order to limit the troops it had posted on Tunisian soil. In fact, the Algerian war was to become among the foremost concerns of the new Tunisian government and may have delayed the process of economic development which was to become the overriding issue during the 1960s.

In February 1958, the French forces attacked the frontier village of Sakiet Sidi Youssef and killed some eighty Tunisians, including children. It took the intervention of the United States and Great Britain to smooth things over between France and Tunisia. Nonetheless, the United States made it clear at this time that it considered North Africa within the French sphere of influence. When Bourguiba returned from an exploratory trip to the United States, having received only minimal economic aid, he had to concede that France remained the "interlocuteur valable" for Tunisia on the international scene.[92]

On the French scene, in May 1958 DeGaulle came to power and on 30 January 1961 he received Bourguiba at Rambouillet. The idea was to test the lay-out for Algerian autonomy on terms similar to those that had been worked out for Tunisia. Bourguiba was encouraged to believe that he was being considered as future leader of a united Maghrib.[94] But Bourguiba was placed in a dilemma. He could not allow the stationing of French troops on Tunisian soil and, at the same time, aspire to being acknowledged as a leader of the Maghrib as a whole. The French authorities either did not understand his dilemma or had other priorities. Consequently, when the Bizerte crisis reached its apogee in June 1961, they did not evacuate their troops but only gave assurance of a future withdrawal, which was effected only in 1964, after the Algerian war had ended.[94] If the French had withdrawn from Bizerte in 1961, this might have lifted Bourguiba to such a level of authority that Tunisia could have become a partner in the Evian treaty and a different Algeria would have emerged from the war of liberation. But this was not to be. Bourguiba was thus left to reconcile himself to being a leader within the confines of Tunisia itself.

As for relations with the United States, it was only in the early 1960s, following the election of President Kennedy, that the United States reversed its policy of non-intervention in the "spheres of influence" of its N.A.T.O. allies and aid was channelled to Tunisia.[95]

As explained earlier, political independence was only an intervening phase in the more fundamental processes of state- and nation-building.

These processes thus linked Bourguiba with the reformists of the late nineteenth century who had begun the task. It is in this spirit of Reformism that a new Code of Personal Status had been promulgated in August 1956 and the court systems united. The Code of Personal Status, aside from its implications for women and for the family unit, meant that all branches of law now came under the purview of the Tunisian state.[96] The reform of the law was accompanied by a reform in the court system such that the Sharî'ah courts were amalgamated under the aegis of the national judiciary. In some ways as a logical consequence of these measures, the Zaytûnah was truncated of its role in preparing jurists for the Sharî'ah system and became simply the Theology Faculty of the University of Tunis.[97] With the promulgation of the Constitution in 1959 and the election of Bourguiba as President, one may consider that the process of state-building had been achieved in Tunisia by the early 1960s. But a modern state, based on the consent of the polis, could be maintained only through the process of nation-building which required the development of all aspects of society, particularly the economic.

As the 1950s were coming to an end, and the Youssefist challenge to Bourguiba's conception of the Tunisian state had been met, another challenge began to appear in the obvious question of who was to plan the blue-print for a coherent project of nation-building. Bourguiba's experience with Ben Youssef had led him to place great value on national unity and, in his vision, this could be safe-guarded only by means of a unified organ, the Néo-Destour Party. But, rather unique among newly-independent countries, Tunisia had emerged from the struggle for independence with a strong trade union. Ben Salah, in contrast to Bourguiba, saw the U.G.T.T. as the instrument for the construction of a viable political community.[98]

It is not clear whether Bourguiba agreed or disagreed with Ben Salah's project for a planned "socialist" economy on grounds of principle. Consistently with his étapist philosophy, it is more probable that he disagreed with the timing and, even more fundamentally, with the means of effecting such a project. Bourguiba's early concern with economic issues during his journalistic phase between 1929 and 1934 would lead us to conclude that he was in sympathy with the progressive elements in Ben Salah's project, but only to the extent that (1) the planning promised to provide a gradual evolutionary, rather than revolutionary, economic and social transformation, and (2) that it did not violate the basic fabric of Tunisian society.

Having built the basic structures of the State using the pre-eminence of the Party as their insurance, Bourguiba felt that it was time to turn to the task of nation-building. He, therefore, invited Ben Salah to implement precisely the economic blue-print which he had rejected in the 1950s. Bourguiba also accepted the idea that to build a modern nation required, over and above the economic aspects of the process, change in "traditional" values. In the name of modernization and the need to improve production, Bourguiba went to the extent of asking Tunisians to stop fasting the Holy Month of Ramaḍân. Yet, these same "traditional" values led him to offer Islamic justifications for this innovation. The struggle for modernization was a type of <u>jihâd</u> and, according to Islamic tenets, the Ramaḍân fast may be broken in times of struggle.[99] Strong measures were taken to impose both a new economic plan and a new cultural policy until 1969. At that point, Bourguiba seemd to reverse gears and threw out Ben Salah.

The above study of "personnalité" provides a key to the puzzling double reversal effected by Bourguiba during the 1960s. In fact, once Ben Salah agreed to work within the Party and government, rather than the trade union, he was quickly put in charge of implementing that same project which had supposedly turned Bourguiba against him in December 1956. But when Ben Salah accelerated the pace of change and threatened the continuity and the coherence of the Tunisian social fabric, he was summarily dismissed in 1969. This concern for "national unity" or the coherence of the Tunisian "personnalité" explains Bourguiba's continuous attempts to keep the main national corporatist organizations - the U.G.T.T., the U.N.A.T., the U.T.A.C., the U.G.E.T., and the U.N.F.T.- under the control of the one legitimate organ of the nation, the Néo-Destour Party.

> La concentration de toutes les couches de l'opinion dans ces divers mouvements permet ainsi au Néo-Destour de tenir les rênes de toutes les activités du pays. A ses ordres, des grèves se déclencheront ou des travaux acharneś seront entrepris. A ses ordres et en quelques heures, la levée en masse de la nation pourra être décidée.[100]

Even the Néo-Destour Party itself was re-organized in 1958 in order to construct national unity and to channel change according to Bourguiba's views of the Tunisian "personnalité", of continuity through change.

There is a great degree of inter- changeability between the government and the Party, due to the necessity of maintaining the "complexe unifié, integré et hierarchisé",[101] which may be considered as a concomittant result of the "acting organ", as a necessary element of the Tunisian national "personnalité". Similarly, the Party had followed a policy of being present in all "national organizations" which are thus considered as extensions of the Party rather than as autonomous entities representing corporate interests.

The Constitution was finally proclaimed in 1959. The main criticism made of the Tunisian Constitution is that the separation between the Executive and the Legislative branches is not clear-cut. According to Article 28, the right to initiate bills is shared between the President and the Assembly. Article 47 allows the President to by-pass the Assembly through the use of referenda. Finally, through Article 52, it is the President who promulgates the law. The Constitution sanctified the position of the Head of State as the symbol of national unity and of popular sovereignty; in other words, of the Tunisian "personnalité".[102] In 1959, Bourguiba was the only candidate for the presidency and obtained 1,005,763 out of 1,007,959 votes or practically 99.8 percent.[103]. As usual in Arab countries, the process was closer to being a bay^ʿah (promise of allegiance) than an election by majority. On 19 March 1975, an amendment was added to Article 39 of the Constitution which proclaimed Bourguiba President for life; in effect, he became the constitutional incarnation of the Tunisian "personnalité".

By focusing all political legitimacy in his own person, Bourguiba created a dilemma. On the one hand, such a focus was aimed at keeping in view the memories of a successful struggle for independence and the visions of future modernization. On the other hand, the social disparities of the present could not be hidden. There arose a credibility gap between political discourse and social realities.[104] At that point in time, Islamic symbols began to be used, once more, by a variety of groups to express their opposition to this monolithic view of the Tunisian nation-state. Another phase in the relationship between Islam and politics in Tunisia began when Hind Chelbi presented herself before Bourguiba on the Night of Power (laylat al-qadr) wearing a new version of the veil. Islam was then to provide the sources for the symbols needed to express opposition or, in other words, to play the role of de-legitimizing factor.[105]

Chapter VI

CONCLUSION

A QUESTION OF BIOGRAPHY AND HISTORY[1]

There is more to biography than the life of an individual. A life-story is not just one of an infinite number of possible monographs which add up to history. A historian who thinks so merely accumulates and never achieves any meaning. We must not think that Habib Bourguiba, for example, is a microcosm with all of modern Tunisia locked in his archetypal mind. Many Tunisians disagreed with him, at one or all of his life's stages. His opponents, however, no less than his followers, can be comprehended in Bourguiba's story, as they were all linked in a continuous dialogue. A historian, therefore, can do more than list antagonistic ideas, he can link them. Biography can be extrapolated to history, society derived from the individual.

As Bourguiba's own story illustrates, an individual playing a leading role in society cannot help but have an intellectual commitment to history, the collective memory[2] of past dialogues and of the meaning of past social formations, and an intellectual commitment to value, the collective project for a meaningful society in the future. As he plays out his role, he needs to make sense of the ongoing dialogue in terms of a meaningful past so that he may link his present to a meaningful vision of the future. A stable society is one whose members perceive a coherence between their past and their future as these are mirrored in the culture they are creating in the present. In its great ages, Ifrîqiyâ had been such a society. Its inhabitants, or at least those who were articulate, had appreciated their civilization not only because they were born in it but because they thought it held value. In the late nineteenth century, however, history and value were torn apart in many Tunisian minds as domination led them to question their own worth. Bourguiba began his career in the 1920s as one who was straining against his tradition intellectually, seeing value elsewhere, but still emotionally tied to it, held by his history.

A person who feels such a tension will seek to ease it and Bourguiba tried to resolve the conflict between history and value. His device was to rethink the Arab-Islamic tradition so that the Tunisian "personnalité" of which he was a part and which was a part of him, should include what he valued in the West as it encompassed what was of value in the Arab-Islamic heritage. Identity or personality, according to Bergson, maintains its uniqueness and its indivisibility precisely because it is the locus of change and movement.[3] What this means for Habib Bourguiba and for his biographer is this: Bourguiba's political action expresses a continuous adjustment of changing perceptions of the outer world to an inner need relatively fixed, in terms of the common dialogue he inherited and of the common dialogue he is transmitting. This need may be expressed as the need for a satisfying answer to a persisting question. When we know this question, we would come as close as we can to glimpsing his identity, to piercing through to the persisting Bourguiba who binds together, by his thinking them, ideas which seem outwardly disconnected. It is the question which would impose unity on all these perceptions informing his actions and the actions of other Tunisian leading figures anterior to, contemporary with and heirs of Bourguiba.

The question can be found by hypothesis. What question, we may ask, is the one question to which Bourguiba's political ideas and behavior could be construed as an answer? If we find this question, we find the unifying principle which works to give coherence to his ideas. And this principle, deduced from biography, would be a key to the Arab-Islamic intellectual history in which Bourguiba plays his part. For there are two unities imposed upon ideas in history, and knowledge of one can mean knowledge of the other. First, the personal identity of a single individual - biography - gives a unity to different ideas thought, horizontally through time, by at least one individual. Second, contemporaneity, the vertical in time, gives unity to different ideas thought by many individuals. And if there exists a common point of intersection between these two sets of ideas, the unifying principle in the case of the individual and in the case of his contemporaries will be the same. If there is one question to which each of society's simultaneous ideas can be construed as an answer, and if it is the same question as the one behind the successive ideas of the individual, then we can translate from the individual to the society. When we recognize Bourguiba's question, we grasp the meaning of anti-Bourguiba ideas. For the thought of Bourguiba's antagonists is as much an answer to his question as his own thought is.

Hypothetically, this could be the possible question: "How could an inhabitant of Tunisia be reconciled to the observable dissipation of his inheritance, his "patrimoine", both material and cultural?" Or, in other words, "how could a Tunisia in full process of Western political domination feel itself on par with the West or, at least, with France?" This question is the inner link between Bourguiba and Islamic conservatives, on the one hand, and between Bourguiba and Western assimilationists, on the other hand. Arab intellectuals who had been alienated from their Arab-Islamic tradition by Western domination could yet not rest easy with the kind of Westernization which seemed to enjoin upon them a spirit of humility.; For them, the existence in the West of revolutionary ideas, critical of the very civilization which had impinged on their land, offered one way out. When these "revolutionary" ideas insisted on the value of the specific culture of each society as a necessary dimension of legitimacy and, therefore, as the means for mobilizing the masses, they justified that dual play on the Arab-Islamic and French-Western cultural modes at which Bourguiba became a past master.

No longer had Tunisia either to cling to a moribund system or to defer respectfully to a France of unchallenged prestige. Before the First World War, roughly in the early decades of the twentieth century, Tunisian nationalists did not hesitate to abandon Islamic themes and to accept Westernization in the name of progress, as illustrated by Thaalbi's first book, which earned the opprobium of the traditonalists for its unabashed embrace of Western values. This attitude enabled them to view Westernization simply as a means to achieve progress within the framework of a non-culturalistic Tunisian nationalism. Tradition could be flouted to strengthen the nation; for nation, not culture, was the unit of equivalence. The issue was not between

Arab-Islamic and French-Western civilizations but between the progress of the Tunisians and the progress of the French. This position yielded to a second stage, following the First World War when the hope for progress in "association" with France was shaken. The enormity of the Great War created the need to measure the admiration of the West by the realisation of the limits of Western progress. As the Arab-Islamic civilization had achieved great heights and as it had lost its pre-eminence, so had hopes in the Western formula for progress been shaken. In reaction, Tunisian nationalists insisted on the value of Islam and Islamic traditions, as such, without any understanding of the dynamic forces of the Arab-Islamic heritage.

These inconsistencies represented pressure on the future. They made Tunisian nationalists move to a new position, in a second phase, whenever they were able to think that Western civilization was discredited: in 1918, with the First World War; in 1929, with the Great Depression and in 1945, following the Second World War. At these points, Islam and the Arab-Islamic civilization were the credible haven which protected the Tunisian "personnalité" from the storms of discredited assimilation.

> ...many évolués are the victims of an upbringing which makes them only superficially modern and only superficially Moslem. They have discovered only the utilitarian side of Western culture and not the spiritual and intellectual center which has made utilitarian success possible. They confuse means and ends. On the other hand, they tend to see their own Islamic culture in its uncreative, ossified, passive side - that which made it possible for the Arabs to be easily dominated in the past. And in repudiating assimilation to the West, these évolués defend the worst of their traditional culture, instead of the principles of rationalism and humanism which once made Islam a dynamic and creative culture. They confuse the word, the symbol, with the reality that once lay behind it. Their responsibility, their "vocation", is to rediscover the reality rather than only the form of their past, and the reality and not only the surface of the modern Western world.[4]

Bourguiba never moved to a third phase where he would oppose French-Western and Arab-Islamic ideals. He never fell into the trap of simplifying the conflict as one between a "materialistic" West and a "spiritual" East. Beyond the advancement of science and the conquest of the material, Bourguiba acknowledged a debt to Western "humanistic" (or specifically, personalist) values. At the same time, Bourguiba did not underestimate the economic relations, the social institutions, and the psycho-social structures which had received the sanction of Islam.

RELIGION AND POLITICS

Generally speaking, relationships between religion and politics in the Arab world have varied throughout history. Religion has often been a force upholding the status quo, reinforcing the stability of society and enhancing political quietism - the "opium" of the masses. And yet, religion has also been an important force easing political and socio-economic change, providing the ideological justifications and the social cohesion necessary for change and even for revolution.[5]

As a system of "collective representations", religion serves to give meaning to the ultimate questions challenging man. Developed across time, it provides some of the most basic values which undergird a society's coherence.

> ...society by virtue of its order and predictability protects the individual from the terror of chaos and meaninglessness. It tells him who he is, where he's from, what he's a part of, and what he can expect.... People's understanding of reality is then neither arbitrary nor limited to their experience and understanding. It is neither historical nor temporal. It is universal. It is cosmic. It is truly the way it is - in the universe.... The ultimate authentication for the societal reality, as members of a society see it and know it, derives more from overpowerful sources than the historical effects of human beings.... Religion is the human enterprise by which a sacred cosmos far transcends human beings, it also includes them and helps give man a meaningful place within the ordered universe. Above all, it protects man from the terrible

alternative of chaos and tentativeness.[6]

Religion thus becomes an integral part of the presuppositions and cultural premises which are so ingrained within the society and the individual that they are taken for granted. As such, religion influences language and communicative exchange which are part and parcel of all components of culture and of productive relations.

Within the Marxist school, Engels at least held that religion could play a revolutionary role in reaching the masses[7] as much as it could function as an "opium". This ambiguity of religion is part of its strength as ambiguity permits it to transcend the space-time limitations of the immediate moment and to become relevant universally and through history. In fact, the imprecision and vagueness of most moral codes may be necessary for their usefulness and survival just as the open-ended character of constitutional provisions is an essential condition for the adaptation of a political order to changing circumstances. The fact that most religious doctrines are open to different readings does not mean that the content of these tenets is entirely irrelevant to their relationship with politics. Though all religions have both quietistic and revolutionary potentials, the proportions in which different implications are present at different times vary. The variation is not eternal, even within each doctrinal system, because other factors may intervene, such as the organizational framework developed, the leadership invoked, and the "situational factors" not directly related to the religious doctrine or its institutions.[8]

Beyond these extraneous factors of change, each religious tradition has limits bounding it such that if it changes beyond these limiting conditions then it would lose that uniqueness which identifies it, its "personnalité". Perhaps the metaphor of a symphony illustrates best this point. Any religious doctrinal system may be considered to be composed of minor and major chords which may be played in different keys by different instruments but which are all recognizably of the whole symphony.

In the study of Arab and Islamic history, Orientalists have generally tended to argue that "Orientals" are guided in their behavior by irrational religious motivation. Reacting against this blanket treatment of "Orientals" as exotically different beings beyond the reach of rational social theory, Mahjoubi' attempts to demonstrate that there existed a strong link between socio-economic conditions and the evolution of the Tunisian nationalist movement. In his view, the determining factor in the history of the Tunisian nationalist movement is undoubtedly economic. Other factors, such as religion, played only supportive roles and only when the economic situation was already explosive.

This was the case in November 1911, during the first violent confrontation in the capital of Tunisia between the Muslim population and the colonial authorities. According to Mahjoubi, it was economic dissatisfaction which exploded when the authorities decided to survey the Djellaz Islamic cemetery. Thus, religion played the role of "trigger" for an already cocked situation. The hostility of the Muslim population was specifically directed against Italian settlers not simply because they were Christians and not simply because Italy had invaded Tripolitania and was at war with the Ottoman Empire, defender of Islam. The hostility was engendered, in fact, because of the struggle over jobs which a deterioration of the economy had exacerbated. The same strife was again at the bottom of the tramway boycott of 1912, provoked when an Italian conductor ran over a Muslim child. The Muslim employees of the tramway company demanded pay and access to jobs equal to their Italian counterparts. Again, the religious factor played the role of trigger in an already charged situation.

Similarly, and contrary to appearances, the religious factor was not at all a determinant variable in the radicalization of the Tunisian nationalist movement during the 1930s. In effect, the problem of naturalization and the burial of naturalized Tunisians in Muslim cemeteries was not a new problem. Decrees as early as 1887, 1889, 1921 and the law of 20 December 1923 had opened the doors to French nationality. Moreover, several naturalized Tunisian Muslims had been buried in Muslim cemeteries during the intervening years without any trouble. In the question of burials, the Tunisian people did not boycott such naturalized Tunisians whom nationalist leaders considered as renegades from Islam. Opposition to the burial of naturalized Tunisians in Muslim cemeteries was <u>not</u> an issue until the 1930s.

It then became an issue because the economic situation of the Tunisian population had deteriorated in the face of the Great Depression and had become explosive. The events provoked by the Eucharistic Congress and the problems of naturalization which were formulated as religious issues occurred, in fact, at a moment when Tunisia was suffering a serious economic crisis. The effect of the economic factor was even more decisive when, in periods of crisis, it accentuated the antagonism between "natives" and "colonists" at the same time that it also de-emphasized the contradictions internal to each group.

As a consequence, during the 1930s, those fractions of the Tunisian élite which had collaborated with the Protectorate authorities became conscious of its inherently discriminatory policies which were placed in relief by the economic crisis. These fractions then realized that their interests were not necessarily compatible with the Protectorate. They therefore turned to the nationalists and rejoined their ranks. The principal contradiction in Tunisia was revealed to be the opposition between the entirety of the "native" population and the entirety of the "colonists". All antagonisms within the "native" population appeared negligible and the Tunisian nationalist movement was assured of a greater social cohesion. Thus, national solidarity overtook all concerns for class struggle.

The same phenomenon developed within the European colony in Tunisia. Antagonisms between the two principal factions of the colony, the land settlers and the functionaries, was reduced during the 1930s. Until then a basic contradiction had existed between the two as they had disputed the allocation of the Tunisian state budget; the settlers had wished to reduce the number of civil servants in order to have a greater share of the public budget allocated to the financing of their settlements. In their opposition to the propertied settlers, the French functionaries had joined the ranks of the left and had lent support to the Tunisian nationalists, at least to the moderate wing of the nationalist movement. Eventually, the rise and development of a Tunisian class of bilingual professionals threatened to compete with the French functionaries for public service jobs. Consequently, the French functionaries began to abandon their liberal and leftist affiliations and to gradually ally themselves with the settlers against the Tunisian nationalists.

Mahjoubi therefore concludes that, in the final analysis, the determinant factor in the evolution of the Tunisian nationalist movement from 1904 to 1934 was essentially economic and that political, cultural, religious and psychological factors had only triggering effects.

In comparison, Kraiem and Sammut[10] focus on consciousness and, consequently, argue that religion played an important role as the fundamental factor in defining national identity. For the Muslim Tunisian, the Protectorate was simply another phase of the crusading spirit against Islam; it was a military, economic, political and ideological invasion of dâr al-islâm (the realm of Islam) by conquering Christians. The French authorities' seeming adherence to liberal humanist principles, to the respect of all religions and of all sacred sites, to promises of conserving the legal institutions of the country were soon understood by Tunisians to be simply cover-ups for the real objectives of the colonizers. Political power was rapidly confiscated by the French Resident General who established a parallel administration leaving the Tunisians with high-sounding titles but no real power. Colonial capitalism, through systematic spoliation, deprived Tunisian owners of most of the cultivable land and monopolized the mining resources of the country. In short, Tunisians became spectators to their own pauperization for the benefit of a conquering minority. This minority also developed an ideology to cover up its "high-law" robbery based on the myth of a superior race burdened with the mission of spreading civilization and progress among barbarous populations incapable of transcending their fanaticism.

In considering the role of Islam as a source for an ideology countering this process, Kraiem and Sammut set up the Marxist schema in which Islam, like all religions, is part of the dominant ideology and serves the interests of the dominant classes by maintaining the lower classes in their exploited positions. They then question the validity of such a thesis for pre-capitalist societies or for societies under colonialism where class struggle is placed in the background with respect to the fundamental contradiction between colonizer and colonized. Kraiem and Sammut then continue by distinguishing two Islams. According to them, the representatives of "official" Islam accepted to collaborate with the Protectorate authorities while the masses opposed the Protectorate under the banner of "popular" Islam.[11]

Conclusion

For Kraiem and Sammut, this "popular" Islam cannot be considered a mystifying ideology since it permitted the disinherited social classes to achieve consciousness of their objective condition. They then proceed to argue that, until the Second World War, the representatives of "official" Islam, who were basically the bourgeoisie of the capital and who manned the Zaytûnah administration and faculty, did not oppose the spoliation of the ḥabûs properties or the naturalization decrees. This attitude of submission was accompanied, among the majority of the ʿulamâʾ, by a conservative attitude towards any reforms which led them to oppose the innovative opinions of Abû al-Qâsim al-Shâbbî on Arabic poetry and of al-Ṭâhir al-Ḥaddâd on the situation of the working class and of woman in Islamic society.

In contrast, "popular" Islam was an ambiguous phenomenon, which rarely expressed itself in purely religious terms. It played a fundamental role in expressing various issues: from the struggle for land, or the struggle against the privileges accorded the colonists, to a generalized resistance against colonial penetration. Popular Islam then manifested itself in the form of spontaneous populist demonstrations characterized by violence and bloody repression. The causes of these explosions were varied but the religious factor was nevertheless essential. According to Kraiem and Sammut, this popular Islam was also represented by the Zaytûnah students who usually were recruited from the interior provinces or from the provincial petite bourgeoisie, in contrast to their teachers who were usually of the grande bourgeoisie of the capital. The Zaytûnah students, without access to the French language or the modern sciences, realized only too well that the French Protectorate system prevented them from normal integration within the economic, social and political circuits of the country. Consequently, the Zaytûnah students did not hesitate to join and even to lead any demonstrations of popular Islam.

Kraiem and Sammut then cite the Djellaz riots as a typical example. They acknowledge that this was a reaction against the policies of land dispossession but point out that Islam provided the necessary base for a popular ideology against this systematic dispossession. The Djellaz cemetery became the junction between two symbols: the burial site of the ancestors and the religious ḥabûs. Thus it was the point at which land and religion met with the ancestors representing the collective memory of a past national community whose fundamental values continued to be perpetuated across the centuries. In their view, during the history of Tunisian resistance to colonial domination, there was always a defense of Islamic values at the base of all political discourse mobilizing the masses. These popular demonstrations were undertaken against the violence visited by France on the symbols of Islam considered as the principal constituent of the Tunisian "personnalité". These views echo the opinion of Jacques Berque;

> ...il entre dans l'appropriation européenne des signes du pays...toutes sortes d'éléments.... Le nouveau venu se porte, dans cette réalité, à ce qui lui en reste dérobé. La conquête de la chose ne fait qu'aviver, et désespérer son appétence à l'égard de la personne adverse. Personne, dans la mesure où elle me résiste. Objet, dans la mesure où je l'atteins, et crois l'asservir. Cet "indigène", et avec lui tout ce qui le touche; ses nourritures, son champ, je veux littéralement me <u>l'approprier</u>. Mais toujours une part de lui m'échappe, fût-il devenu mon serviteur, mon goumier, mon ouvrier, ma "fatma". Contre l'aliénation, il maintient sa personne, dans des zones de lui où je ne parviens pas: sa foi, sa sexualité, sa violence aux aguets, son espoir. Or cette obscurité qui l'oppose à moi, malgré les conquêtes de mon administration, de ma science, de mon agriculture, de mon projet dans tous les domaines, ce que je ne perce pas, que je ne possède pas, et que je convoite et regrette: est-ce ce qui demeure de "barbarie" ou est-ce un refuge de la liberté humaine?

And, he seems to answer his own question in the following terms:

> Or ce refus, au fur et à mesure que le brisent des forces supérieures, se réfugie dans une catégorie de la vie qui s'en fait la plus sûre dépositaire: je veux dire, la religion.[12]

From this perspective, Islam, during the colonial period, had two functions. It demystified colonial policies and served as a means of raising the consciousness of the masses so as to mobilize them for the struggle against foreign domination.

It lent refuge to that part of the Tunisian "personnalité" beyond the reaches of colonial domination and recuperated the attributes of "liberté humaine" for a community perceived to be Tunisian as opposed to French and Muslim as opposed to Western.

Kraiem and Sammut contrast the historic role of Islam with that of Christianity. While Christianity did not itself create a state or a nation but inserted itself within already existing political structures, Islam gave birth to a state and a nation. Despite its extraordinary expansion across a variety of populations, Islam was able to function as an assimilating ideology reinforced by the parallel spread of the untranslatable language of the Qur'ân, Arabic. By its very essence, Islam is universal and could not reconcile itself to the dissection of the Muslim community into distinct and sometimes hostile political entities. It would therefore seem to be in contradiction with the rise of narrower loyalties. It is only through the study of the influence of Western thought as much as of Islam that the emergence of a narrowly Tunisian nationalism could be elucidated.

In their subsequent description of the development of this Tunisian nationalism, Kraiem and Sammut present a variety of Western theories of nationalism followed by a narrative account of the historic evolution of Tunisia from the status of a province of the Ottoman Empire, the Islamic realm par excellence, to an autonomous political entity even before the advent of the Protectorate. Nonetheless, they assert, it was only with the end of the First World War when the Ottoman Empire disappeared that the second generation of Tunisians living under the Protectorate became conscious of a move away from Islamic unity towards a specifically Tunisian nationalism. This development was expressed in its strongest terms in La Tunisie Martyre where Islam and its corollary, the Arabic language, were reduced to being components of the Tunisian "personnalité", in opposition to the French.

Parallel to the rise of this particularist nationalism, the interwar period also witnessed the development of Arab nationalism. Kraiem and Sammut describe the rise of Arab nationalism as "le phénomène le plus spectaculaire de la vie politique d'après-guerre".[13] At this junction in time, official Islam allied itself with popular Islam as the Zaytûnah shaykhs worked hand-in-hand with the

U.G.T.T. But this alliance was not to last long as the U.G.T.T. shifted its support, during the 1952 test of strength, away from the F.M.S. and away from the Arabism of the ʿulamâʾ and of Ben Youssef towards Tunisian nationalism and Bourguiba. Kraiem and Sammut therefore conclude that the concept of a particularist Tunisian "personnalité" had prevailed.

> Cependant, ce sont la Nation [tunisienne] et le phénomène nationaliste qui ont prévalu durant cette période historique de la Tunisie coloniale au détriment des intérêts de classe sociale qui étaient sauvegardés dans la mesure où ils entraient dans un processus de lutte nationaliste. Le communisme, le syndicalisme, le mouvement réformiste musulman n'ont pu développer leur action que dans le cadre d'une lutte nationaliste valorisant la Nation. C'est le nationalisme [tunisien] qui a imposé sa marque au communisme, au syndicalisme et à l'Islam réformiste qui étaient d'ailleurs des éléments constitutifs du nationalisme tunisien. Les partis politiques nationalistes tunisiens ne pouvaient d'ailleurs pas mener une action valable sans eux.[14]

PERSONALITY AND TIME

Thus, we see how Bourguiba's life-story leads to a history outside it. The question which was extracted from beneath his answers is a question which was asked by Béchir Sfar's generation and by Bourguiba's contemporaries. This knowledge, however, brings us only half the distance from biography to history. For history involves a society in time as well as in space. From a study of Bourguiba, an individual in time, we were able to make our way to the fundamental question besieging a whole society.

What can, indeed, the passage of time mean to it? If Bourguiba's thoughts, throughout his life, are threaded on a single question, and if his contemporaries, young and old, and all future generations seem to be drawn to the same question: then men's (as well as women's) minds would stand still forever. Yet, paradoxically enough, the question which does persist in passing time does also, somehow, change in it. It is the kind of change - toward anachronism, encroaching death in persisting life - which only history makes.

Contemporaries are yoked to the question, but this change in the question, its becoming anachronistic, redeems them from its treadmills.

How? As an individual thinker leads us to discover the question, so he can lead us to comprehend the change. In the late nineteenth century, Afghânî had insisted on action, in the form of pursuing the unity of the Islamic ummah, as being of greater value than faith in the struggle against Western domination. When Bourguiba, several decades later, rebelled against both the Destour and the Socialist parties, in the name of the Tunisian nation rather than the Islamic ummah, he was expressing what would have been the same idea if the significance of time could be denied. But every idea is transformed by time itself, and not because its positive content changes but just because it fails to change as time passes and limiting conditions evolve. For an idea can be grasped in its relation to its contemporary alternatives just as much as in relation to its past. Every affirmation includes within itself a rejection of something else possible. A man's convictions are a choice among alternatives[15] and alternatives change in time.

An anachronistic idea is one which is an answer to no living question. When we recognize anachronism in the answer, we cannot fail to recognize change in the question; and the change is a growing irrelevance to the facts of life. This change is the process of intellectual history. The successive different ideas of the individual thinker yield the question which links his contemporaries. And the successive "same" ideas of the individual thinker and his successors yield the secret of its change, if any, across time.

Since the history of ideas is not exhausted in one anachronism, and since ideas demand some question behind them, this change in the question, this gathering irrelevance, has a corollary; the gradual emergence of a new and relevant question. That is why alignments of ideas in contemporaneity are always dissolving. As the question which they share becomes more and more irrelevant, the idea which answers that question alone loses currency, while the idea which has reference to the new question as well persists.

Who are the ones who come to hold this versatile idea, this answer to both a fading question and a relevant, newly emerging one? They are, for the most part, of the younger generation, the younger contemporaries of the old thinker, who had discovered for us his contemporaries' question, who had revealed to us the nature of its change and who could show us too, if and how his generation comes to be superseded.

The basic question posed by Bourguiba and his generation, as it had been posed by Béchir Sfar's generation, was "how could they, as Tunisians, undergoing the full process of French domination, still retain their self-value?" The answer was found in adopting a revolutionary concept, "personnalité", which lent support to a conception of Tunisian nationalism based on the legitimacy of the nation identified by its cultural dimensions, both religious and linguistic. The revolutionary concept had been developed within the French intellectual tradition but, inherently, called for an emphasis on cultural differences as these had developed in history in order to justify the independent status of the state and nation. With political independence, the need to emphasize the Islamic and Arab dimensions lost some of its immediacy in the struggle to give priority to modernization and progress, as such. In fact, these dimensions were drawn into the background in order to maintain Tunisia distinct from its Arab-Islamic neighbors. But, faced with the inability to overcome economic dependence and to achieve economic equity in partnership with the West, the Islamic and Arab dimensions are re-emerging once more. The re-newed emphasis on these dimensions of the Tunisian "personnalité" are part of the attempt to balance dependence on the West with dependence on the Arab-Islamic East.

TWO ANSWERS

Although the concept of personality has been criticized by contemporary students of psychology and although it has fallen into disuse in the legal field,[16] yet it is still prevalent in the Arabic political literature. The actual relevance of the concept of shakhṣiyyah in Arabic political discourse is indicative of the continuing process of state- and nation-building, of the continuing search for legitimacy in the Arab world and for the continuing effort to respond to the felt need to assert some form of coherence to the multiplicity of problems and of failures.

Conclusion

During the period of political domination, the issue of legitimacy in nationalist discourse revolved around the definition of the political community in relationship to the dominating power. In the case of Tunisia and during the greater part of Bourguiba's life, the nationalist discourse was a function of the legal relationship imposed by France on Tunisia, the Protectorate, and of the colonial ideology. Political independence did not automatically sever economic and cultural ties between the two. Nationalist discourse, focusing on nation- or state-building, came under the influence of ideological developments in other Arab and Islamic countries as much as it came under the influence of continued links with France. The sense of failure persists on two levels: the continued inability to establish a minimal measure of social equity and the continued inability to achieve economic independence.

Three main currents of ideology may be distinguished in the Arab world: the particularist nationalisms framed by pre-colonial or colonial states, Arab nationalism and Islamic integralism. All these currents admit that the source of political legitimacy lies within the people or the nation.[17] The primary difference among the three currents is how they define the political community which constitutes the nation, source of legitimacy. None of these currents has achieved a purely territorial definition of nation since all of them take as their point of departure a cultural definition of the people who have right of entry into the political city. In the case of Islamic integralism, the ruling criterion is allegiance to Islam while in the case of Arab nationalism, the primary criterion is the Arabic language and, only as its corollary, an intimate relationship with Islam.

In point of fact, for Michel Aflaq, one of the most important protagonists of Arab nationalism, Islam was the highest expression of the genius of the Arabs and was the means which preserved and spread the Arabic language from the Gulf to the Atlantic. In this conception, Islam is an important dimension of the Arab personality but only one among others. This version of Arab nationalism comes close to that current of Islamic integralism which accepts the idea that linguistically defined nations exist within the Islamic community and that Arab unity is a prerequisite for Islamic unity.

At first sight, it might be expected that particularist nationalisms would take their point of departure from a territorial definition. This has not been the case except, perhaps, in recent developments in Palestinian nationalism where the issue of the land has become overwhelmingly crucial. Local nationalisms, such as the Tunisian or the Egyptian, also used cultural criteria to justify their options and, thus, the premise of a Tunisian, or Egyptian, or Lebanese, shakhṣiyyah and, concomittantly, the relationship of Islam to such a narrowly-defined shakhṣiyyah become fundamental. In the case of Tunisia, the mainstream current which builds upon the bases laid by Bourguiba is represented in the works of Mohamed Mzali, the present Prime Minister, and Béchir Ben Slama, present Minister of Cultural Affairs, who jointly edited the journal, Al-Fikr, where the concept of shakhṣiyyah and its implications were debated at great length.[18]

The concept of shakhṣiyyah reflected by Al-Fikr journal is premised on the historical continuity of a Tunisian entity conditioned by its geographical position between "East" and "West". Through the West, it achieves consciousness and control over reality and acts in a rational and realistic fashion. Through the East, the Arab-Islamic classicism of Tunisia, which forms its subconscious (dafâʾin), is reached. These views are systematically developed by Ben Slama in his exposé on the historical theory underlying the Tunisian nationalist movement, where he explicitly states that every leader of the Tunisian nationalist movement held, consciously or unconsciously, a specific perception of the history of Tunisia which influenced his views of independence.[24]

> History is not merely a branch of knowledge among other branches of knowledge... it is essentially a pillar upon which was based the struggle for [freedom] and honor.[19]

Nonetheless, Ben Slama is torn between two options. On the one hand, he wishes to demonstrate that a Tunisian entity existed from time immemorial or at least before the imposition of French domination and bases himself on the views of Béchir Sfar.[20] On the other hand, Ben Slama is tempted to go along with the view presented by Abdelwahab Bouhdiba who proposes that the Tunisian nation came into being only as a result of Bourguiba's action.[21] Ben Slama reconciles these two apparently opposite views by distinguishing between the objective existence of a Tunisian entity and its self-consciousness as a nation[22] which is implicitly credited to the action of Bourguiba.

Ben Slama traces this process from "tribal then racial solidarity through religious sentiment which changed into the feeling of belonging to the Islamic nation until it turned into a patriotic feeling which soon became nationalist in the full sense of the term."[23] But this was not a simple unilinear evolution as Ben Slama observes the continued tension between "patriotism" (waţaniyyah) in terms of Tunisia and "fraternity" (ukhuwwah) based on Arab and/or Islamic solidarity.

> The problematic today with respect to the Arab peoples [note the plural, shu'ûb] and their governments is how to achieve a reconciliation between the patriotism which has transformed a small fatherland from a mere homestead into a nation protecting its existence, defending its sovereignty and its unity and the concept of fraternity (ukhuwwah) which is a concrete reality and a feeling existing in every Arab and every Muslim.[24]

For Ben Slama, patriotism within the Tunisian framework cannot be maintained if the Arab-Islamic dimension is not preserved.

> ...we should make a note which has importance for all the Arab peoples [note the plural shu'ûb again], including the Tunisians, namely that it is impossible to strengthen patriotism...except if that fraternity is preserved in some form or the other...otherwise, we will see dangerous developments none of us would accept, such as the denial of patriotism itself - in other words, a denial of the nation - and the pursuit of other ideologies, such as internationalism or other tendencies which are not based on realism or idealism.[25]

Conversely Arab and/or Islamic unity cannot be aspired to except through the strengthening of the existing local states.

> ...there can be no humanist fraternity in the Arab world if this [humanist fraternity] did not lead to the growth of the Arab-Islamic fraternity which is one of the conditions of its existence and this [Arab-Islamic fraternity] cannot develop if it did not harmonize with [the various] patriotisms.[26]

Finally, Ben Slama proposes a program in order to effect the reconciliation between the two poles of the tension. On the cultural level, the ability to innovate is the most crucial aspect and is conditioned by language. If a language other than Arabic becomes the language of innovation in Tunisia then it would be difficult indeed to establish any reconciliation between Tunisian patriotism and that fraternity which would establish links between all who are part of the Arab world. Such links are necessary as the means to provide security against the invidious domination of the Great Powers. When the Arab-Islamic culture achieved political significance during the seventh and eighth centuries, the Arab-Islamic civilization it created was based upon the unity of "a nation within nations" (ummah fî umam). But that period is over and now is the period of "nations within a nation" (umam fî ummah) where patriotisms seek fraternal links but refuse the assimilation of a nation within nations.[27]

In contrast, Hichem Djait distinguished between a "personnalité politique nationale", Tunisian, and a "personnalité historique idéologico-culturelle", Arab-Islamic, and posed a dialectic between these two "personnalités".

> Ainsi, ce qui caractérise l'être arabe actuel, c'est une profonde dualité entre la structure de la société, de l'Etat et de l'économie (évoluant dans la sphère nationale) et une conscience culturelle et politico-idéologique (évoluant au niveau de l'ensemble arabe). En tant que tirée vers le passé par son contenu et ses fidélités, celle-ci demeure fixé sur la personnalité arabo-islamique.[28]

From this perspective, Djait considered the naturalization controversies of the early 1930s as an expression of the combination of the two "personnalités". Since he presupposed the separation of the two levels, the national and the cultural, he concluded that such a combination was false. According to Djait, doctrinal Islam attaches individual belief to individual acts and, thus, he broke the eventual link between Islam and the Tunisian "nation" and allowed the possibility of being Muslim and French simultaneously.

> ...pour exprimer une réalité confuse et pourtant profonde, l'on a donc eu recours au seul langage qui soit familier, qui ait eu un sens clair et distinct, celui-là même qui est sécrété par la personnalité idéologico-culturelle. Il en était de même en Tunisie: ceux qui ont été fusillés, ceux qui exposèrent dans les manifestations leur poitrine aux balles de l'armée et de la police coloniales, l'immense rumeur populaire qui les bénissait, les exaltait et appelait sur eux la miséricorde de Dieu, usaient du terme de Djihad et se référaient à ce verset du Coran: "Et ne crois point que ceux qui ont été tués pour la cause de Dieu sont morts! Bien plutôt ils sont vivants et nourris auprès de leur Seigneur." Est-ce à dire que les masses populaires pensaient vraiment que le combat pour l'indépendance fût avant tout un combat pour une foi qui aurait été fondamentalement menacée dans son être? Ou bien s'agissait-il de l'habillage d'un sentiment nouveau, en l'occurrence le sentiment national moderne, par une terminologie ancienne qui, à son tour, réveille des gestes et des attitudes séculaires, le tout s'entremêlant et s'entre-dynamisant dans une puissante confusion?
> Le problème, de taille, révèle l'ambiguité de toute action historique.[29]

Consequently, Djait posited that a separation could exist between the "personnalité politique nationale" and the "personnalité historique idéologique-culturelle" and, moreover, that the relationship between the two is conditioned by history. These premises indicate that he could have envisaged a time when even the cultural consciousness of Tunisia would move beyond Islam and its Arab-Islamic civilizational heritage.

> En effet, la relation de la personnalité de base au devenir historique est double, selon l'ambiguité même de l'historicité qui est au fond l'ambiguité de l'humain à la fois nature

> et liberté. En premier, la personnalité de base est liée à l'histoire en ce qu'elle est déterminée par elle. De deux façons, et d'abord indirectement: elle est déterminée par l'histoire dans la mesure où elle est déterminée par les institutions primaires, qui sont historiques.... Et l'histoire aide ici à concevoir non seulement ce qui agit sur la personnalité de base, mais comment cela agit.... Mais il y a plus: la personnalité de base est directement atteinte par l'histoire.[30]

Djait's assertion of an Arab-Islamic "personnalité idéologico-culturelle", practically synonymous with "personnalité de base" in Tunisia did not lead him to assert an Arab-Islamic "devenir". He posited a separation between "religion" and "politics" by proposing the continued separation of the "personnalité politique nationale", embodied in the historic states such as Tunisia, and of the "personnalité historique idéologico-culturelle", formed mainly by Islam and the Arab-Islamic civilization, in a relationship of creative tension. Djait retreats somewhat from this position following the Islamic revolution in Iran which aimed at subjecting the political sphere to the religious exigencies of Islam. He does not fall into the extreme position as he notes the originality of the Islamic revolution within the confines of the law; "combien la Révolution islamique est neuve par son élan fondamental, mais combien aussi elle reste prisonnière du carcan de la Sharī'ah". This hesitation might be due to the chronic "timidité des 'ulama' face à la sphère politique pure".[31]

A comparison of the works of Djait and Ben Slama uncovers an ironic situation. Djait wrote in French to defend the existence of an Arab-Islamic "personnalité", considered separate from but of equal importance to the political realm, while Ben Slama wrote in Arabic to defend the openness, to the West, of the Tunisian shakhṣiyyah, comprehending Arab and Islamic dimensions. But perhaps there is some logic to this irony; Djait did not feel the need to defend the Arab-Islamic "personnalité" to an Arabic-speaking audience and Ben Slama did not feel the need to defend the openness of the Tunisian shakhṣiyyah to a French-speaking audience. Moreover, the project which Djait proposed, if carried to its ultimate logic, would lead to secularism where religion, basis of the "personnalité idéologico-culturelle", would be separate from politics, basis of the "personnalité nationale". In contrast, the project proposed by Ben Slama could not envisage the complete separation of religion from politics since he recognizes the influence of culture, formed by religion, in the definition of the legitimate political community.

The loss of the juridical aspect of the concept of "personnalité" had led Djait to conceive of a duality between the "personnalité politique nationale" and the "personnalité idéologico-culturelle", both considered only from the perspective of psycho-sociology. But, for Bourguiba who was trained as a lawyer precisely during that period when the juridical aspect of the concept of "personnalité" was carried to its ultimate in French legal thought, a divorce between the two could not be accepted. For Bourguiba, the cultural definition of the legitimate political community meant that the "personnalité historique idéologico-culturelle" was the very basis for the legitimacy of the "personnalité politique nationale".

In contrast to Djait, Ben Slama took as point of departure the existence of the Tunisian "personnalité" in action throughout history. Simultaneouly, he argued that an authentic Tunisian "personnalité" could not continue to exist without its Arab and, by extrapolation, its Islamic dimensions.

> It has never been possible to separate the issue of Tunisification from the issue of Arabization or vice versa, on condition that the term "Arabization" does not carry [any connotations] of specific political tendencies contrary to the will of the Tunisian people to remain Tunisian; in other words, in control of... their destiny and [not] melted into another people whoever that may be.[32]

ISLAM AND LEGITIMACY: NO NEW QUESTION

The four Tunisian authors discussed above represent elements of continuity with Bourguiba's views, confirming the validity of our hypothetical question. All argue that, at one point in time or another, the Tunisian nationalist movement considered Islam as a necessary dimension for the Tunisian identity distinct from the dominating power and fundamental to the legal implications of the relationship between Tunisia and France. Mahjoubi argued that Islam was the "trigger" exploding the economic and social crises which were the determinant factors in the evolution of the Tunisian nationalist movement. Kraiem and Sammut did not argue that Islam was a determinant factor in the history of the Tunisian nationalist movement but held that it served as the means of mobilizing the masses. It acted as a demystifying ideology countering the "mission civilisatrice" proposed by the Protectorate authorities and revealing the fundamental contradiction between the colonized society and the colonizing power, during the period of political domination.

Following independence in 1956, the continued inability to overcome social inequity or to break the relationship of dependence on France would not permit an undisputed legitimacy to a particularist Tunisian entity. First challenged by Arab nationalism during the 1960s then by the resurgence of integralist Islam during the 1970s, the legitimacy of a particularist Tunisian nationalism centered on a Tunisian nation and on its organ, the Tunisian state, is still in question. The works of Djait and Ben Slama are in response to these challenges and, in many respects, they propose similar solutions. Both take as point of departure the continued existence of limited "national" states such as Tunisia and both suggest the strengthening of the Arab and Islamic dimensions on the cultural level alone.

The difference between them is that Djait believed it possible, at least at the time of writing his book, to keep the cultural sphere separate from the political sphere. The implications would seem to be that unity, both the Arab and the Islamic versions, may be pursued on the cultural level alone without affecting the political level. But such a solution - in its attempt to separate religion, still a fundamental component of culture in the Arab world, from politics - requires one of two solutions: either a shift from the principle of "personnalité" to the principle of territoriality or, even more difficult, the elimination of religion as a generative component of culture. As long as religion remains the source of societal values, the shift away from the principle of "personnaliré" would strip the Tunisian state of its legitimacy based, as explained above, on the concept of a Tunisian "personnalité" in which Islam and the Arab-Islamic heritage are fundamental dimensions. These cannot be eliminated from politics without radically altering the bases of political legitimacy.

As a consequence, Ben Slama insisted on the continued link between the cultural and the political spheres. He argued that only by reinforcing the Arab-Islamic dimension, largely shaped by Islam and the Arabic language, of the Tunisian "personnalité" could the legitimacy of a Tunisian entity be maintained in the face of rival ideologies. Ben Slama is presently Minister of Cultural Affairs while Djait is Professor of History at the University of Tunis.

The events of 26 January 1978, when the U.G.T.T. struck and mass demonstrations led the police to open fire on the crowds, were stark warning of the social inequalities underlying the giant steps that Tunisia had taken towards dependent development. Two years from that date, in January 1980, armed rebels took over the main points in the town of Gafsa and the army had to be called in.[33] Once more, Tunisians shed Tunisian blood. There could be no doubt that the economic, social and political policies of the Bourguiba political order, as defined by Nouira, were being questioned and the legitimacy of the Tunisian state was being challenged. The basic question was still being asked but the limiting conditions (the context) had changed: "How can Tunisians, undergoing the full process of dependent development, still retain their self-value?"

The events of January 1978 and 1980 pointed out the need to broaden the political base of the Tunisian state in order to limit the starkness of class distinctions. As described above, the pressure in 1978 came from the U.G.T.T. and, in 1980, Gafsa represented the disaffection of the Tunisian south from where many of the working class originate and where the most important mines are located. These classes and regions, in general, lack the complete bilingualism necessary for full entry into the Tunisian political process as long as Tunisia is in a relationship of dependency on France. As a consequence, dependency on France is linked to political and social inequity.

The failure of the socialist experiment of the 1960s had created a credibility gap between the discourse and the action of the Tunisian government. Seemingly insensitive to this gap, this dissonance, the Tunisian government did not tolerate any opposition and attempted to prevent any political discourse but its own.[34] Moreover, this gap reinforced the dissonance between the three conceptions of the political community - the Tunisian, the Arab and the Islamic - such that they appeared contradictory rather than complementary. One may see an ironic double dissonance here. On the ideational level, one may view the Tunisian "personnalité" as contradictory to the traditional Arab-Islamic "personnalité" as the basis of legitimacy. But, this possible contradiction only exploded through the gap between the promises inherent in the official discourse and the actual state of affairs. It is not because "modernization" is inherently un-Islamic or because Islam is inherently anti-modern.[35] "Modernization" created its own contradictions between discourse and action, its own dissonance. In other words, the "modernization" experiment in Tunisia has not yet succeeded either in fulfilling its promises of economic independence and social equality or in the creation of a new coherent system of values. Only Islam remained as the cultural source from which symbols could be drawn to respond to the double issues of the collective identity and social inequality. The partnership worked out between the Destour Party and the U.G.T.T. in the November 1981 elections could only have been achieved within the framework of a tilt away from dependency on France and towards the Arab-Islamic dimensions of the Tunisian "personnalité".

Bourguiba was born into the Arab-Islamic tradition. If he could have adhered to it unquestioningly, it would have guaranteed the dignity of his Arab-Islamic personality. But this was not to be as Tunisia fell under French domination. Any new credo had to offer value and to seem besides (else, why change?) intellectually more respectable. When, in his first stage, he tended towards unstinting admiration for France and for the West in general, he did not do so in hatred of his Arab-Islamic tradition but in despair of its defense. And when the Great Depression showed that the West was not infallible or impregnable, this lifted that despair from him and it was wholly natural that he should discover revolutionary value in the Islamic dimension of the Tunisian "personnalité".

Thus we see that just as no idea is, as it were, an isolated point in space, definable alone without reference to simultaneous existences, so no idea is an isolated point in time. There are no such isolated points, there are only potentialities working themselves out in process. Immediate fact is more than what the senses can apprehend. Just as its contemporary alternatives are immanent in the idea, immanent in it also are its past and future. So how does the idea of a Tunisian "personnalité" incorporate the potentialities of Islam?

One of the most important political thinkers in the contemporary Arab world, Abdallah Laroui, concedes that religion as part of the "traditional logic" may justify revolutionary aims but he warns that such use may weaken progressive forces as they have to compromise with conservative social forces. The ambiguity of religious doctrines then becomes a trap in which conservative social forces preserve the past and block the future.

> There is no doubt that the current which uses traditional logic to justify objectives of liberation represents the majority in Arab countries since the Second World War. Despite a unity of objectives... this current may be divided into two tendencies: one truly originates from the need for liberation and adopts traditional logic in order to increase its chances of achieving its program for liberation by immersion in social reality. The second tendency (which holds the majority) originates from the need to preserve the traditional heritage and values.... Within the sphere limited to culture, temporarily [considered] in abstraction from its social roots, do we not have the right to affirm that the ideological structure... was fundamentally weak because it used a traditional [mode] for the justification of true political positions (liberation, socialism, unity)? By preserving the traditional approach, it also preserved the justifications for the resurrection of conservative forces which had applauded the critique of imported ideologies and had seemed to care for the objective of liberation [but actually] cared only for traditional customs. Was it not natural that the progressive forces should lose everything when conditions altered? They did not achieve liberation and did not even guarantee its means (socialism and unity) when the traditional approach, which they had believed to be the means of popular unity and of [the assertion of their] distinctive

> [identity], became an effective means to reconciliation with the alien. Was not the victory of the conservative wing guaranteed from the very beginning?[36]

Social injustice and dependency still pose a threat to the stability of the Tunisian state. The apparent contradiction between the Arab-Islamic and the Tunisian "personnalités" created cultural dissonance such that the issues of economic dependence and social inequality became part of the problem of political identity. Consequently, the question still continues to be asked.[37]

Notes

CHAPTER 1

[1] An exception is Samir Amin; see in particular his Sociétés précapitalistes et capitalisme (Paris: Anthropos, 1978).

[2] Elbaki Hermassi, Etat et Société au Maghreb; Etude Comparative (Paris: Anthropos, 1975), 9. An example of the undifferentiated application of practically all these meanings is to be found in Peter Gran, The Islamic Roots of Capitalism in Egypt, 1760-1840 (Austin: University of Texas Press, 1979). This minor remark should not detract from the value of the book which must be credited for breaking important new ground in the revision of eighteenth and nineteenth century history of Egypt in particular and of the Middle East in general.

[3] Jean Duvignaud, "Classes et conscience de classe dans un Pays du Maghreb: La Tunisie", in Cahiers Internationaux de Sociologie XXXVIII (1965), 187.

[4] Harold Lasswell, Politics: Who Gets What, When and How (New York: Meridian Books, 1958).

[5] Marvin Harris, The Rise of Anthropological Theory: A History of Theories of Culture (New York: Thomas Crowell, 1968), 571 and 575.

[6] See the comments on this process in Bassam Tibi, Arab Nationalism: A Critical Inquiry, edited and translated from German by Marion Farouk-Sluglett and Peter Sluglett (New York: St. Martin's Press, 1981), 22-26, 34, 49, which are based on Richard F. Behrendt, Soziale Strategie fur Entwicklungslander, Entwurf einer Entwicklungsstrategie (Frankfurt/Main: S. Fischer, 1965), 250.

[7] Emile Durkheim, The Elementary Forms of Religious Life (1915), translated from French by Joseph W. Swain (London: Allen & Unwin, 1964). David E. Apter, in The Politics of Modernization (Chicago: University of Chicago Press, 1965),

attempts to make explicit the connections between systems of "collective representations" and legitimacy. He conceives of a spectrum between two poles: the secular libertarian polis and the sacred collectivity. The first is based on the legitimacy of instrumental values such that authority depends on the persuasive nature of information and emphasizes responsibility. The opposite pole is based on the legitimacy of intrinsic or consummatory values such that authority depends on the coercive power of a hierarchical structure. The power of these intrinsic values derives from their "sacred" nature and, more often than not, from their function as referents for self-identification.

[8] Keith H. Basso and Henry A. Selby (eds.), Meaning in Anthropology (Albuquerque: University of New Mexico Press, 1976), 2. and, particularly, David M. Schneider, "Notes toward a Theory of Culture", in Basso, Meaning, 197.

[9] R.H. Hook, (ed.) Fantasy and Symbol: Studies in Anthropological Interpretation (London: Academic Press, 1979), 9.

[10] Janet L. Dolgin with David S. Kennitzer and David M. Schneider, (eds.), Symbolic Anthropology: A Reader in the Study of Symbols and Meanings (New York: Columbia University Press, 1977), 6.

[11] Dolgin, Symbolic, 16.

[12] Hamid Algar, Ervand Abrahamian and Nikki Keddie; see Edward Said, Covering Islam: How the Media and the Experts determine how We see the Rest of the World (New York: Pantheon, 1981), 173.

[13] Abdelkader Zghal, "Le Retour du sacré et la nouvelle demande idéologique des jeunes scolarisés: le cas de la Tunisie", Annuaire de l'Afrique du Nord (1979), 41-64.

[14] Toshihiko Izutsu, The Structure of Ethical Terms in the Koran (Tokyo: Keio Institute of Philological Studies, 1959); God and Man in the Koran: Semantics of the Koranic Weltsanschauung (Tokyo: Keio Institute of Cultural and Linguistic Studies, 1964); The Concept of Belief in Islamic Theology: A Semantic Analysis of Iman and Islam (Tokyo: Keio Institute of Cultural and Linguistic Studies, 1966-67); and Ethico-Religious Concepts in the Quran (Montreal: McGill University Press, 1966). Incidentally, Northrop Frye in his Anatomy of Criticism; Four Essays (Princeton: Princeton University Press, 1957) used tools developed in Biblical studies for literary criticism. The relevant articles where I experimented with this approach are Norma Salem, "A Partial Reconstruction

of Michel ʿAflaq's Thought: The Role of Islam in the Formulation of Arab Nationalism", The Muslim World LXVII/4 (October 1977), 280-294, and "The Sacred and the Profane: Sâdât's Speech to the Knesset", The Middle East Journal 34/1 (Winter 1980), 13-24. Mârlîn Naśr also used "semantic field analysis" in her book, Al-Taşawwur al-qawmî al-ʿarabî fî fikr Jamâl ʿAbd al-Nâşir (1952-1970); dirâsah fî ʿilm al-mufradât wa-al-dalâlah [The Arab Nationalist Conception in the Thought of Jamâl ʿAbd al-Nâśir (1952-1970): A Study in Lexicology and Semantics] (Beirut: Markaz al-wahdah al-ʿarabiyyah, 1981). The author presents an impressive theoretical defense of this approach; see in particular her first chapter, "Madkhal ilâ muqârabah ʿilmiyyah li-al-fikr al-qawmî al-ʿarabî: manâhij taḩlîl fikr ʿAbd al-Nâśir al-qawmî" [Introduction to a Scientific Approach to Arab Nationalist Thought: Methods for the Analysis of the Nationalist Thought of ʿAbd al-Nâśir], 19-74. The author is conscious of the dangers of narrow adherence to any specific methodology which threatens to strangle the innovative jump to new discoveries (p.62). Also tobe noted is Chapter Seven of the book, "Al-Şilât al-dîniyyah wa-al-ḩadîthah wa-al-thaqâfiyyah fî al-khiţâb al-qawmî al-nâşirî" [The Religious, Modern and Cultural Connections in the Nationalist Nasirite Discourse], 343-371.

[15] Ali Merad, "L'idéologisation de l'Islam dans le monde musulman contemporain", in Jean-Claude Vatin and Ernest Gellner, Islam et Politique au Maghreb (Paris: Editions du C.N.R.S., 1981), 154. The book was published in late 1981 and I was able to obtain a copy only in May 1983, after having basically completed my own work. All references to the book did not, therefore, inspire but simply gave further weight to the perceived importance of Islam as a source of symbols for political discourse since so many researchers together, yet independently, worked on the topic. In many of the papers, the authors lament the lack or poverty of intellectual tools for the analysis and comprehension of the problem.

[16] Harry E. Barnes, The New History and the Social Studies (New York: Century, 1926), 31.

[17] "Biographical Literature", Encyclopaedia Britannica (1974), 1006.

[18] James L. Clifford, From Puzzles to Portraits. Problems of a Literary Biographer (Chapel Hill: University of North Carolina Press, 1970), 83-98. Also see Robert Gittings, The Nature of

Biography (Seattle: University of Washington Press, 1978), 58-62 and 83.

[19] A.O.J. Cockshut, Truth to Life; The Act of Biography in the Nineteenth Century (New York: Harcourt, Brace, Jovanovich, 1974), 13. Catherine D. Bowen, Biography: the Craft and the Calling (Boston: Little & Brown, 1968), 43. Thomas E. Berry, (ed.), The Biographer's Craft (New York: Odyssey Press, 1967).

[20] Bowen, Biography, 59.

[21] Merad, "L'Idéologisation" in Vatin and Gellner, Islam, 153. On the importance of legitimacy in the Arab world, see Michael C. Hudson, Arab Politics: The Search for Legitimacy (New Haven: Yale University Press, 1977) and for the Maghrib, John Waterbury, "La Légitimation du pouvoir au Maghreb: Tradition, Protestation et Répression", in Annuaire de l'Afrique du Nord (1977), 411-422.

[22] Sidney Hook, The HERO in History: A Study in Limitation and Possibility (New York: John Day, 1943), 18. Differently put, "Men [and presumably, women] do make their own destinies, but they do not do so just as they please"; see Alastair Davidson, Antonio Gramsci: Towards an Intellectual Biography (London: Merlin Press, 1977), 204.

[23] Habib Bourguiba, Ḥayâtî, Arâʾî, Jihâdî [My Life, My Opinions, My Struggle] (Tunis: Ministère de l'Information, 1978), 52.

[24] Mohamed-Salah Lejri, L'Evolution du Mouvement National Tunisien des Origines à la deuxième guerre mondiale, 2 volumes (Tunis: Maison tunisienne de l'Edition), I, 15-16.

[25] Ibid., 265-266.

[26] On the balance between the "West" and the "East" in the conception of Mohamed Mzali (presently Prime Minister) and of Béchir Ben Slama (presently Minister of Cultural Affairs), see Halim Barakat, "The Tunisian Al-Fikr: Polarities of the East and the West" (paper delivered at the Conference on North Africa Today: Issues of Development and Integration held at Georgetown University on 22-23 April 1982). Barakat avoids the term "personality" and prefers the term "character", thus placing himself exclusively within the field of psycho-sociology and ignoring the legal implications of the term "personnalité".

[27] "Les Réactions à l'occupation française de la Tunisie en 1881", premier séminaire d'histoire du Mouvement National, organisé par la Commission d'Histoire du Mouvement National, du Ministère de l'Enseignement Supérieur et de la Recherche

Scientifique, Sidi Bou Said, Tunis, 29-31 mai 1981.

[28] Camille Bégué, Le Message de Bourguiba: Une Politique de l'Homme (Paris: Hachette, 1972), 19.

[29] Ibid., 37 n. 1.

[30] Ali Dimassi, Habib Bourguiba; l'Apôtre de la Liberté tunisienne (Tunis: Ali Dimassi, 1979), back cover.

[31] ʿAbd Allah, Ḥarakah, back cover.

[32] Norma Salem, "Michel ʿAflaq: A Biographical Study of His Approach to Arabism" (Unpublished M.A. thesis, McGill University, Institute of Islamic Studies, Montreal, Quebec, 1975); "Partial" in Muslim; and "Michel ʿAflaq: A Biographical Sketch", Arab Studies Quarterly II/2 (Spring 1980), 162-174.

[33] Habib Bourguiba, "Le Voile", an article he first published in 1929 in L'Etendard Tunisien; see Histoire du Mouvement National. Vol. 1. Habib Bourguiba: Articles de Presse, 1929-1934, edited by Chedli Klibi and published by the Tunisian Ministère de l'Information in 1967, 1-5.

CHAPTER 2

[1] L. Carl Brown, "Part One: An Appreciation of The Surest Path", in The Surest Path: The Political Treatise of a Nineteenth Century Muslim Statesman, A Translation of the Introduction to the Surest Path to Knowledge concerning the Condition of Countries by Khayr al-Dîn al-Tûnisî (Cambridge: Harvard University Press, 1967), 15.

[2] Henri de Montety, "Old Families and New Elites in Tunisia", in Man, State and Society in the Contemporary Maghrib, edited by I. William Zartman (New York: Pall Mall, 1973), 171-180; André Demeerseman, "Catégories sociales en Tunisie au XIXe siècle d'après la chronique de Ahmad Ibn Abi d-Diyaf", Institut des Belles Lettres Arabes XXX/117 (1967), 1-12; XXXII/123 (1969), 17-36, 124, 241-272; XXXIII/125 (1970), 69-101, is more of a philological than a sociological study and not even a good one at that, since the author commits many errors (e.g. he confuses aʿlâm with ʿulamâʾ in the belief that they are two plurals of the same singular ʿâlim, p. 73). Duvignaud, "Classes", is too general. Mustapha Kraiem, La Tunisie Précoloniale (Tunis: Société Tunisienne de Diffusion, 1973), II, 103-204; L. Carl Brown, The Tunisia of Ahmad Bey, 1837-1855 (Princeton: Princeton University Press, 1974); and Nicholas S. Hopkins, "Traditional Tunis and Its Transformations", in S. Benet et al., (eds.), The

Impact of Modernization on Peasant Societies (New York: New York Academy of Sciences, 1974), have the most insights.

[3] The special issue of Daedalus (Spring 1968) entitled "Historical Population Studies" addresses itself to this problem but mainly from the perspective of demography. The book by Peter Laslett, The World We Have Lost (New York: Charles Scribner's Sons, 1965) examines the issue of demographic change and social mobility in history. For the Middle East in general, Roger E. Owen and Thomas Naff, (eds.), Studies in Eighteenth Century Islamic History (Carbondale: South Illinois University Press, 1977) cast doubt on the assumption of static social structures before the arrival of the West in the guise of Napoleon's invasion. Also see Hermassi, Leadership 22ff. Gran, Islamic, attempts to prove that elements of social change, presaging the bourgeois and industrial revolutions, already existed in Egypt before Nepoleon's arrival. For North Africa, see the argument in James Allman, Social Mobility, Education and Development in Tunisia (Leiden: Brill, 1979), 19-28, flawed by his over-reliance on Ibn Khaldûn's model and his belief that a "dynamic middle class never arose in North Africa in the Middle Ages" (p. 22). In the case of Tunisia, it has been shown that at least during the nineteenth century and for at least one social category, the ʿulamâʾ, recruitment from other social categories was greater (59 percent) than recruitment from the same category (41 percent); see Arnold H. Green, The Tunisian 'Ulama 1873-1915: Social Structure and Response to Ideological Currents (Leiden: Brill, 1978), 75 and 119. The circulation of this élite was greatest between the ahl al-ʿilm, the ahl al-makhzan and the baladîs. The mamlûks were in a more ambiguous situation as, through the nineteenth century, they were tending towards assimilation though the memory of their origins was still evoked while the âfâqîs were the least favored in terms of the circulation of this élite; ibid., 85. Another interesting study of social change in Tunisia is the book by Sophie Ferchiou, Techniques et sociétés: exemple de la Fabrication des Chéchias en Tunisie (Paris: Mémoires de l'Institut d'Ethnologie, 1971). The author shows that, whereas in the early nineteenth century, the shâshiyyah industry "ferait honneur à une nation européenne" [Thomas MacGill: An Account of Tunis, of its Governement, [sic] manners, customs and antiquities, especially of its Productions, manufactures and

commerce (Glasgow and London, 1811) as quoted by Ferchiou, Techniques, 97], it was unable to resist the penetration of cheaper products under the Protectorate which favored French goods and it was practically destroyed during the 1932 economic crisis. The author succeeds in linking "techniques" to "social formation" and in tracing the evolution of the two under "normal" conditions and under constraints of the Protectorate.

[4] Nicola A. Ziadeh, Origins of Nationalism in Tunisia (Beirut: American University of Beirut, 1962), 9.Also see Abdurrahman Cayci, La Question tunisienne et la Politique ottomane, 1881-1913 (Erzurum: Ataturk Universitesi, 1963) and Robert Mantran, "L'Evolution des relations entre la Tunisie et l'Empire Ottoman du XVIe au XIXe siècle", Cahiers de Tunisie, nos. 26-27 (1959), 319-333.

[5] Paul Brenner, "The Origins of Capitalist Development: A Critique of Neo-Smithian Marxism", New Left Review 104 (1977), 25-92. The political position he jumps to -- of "the necessary interdependence between the revolutionary movements at the 'weakest link' and in the metropolitan heartlands of capitalism" -- is yet to be vouchsafed in our contemporary situation.

[6] See Paul Sebag, La Tunisie: Essai de Monographie (Paris: Editions Sociales, 1951), 215. Similarly, Carmen Sammut "L'Action des Jeunes tunisiens: Réformisme d'Assimilation ou nationalisme d'émancipation", Revue d'Histoire Maghrébine 10-11 (1978), 76, 142, 147, states that even the nationalist "feeling" was a result of the French imperialist penetration and that the Young Tunisians, almost thirty years following the occupation, were burdened with the task of "forming" the Tunisian nation. In the same vein, André Raymond and Jean Poncet, La Tunisie, 2nd edition (Paris: Presses universitaires de France, 1971), 54, who hold that the formation of a Tunisian bourgeoisie was a "fruit" of the Protectorate. Also see Jean Ganiage, Les Origines du Protectorat français en Tunisie, 1861-1881 (Paris: Presses universitaires de France, 1959).

[7] I add the "where" to Lasswell's definition in order to indicate that, at least for the Tunisia of the nineteenth century, the "nation-state" framework is not to be taken for granted; cf. his Politics.

[8] By the Constitution of 1861, the Tunisian nationality was separated from the Ottoman; see Ibrâhîm ʿAbd al-Bâqî, Al-Jinsiyyah fî qawânîn duwal al-Maghrib al-ʿarabî al-kabîr; dirâsah muqâranah

[Nationality in the laws of the States of the Great Arab Maghrib; A Comparative Study], (Cairo: Maṭbaʿat al-Jabalâwî, 1971), 61.

[9] Pierre Grandchamp, Etudes d'histoire Tunisienne XVIIIe-XXe siècle (Paris: Presses universitaires de France, 1966); Bice Salama, L'Insurrection de 1864 en Tunisie (Tunis: Maison tunisienne de l'Edition, 1967) and Khalifa Chater, Insurrection et Répression dans la Tunisie du XIXe siècle: La Mehalla de Zarrouk au Sahel (1864) (Tunis: Publications de l'Université de Tunis, 1978). See also Ganiage, Origines, 11-69, 181 and 277-340, Raymond and Poncet, Tunisie, 24; Lejri, Evolution, 33-51 and particularly 43n; ʿAbd al-Bâqî, Jinsiyyah, 55ff.

[10] Cf. Bryan S. Turner, "Ideology, Nationalism and the Superstructure", Marx and the End of Orientalism (London: George Allen & Unwin, 1978), 53-56.

[11] L'Afrique du Nord en Marche: Tunisie, Algérie, Maroc (Paris: Payot, 1964) and L'Evolution Politique de L'Afrique du Nord musulmane, 1920-1961, (Paris: Armand Colin, 1962) on the one hand and Lejri, Evolution, I, 12 and Muḥammad al-Fâḍil Ibn ʿAshur, Al-Ḥarakah al-adabiyyah wa-al-fikriyyah fî Tûnis [The Literary and Intellectual Movement in Tunisia], on the other hand.

[12] Stuart E. Brown, "The Young Tunisians" (Unpublished Ph.D. Dissertation, Institute of Islamic Studies, McGill University, Montreal, Quebec, 1976).

[13] Green, 'Ulama, 130. For the text of the Treaty, see ʿAbd al-Bâqî, Jinsiyyah, 457-459.

[14] Henri Cambon, Histoire de la Régence de Tunis (Paris: Berger-Leviau, 1948). Also see Green, 'Ulama, 153, and Dimassi, Bourguiba, 130.

[15] For the text of the Treaty, see ʿAbd al-Bâqî, Jinsiyyah, 460-461. For the French text, see Lejri, Evolution, I, 59-60.

[16] For details on the capitalist world system, see Arghiri Emmanuel, L'Echange inégal (Paris: Maspéro, 1969); Samir Amin, L'Accumulation á l'Echelle mondiale; Critique de la Théorie du Sous-développement (Paris: Anthropos, 1970); André Gunder-Frank and Samir Amin, L'Accumulation dépendante et Sociétés pré-capitalistes et capialisme (Paris: Anthropos, 1978); Immanuel Wallerstein, The Modern World System: Capitalist Agriculture and the Origins of European World Economy in the 16th Century (New York: Academic Press, 1974); Daniel Chirot, Social Change in the

20th Century (New York: Harcourt, Brace, Jovanovich, 1977).

[17] Article of the Treaty as quoted by Green, 'Ulama, 130.

[18] As quoted by Dimassi, Bourguiba, 334.

[19] E. Fallot, "Le Functionnement du Protectorat tunisien", in La Tunisie au début du XXe siècle, edited by Maurice Besnier et al. (Paris: F.R. de Rudeval, 1904), 352.

[20] Quoted by Chedly Khairallah, Mouvement Evolutionniste Tunisien, (Paris: Editions Cujas, 1967), III, 43 as cited in La Deuxième internationale et l'Orient, edited by Georges Haupt and Madeleine Rébérioux (Paris: Cujas, 1967). Also see Noureddine Sraieb, "Enseignement, Elites et Systèmes de Valeur: le Collège Sadiki de Tunis", Annuaire de l'Afrique du Nord (1971), 104-135.

[21] Ibn ʿAshûr, Ḥarakah as cited by Green, 'Ulama, 153.

[22] Kraiem, Nationalisme, 17-20 and Lejri, Evolution, 56-89.

[23] André Pautard, Bourguiba, (Paris: Editions Média, 1978), 38; Bourguiba, Ḥayâtî, 3; Tunisia, Habib, 19; Ahmed Kassab, Histoire de la Tunisie; L'Epoque Contemporaine (Tunis: Société tunisienne de Diffusion, 1976) 228; Ahmed Abdessalam, Sadiki et les Sadikiens (Tunis: Cérès Productions, 1975), 198; Tunisia, Habib, 20.

[24] Bourguiba, Ḥayâtî, 3-5. Pautard, Bourguiba, 41, mentions seven instead of eight children in total. The mistake may be due to the fact that Bourguiba never mentions his older sister who remains a mysteriously shadowy figure.

[25] Bourguiba, Ḥayâtî, 4-5.

[26] Tunisia, Habib, 48.

[27] Mohamed-Salah Sfia, in Haupt, Deuxième, 413-414, quoting Salamah Musa. Also see Bourguiba, Ḥayâtî, 32, 7; Dimassi, Habib, 191; Pautard, Bourguiba, 42-43.

[28] Ibn ʿAshûr, Al-Ḥarakah, 174 and Bourguiba, Ḥayâtî, 31.

[29] Dimassi, Habib, 198-199 and also 189.

[30] Bourguiba, Ḥayâtî, 3.

[31] Tunisia, Habib, 19; Bourguiba, Ḥayâtî, 4-6 and 10; Dimassi, Habib, 188.

[32] Bourguiba, Ḥayâtî, 11 and 23. The position of shaykh al-madînah is not simply the equivalent of "mayor" as may be understood in a contemporary European or North American context; in nineteenth century Tunisia, the skaykh al-madînah had replaced the muḥtasib as the link between the central state

and the guilds; see Ferchiou, Techniques, 109 and 144-148. Also note Pautard, Bourguiba, 45 and Bourguiba, Ḥayâtî, 7 and 22. One is left to wonder whether this is the same Mizâlî family as the present Prime Minister, Mohamed Mzali. Bourguiba himself distinguishes between two branches of the Mizâlîs, the aʿyân and the makhzanîs, to both of which he was related; through his grandmother to the first and through his sister-in-law, Ahmed's wife, to the second. See ohamed-Salah Mzali, Au Fil de ma Vie: Souvenirs d'un Tunisien (Tunis: Editions H. Mzali, 1972), 19-20 and Dimassi, Habib, 186.

33 Bourguiba, Ḥayâtî, 22.

34 Dimassi, Habib, 197, gives 17 November 1913 as the exact date; cf. Tunisia, Habib, 21. Imprecision allows Dimassi to state, in one breath, that she was 40 years old when she died (p. 200) and that she was 40 years old when Habib was born (p. 191). This latter alternative would make her over fifty at the time of her death, a respectable age given the life-expectancy in Tunisia at the time. Also see Pautard, Habib, 41.

35 Bourguiba as quoted by Pautard, Bourguiba, 46. Also see Bourguiba, Ḥayâtî, 8 and 21-22 and Tunisia, Habib, 20.

36 Bourguiba, Ḥayâtî, 61.

37 Ibid., 6, 10-11 and Tunisia, Habib, 20. Bourguiba's condemnation of the beylical state, understandable in view of his coup d'état in 1957 in which he established the Republic of Tunisia with himself as President, deliberately points out that one of the reasons for the 1864 insurrection was the expropriation of tribal land which the Bey had undertaken on Khayr al-Dîn's behalf; see Bourguiba, Ḥayâtî, 9. In fact, he has reversed the sequence of events since the expropriation was made after rather than before the insurrection and Bourguiba corrects himself in the following lecture in a fuller rendition of Khayr al-Dîn's role in the history of Tunisia where he then highlights the allocation of the Enfida domains to Khayr al-Dîn after the 1864 insurrection; seeBourguiba, Ḥayâtî, 29.

38 Ibid., 6,9 and 15-17; Tunisia, Habib, 20; Dimassi, Habib, 184 and 188. Pautard, Bourguiba, 41, gives the year 1887 for the appointment. Cf. Abdessalam, Sadiki, 195.

39 Tunisia, Habib, 48 and Bourguiba, Ḥayâtî, 5 and 15.

[40] Tunisia, Habib, 19 n. 1. Allman, Social, 29. Moncer Rouissi, Population et Société au Maghreb (Tunis: Cérès, 1977), 49, and, especially, Abdelkader Zghal, "Les Effets de la Modernisation de l'Agriculture sur la Stratification sociale dans les campagnes tunisiennes", Cahiers Internationaux de Sociologie XXXVII (1965) 201-106, based on Ibn Abî al-Ḍiyâf, focus on the social stratification and its transformation in Tunisia and are particularly valuable. Also see Jean Ganiage, "La Population de la Tunisie vers 1860: Essai d'évaluation d'après les registres fiscaux," Etudes Maghrébines: Mélanges Charles-André Julien (Paris: Presses universitaires de France, 1964). See map in Jean Poncet, La Colonisation et l'Agriculture européenne en Tunisie depuis 1881: Etudes de géographie historique et économique (Paris: Mouton, 1961), 133. On iqṭâʿ, see EI[2] and Claude Cahen, "L'Evolution de l'Iqṭâʿ du IXe au XIIIe siècle", in Annales Economies, Sociétés, Civilisations, VIII/1 (janvier-mars 1953).

[41] The following description of land tenure in Tunisia is based mainly on Poncet, Colonisation, but also see Robert Jambu-Merlin, Le Droit Privé en Tunisie (Paris: Librairie générale de droit et de jurisprudence, 1960), 304-338. An illustration of many scholars' lack of intellectual tools necessary to the fields of Islamic law and economic history is Dimassi's reading of Poncet (without acknowledgement), where he classifies the beylik (or the Bey's) lands as milk whereas there were two categories of these lands, and in both cases, beylik was closer to hanshîr with the tribute going either to the Bey's private purse or to the public treasury. The distinction between these two budgets is clearly made in the Arab-Islamic historical experience of government as early as the Abbasids; see Dominique Sourdel, La Civilisation de l'Islam classique (Paris: Arthaud, 1968). On the relationship between land tenure and the Tunisian nationalist movement, see Ziadeh, Origins, 39-45; Kassab, Histoire, 39-97, and Poncet, Colonisation, in general. Mahjoubi, Origines, 28-29, quoting Sebag, Tunisie, 40, goes to the extent of dating the beginnings of the Tunisian nationalist movement to 1904 when the French Courts rendered sentence on the claims of Tunisian tribes to the land: "La première condition pour être propriétaire c'est d'exister; or, en Tunisie les tribus, comme personnes juridiques, n'existent pas."

[42] By that time, ḥabûs land constituted almost a quarter of cultivable land in Tunisia; see Mahjoubi, Origines, 30. It is possible that this tendency for centralization of land control was at the roots of the salafiyyah movement against sufism and sufi institutions, mainly the zâwiyâs.

[43] L. Carl Brown, "The Tunisian Path to Modernization" (Mimeographed paper, Princeton, April 1971), 44 and Julien, L'Afrique, 57 and Sebag, Tunisie, 45.

[44] See Poncet, Colonisation, 151.

[45] Ibid., 140, 152, 190-192 and Mahjoubi, Origines, 14-21, particularly 19-ff; Dimassi, Habib, 96.

[46] Mahjoubi, Origines, 33-41; Kassab, Histoire, 131-174; and Ferchiou, Techniques.

[47] Dimassi, Habib, 135. See also S. Brown, Young, 13; Green, Tunisian, 200; and Ibn ʿAshûr, Ḥarakah, 85-86.

[48] Bourguiba, Ḥayâtî, 16 and Pautard, Bourguiba, 56.

[49] Zghal, "Effets", 203.

[50] Allman, Social, 52.

[51] Bourguiba, Ḥayâtî, 3 and 7.

[52] Ibid., 7-8.

[53] Abdessalam, Sadiki, 195, 196, 198 respectively. Also see Bourguiba, Ḥayâtî, 26.

[54] Caudel, "Société" in Besnier, Tunisie, 283. Also see Mahmoud Abdel-Moula, L'Université Zaytounienne et la Société tunisienne (Tunis: Abdel Moula, 1971), 86; M'Hamed Lasram, "L'Enseignement supérieur musulman; la Khaldounia à Tunis" in Congrès de l'Afrique du Nord tenue à Paris du 6 au 10 octobre 1908; Compte-rendu des travaux, II, 174, as quoted by Mahjoubi, Origines, 117. Also see Mongi Smida, L'Enseignement supérieur en Tunisie (Structures-Régimes- Bourses), (Tunis: Société tunisienne de Diffusion, 1974), 97 and 195.

[55] Sraieb, "Enseignement", 124-125. Also see Yves Chatelain, La Vie littéraire et intellectuelle en Tunisie de 1900 à 1937 (Paris: Geuthner, 1937), 27.

[56] Worked out from figures given by Dimassi, Habib, 112. Also see Sraieb, "Enseignement", 105-106.

[57] Pautard, Bourguiba, 61. See also Allman, Social, 90, based on Montéty, "Vieilles Familles" and Sraieb, Enseignement", 125.

[58] Pautard, Bourguiba, 63, quoting Pierre Rossi, La Tunisie de Bourguiba (Tunis: Editions Kahia, 1967).

[59] Raymond F. Betts, Assimilation and Association in French Colonial Theory, 1890-1914 (New York: Columbia University Press, 1961), 125, quoting the Compte-rendu du Congrès colonial de Marseilles, 1906, 2 volumes (Paris: Guillamin et Cie., 1908). Also see Ibn ʿAshûr, Ḥarakah, 86-91.

[60] L.C. Brown, "Tunisia under the Protectorate: A History of Ideological Change" (Ph.D. dissertation, Harvard University, Cambridge, Mass., 1962), 40. Béchir Ben Slama, Al-Naẓariyyah al-târîkhiyyah fî al-kifâḥ al-taḥrîrî al-tûnisî [The Historical Theory in the Tunisian Liberation Movement], Part I. (Tunis: ʿAbd al-Karîm Ibn ʿAbd Allâh, 1977), 112-140.

[61] Roger Casemajor, L'action nationaliste en Tunisie, du pacte fondamental de M'hamed Bey à la mort de Moncef Bey (1857-1949) (Tunis: n.p., 1949), 88.

[62] Bourguiba, Ḥayâtî, 24; Pautard, Bourguiba, 59; Dimassi, Bourguiba, 200; Mahjoubi, Origines, 47-84 and Sraieb, "Enseignement", 109.

[63] Kraiem, Nationalisme, 106-116. Also see Jambu-Merlin, Droit, 42.

[64] Abdel-Moula, L'Université, 16. Also see S. Brown, Young, 109.

[65] Bourguiba, Ḥayâtî, 11 and Mahjoubi, Origines, 106.

[66] Bourguiba, Ḥayâtî, 11-12.

[67] Dimassi, Habib, 144. Also see S. Brown, Young, 32-33.

[68] Les Revendications du peuple algéro-tunisien, Mémoire adressé au Congrès de la Paix, septembre-décembre 1918, pp. 129-137, as quoted by Mahjoubi, Origines, 146. Also see Mohammed Dabbab, Les Délégations destouriennes à Paris ou la "Question tunisienne" dans les années 1920; Revendications, Manoeuvres, Polémiques, Scission. Textes et Documents (Tunis: Maison tunisienne de l'Edition, 1980), 37. For details on this period, see Mahjoubi, Origines, 139-164. Also see Béchir Tlili, "La grande guerre et les questions tunisiennes; le groupement de la 'Revue du Maghreb' (1916-1918)", Les Cahiers de Tunisie XXVI/101-102 (1978), 31-108.

[69] See L'Afrique française, Chronique de Tunisie (août 1922-1928) quoted by Lejri, Evolution, 180, for the first translation. The second translation is the more prevalent.

[70] Kraiem, Nationalisme, 137.

[71] Bourguiba, Ḥayâtî, 11.

[72] Abdessalam, Sadiki, 198. Compare with ibid., 18 and 21; Tunisia, Habib, 20;

[73] Bourguiba, Ḥayâtî, 24-25.

[74] Ibid., 30.

[75] Ibid., 29; Tunisia, Habib, 21; Jean Lacouture, "Les Options d'Habib Bourguiba" in his Cinq Hommes et la France (Paris: Seuil, 1961), 111; cf. Abdessalam, Sadiki, 77.

[76] See photograph in Tunisia, Habib, 48. Also see Bourguiba, Ḥayâtî, 21.

[77] Ibid., 54.

[78] Sraieb, "Enseignement", 114.

[79] Chatelain, Vie, 271, cites one "Mohamed Bourguiba" among a list of poets whose work appeared after the First World War. Also see Tunisia, Habib, 22.

[80] Pautard, Bourguiba, 62. Also see Bourguiba, Ḥayâtî, 32 and Sraieb, "Enseignement", 118.

CHAPTER 3

[1] René Gallissot, "Le socialisme dans le domaine arabe: Syrie, Liban, Irak, Palestine, Egypte, Maghreb", in Jacques Droz, (ed.), Histoire générale du socialisme (Paris: Presses universitaires de France, 1972), 545-606. On the futility of the Ottomanist option which had been forcefully propounded by Bash Hanba, see Ibn ʿAshûr, Ḥarakah, 99.

[2] Mahjoubi, Origines, 188 n. 61 and 189 n. 62.

[3] The first meeting took place in March 1919, according to Chedly Khairallah, Le Mouvement national tunisien, 1904-1932, as referred to by Mahjoubi, Origines, 202-3. Ziadeh, Origins, 90, states that the first meeting took place in November 1918. Also see Lejri, Evolution, I, 167; Dimassi, Habib, 153; Dabbab, Délégations, 20.

[4] Lejri, Evolution, I, 169. On the early history of contacts between Tunisians and French socialists, see Béchir Tlili, Socialistes et Jeunes Tunisiens à la veille de la Grande Guerre (1911-1913) (Tunis: Publications de l'Université de Tunis, 1974).

[5] Ziadeh, Origins, 91.

[6] Ibid., 104. Of course, such a position is in contradiction with the more usual thesis that colonialism was itself a mechanism for progress; L.C. Brown, Tunisia under, 8.

[7] The book was published by Couve et Cie in 1920; see Ziadeh, Origins, 103 n. 44. But November and December 1919 are also cited; see Dabbab, Délégations, 20. The book was published anonymously but most sources cite Thaalbi as author and Sakka as translator from Arabic to French and the matter is still controversial. In any case, the most pertinent judgement is that "In so far as the book expressed an idea and a programme for the future of Tunisia, it mattered very little who actually wrote it"; see Ziadeh, Origins, 103. For summaries of the major points of the book, see ibid., 89-127, with particular reference to 103-8, and Mahjoubi, Origines, 206-15.

[8] Cited by ibid., 368.

[9] Based on the account of Haupt and Rébérioux, Deuxième, 152 and pp. 31ff as well.

[10] Lacouture, "Options", 109.

[11] The Party had first been identified as "Parti Libéral Tunisien"; see Lejri, Evolution, I, 180 and Mahjoubi, Origines, 218. But Thaalbi had insisted on adding a reference to the Constitution, the Destour. The final translation was carried into the literature in English and the Party has come to be known as the Tunisian Liberal Constitutional Party; see S. Brown, Young, 221.

[12] Mahjoubi, Origines, 240 and 257.

[13] Lejri, Evolution, I, 181. The eight points adopted by the Destour Party in its first program are the following: "(1) the establishment of a legislature (deliberative) assembly composed of Tunisians and French members elected by universal suffrage, with freedom of forming its own agenda and with unlimited budgetary powers; (2) The government to be responsible to the assembly; (3) The powers -- legislative, executive and judiciary -- to be completely separate; (4) Tunisians to be eligible for administrative posts, if they possess the necessary qualifications; (5) Functionaries performing the same duties should receive equal pay, whether Tunisians or French; (6) The formation of elected municipal Councils in all towns of Tunisia; (7) Tunisians should have the right to share in the purchase of lands from the Directorate of Agricultural Affairs (i.e. lands for colonization) and Public allotments; (8) The freedom of the Press, of meetings and of association as a right of the Tunisians"; see Ziadeh, Origins, 93. When the second delegation arrived in Paris in December 1920, "a ninth point demanding that compulsory education should be the right of every Tunisian and the

responsibility of the State in this regard was added to the eight demands"; ibid., 95 and Dabbab, Délégations, 149, quoting Guellaty. From then on, the Destour program included all nine points.

[14] Dimassi, Habib, 234.

[15] Ibid., 155. Mahhoubi, Origines, 237, notes, "Dans la capitale, elle [la délégation] mène une campagne pour une constitution mais aussi contre le projet d'emprunt que les autorités du Protectorat soumettent au gouvernement de la République et surtout contre l'ouverture des habous privés à la colonisation." Also see Dabbab, Délégations, 51.

[16] Dimassi, Habib, 240, quoting Taher Ben Ammar. For details on the delegations, see Dabbab, Délégations, 71-104; Lejri, Evolution, I, 183ff.; Mahjoubi, Origines, 236-53; and Dimassi, Habib, 163.

[17] Mahjoubi, Origines, 309-22 and 327-31. According to L.C. Brown, Tunisia under, 41-2.

[18] Mahjoubi, Origines, 394.

[19] Dabbab, Délégations, 109-110.

[20] Ibid., 22. Also see Mahjoubi, Origines, 276-80.

[21] Ibid., 317 n. 45; Lejri, Evolution, I, 209; Dabbab, Délégations, 110, who also lists one "Materi". Also see Histoire, VI, 29.

[22] Dabbab, Délégations, 183 and 189, respectively.

[23] "Le Devoir de l'élite", published in Tunis-Socialiste, 20 November 1921, as quoted by Dabbab, Délégations, 189.

[24] Al-Tâhir al-Ḥaddâd, Imra)atunâ fî al-sharî(ah wa-al-mujtama([Our Woman in the Law and in Society] (1930), 2nd edition (Tunis: Al-Dâr al-tûnisiyyah li-al-nashr, 1972), 43.

[25] Mahjoubi, Origines, 279.

[26] An indication of the fluidity in their respective membership is the fact that Sadok Zmerli, Figures Tunisiennes: Les Successeurs (Tunis: Maison tunisienne de l'Edition, 1967), 293, claims Hassan Guellaty founded the theatrical group, Al-Adâb, in which Mohamed Bourguiba was active, while Ibn (Ashûr, Ḥarakah, 110, claims Thaalbi founded it.

[27] Mahjoubi, Origines, 265 and 303.

[28] Ziadeh, Origins, 110, notes that "It became customary for many French writers to associate the national leadership with communism."

[29] See Mahjoubi, Origines, 262-3.

[30] As quoted by ibid., 266-7.

[31] Ibid. 301 and 335. Demoralization set in to such an extent that Ben Ayed split off, forming the short-lived Parti Destourien Indépendant; see ibid., 304-9. It is thought that Thaalbi himself was so disgusted that he left Tunisia on 26 July 1923 for Egypt; see ibid., 340.

[32] Ibid., 367.

[33] Ibid., 189. Also see Tlili, "Destour", 142 and Mahjoubi, Origines, 344.

[34] Hermassi, Etat, 125. Quoting the Destour newspaper, Le Libéral, 7 November 1925, Tlili, "Destour", 143, states, "La C.G.T.T., purement ouvrière, ne se rattache donc à aucun parti politique." Also see Dimassi, Habib, 170 and 172-3. There were also some echoes of the Sultan Galiev thesis that the class struggle within any colonized society was meaningless since the colonizing power impoverished all elements of the indigenous society. The struggle was necessarily between the "native" society on the one hand and the colonizing power on the other hand. See al-Ṭâhir al-Ḥaddâd, Al-ʿUmmâl al-tûnisiyyûn wa-ẓuhûr al-ḥarakah al-niqâbiyyahfî Tûnis [The Tunisian Workersand the Beginnings of the Labor Movement in Tunisia] (1927), 3rd edition (Tunis: Al-Dâr al-tûnisiyyah li-al-nashr, 1972) and L.C. Brown, Tunisia under, 102.

[35] Mahjoubi, Origines, 381-2. In defense of the Destour against the Néo-Destour accusation of having abandoned the C.G.T.T., see Tlili, "Destour".

[36] Ibid. 404, for details.

[37] Ibid., 409.

[38] Ibid., 415.

[39] Ibid., 437-8.

[40] Tunisia, Habib, 23.

[41] See Lejri, Evolution, I, 132-7 and Mahjoubi, Origines, 396-8. See Albert Memmi, Statue de sel, (Paris: Gallimard, 1972, copyright 1966) for a semi-autobiographical version of the malaise of a "native" Jew who is led to the new land of French culture and cannot look back. Interestingly, Bourguiba was able to obtain some support for the option of autonomy from Jewish Tunisians following World War II.

[42] Lacouture, "Options", 114. Also see Tunisia, Habib, 23.

[43] Bourguiba, Ḥayâtî, 34.

[44] Dimassi, Habib, 217. Also see Tunisia, Habib, 26.

[45] Dimassi, Habib, 217.

[46] Ibid., 169. Lacouture, "Options", 114.

[47] Ibid., 114-5. Also see Bourguiba, Ḥayâtî, 24.

[48] Ibid., 36; Nathanael Greene, From Versailles to Vichy; The Third French Republic, 1919-1940 (New York: Thomas Y Crowell, 1970), 44. This was also the period when the Cartel des Gauches undertook a savage war against ʿAbd al-Karîm in the Moroccan Rif; see Georges Lefranc, "Le Socialisme en France", in Droz, Histoire, 368-9.

[49] Bourguiba, Ḥayâtî, 42, 43, 49; Tunisia, Habib, 24; Dimassi, Habib, 585; Bégué, Message, 8.

[50] Lacouture, "Options", 114-6. See Albert Memmi, La Dépendance: esquisse pour un portrait du dépendant (Paris: Gallimard, 1979).

[51] Bourguiba, Ḥayâtî, 54; Dimassi, Habib, 465 and Greene, From, 17-8.

[52] On the relationships between Jean Jaurès, Henri Bergson and Charles Péguy, see André Harvey, Bergson, maître de Péguy (Paris: Elzévir, 1948); André Robinet, Péguy entre Jaurès, Bergson et l'Eglise; métaphysique et politique (Paris: Seghers, 1968). Also interesting is Robert Vigneault, L'Univers féminin dans l'Oeuvre de Charles Péguy (Paris: Déclés de Brower, 1967).

[53] Personal interview with Mohamed Sayah, August 1980.

[54] Alfred de Vigny, Oeuvres complètes, préface, présentation et notes de Paul Viallanieux (Paris: Seuil, 1965), 102.

[55] Bourguiba, Ḥayâtî, 28.

[56] Bégué, Message, 37-38.

[57] Dimassi, Habib, 222.

[58] Félix Garas, Bourguiba et la Naissance d'une Nation (Paris: René Julliard, 1956), as quoted by Dimassi, Habib, 222. Also see Félicien Challaye, Péguy Socialiste (Paris: Amoit-Dumont, 1954).

[59] Lacouture, "Options", 116; Tunisia, Habib, 23; Dimassi, Habib, 227.

[60] Ibid., 118.

[61] Tunisia, Habib, 27 and Pautard, Bourguiba, 80 and Bourguiba, Ḥayâtî, 65-6.

[62] Tunisia, Habib, 28-30 and "Le Voile" in L'Etendard Tunisien (11 January 1929); see Histoire, I, 1-6.

[63] Lejri, Evolution, II, 8 n. 2 and 18.

[64] See the article by Bourguiba, "L'Evolution d'un Protectorat", in La Voix du Tunisien on 23 February 1931; Histoire, I, 20-4.

[65] Lejri, Evolution, II, 26.
[66] Bourguiba, Ḥayâti, 67-8.
[67] La Voix du Tunisien (3 May 1930), as quoted by Mahjoubi, Origines, 473.
[68] The open letter from the Destour was followed by some 678 signatures and was published in La Voix du Tunisien (3 May 1930); see Mahjoubi, Origines, 470.
[69] Mahjoubi, Origines, 479.
[70] Ibid., 485ff.
[71] Bourguiba, Ḥayâtî, 71.
[72] Ibid., 68.
[73] "La Voix du Tunisien à la Maison de France", in La Voix du Tunisien (2 July 1931); see Histoire, I, 85.
[74] "Appel à nos camarades destouriens: Prenez garde au transfuge", in L'Action Tunisienne (31 March 1933); see Histoire, I, 274.
[75] Bourguiba, Ḥayâtî, 73.
[76] "Appel à nos camarades destouriens: Prenez garde au transfuge", in L'Action Tunisienne (31 March 1933); see Histoire,I, 273. See also Mahjoubi, Origines, 464.
[77] Tunisia, Habib, 27.
[78] The following description of the Néo-Socialistes is based mainly on Jean Touchard, La Gauche en France depuis 1900 (Paris: Seuil, 1977), 179-188, but also see Daniel Ligou, Histoire du socialisme en France (1871-1961) (Paris: Presses universitaires de France, 1962) and Lefranc, "Socialisme" in Droz, Histoire, 416ff. For a short description of the Radical Party in France in the 1930s, also see Touchard, Gauche, 102-138.
[79] Mahjoubi, Origines, 488.
[80] Bourguiba, Ḥayâtî, 73-4; Mahjoubi, Origines, 487 and 537-9.
[81] Ibid., 487, quoting Lisân al-Shaʿb (26 December 1923) as cited by Yahya El-Ghoul, "Naturalisation française et mouvement national tunisien" (Unpublished thesis, University of Tunis, 1973), 124 and based on Ahmed Tewfik al-Madani, Hayât Kifâḥ [A Life of Struggle], 281.
[82] Mahjoubi, Origines, 540-569. Also see Habib Bourguiba, "La Famine en Tunisie", in La Voix du Tunisien (13 June 1931) and "La Protection du marché intérieur", in L'Action Tunisienne (14 November 1932), reproduced in Histoire, I, 62-79 and 110-5 respectively.

[83] Bégué, Message (Paris: Hachette, 1972) 13-4. Also see Poncet, Colonisation, 254, 290, 305; Mahjoubi, Origines, 560-1; Bourguiba, "Le Budget Tunisien: Droits de douane et politique douanière", in L'Action Tunisienne, (8 November 1932) reproduced in Histoire, I, 105-10; Kassab, Histoire, I, 104-119.

[84] See Poncet, Colonisation, 256 and 287.

[85] Zghal, "Effets", 204. The work of Zghal is seminal to an understanding of the socio-economic forces within Tunisia; see in particular his articles, "Nation-building in the Maghreb", International Social Science Journal 23 (1971), 435-451; "Mouvements paysans en Tunisie", Cahiers int. hist. écon. soc. 8 (n.d.), 337-345 and with Mohamed Chérif, "The reactivation of tradition in a post-traditional society" Daedalus 102i (1973), 225-237.

[86] Bourguiba in his open letter to M. Guernut, Vice President of the Committee on Human Rights, in L'Action Tunisienne (5 May 1933); see Histoire, I, 100-2 and 276-81.

[87] Bourguiba, "La Tunisie Française reprend sa vieille tradition", in L'Action Tunisienne (15 April 1933); see Histoire, I, 306-11. Also see Mahjoubi, Origines, 597-600.

[88] Bourguiba, "Inconscience ou cynisme?", in L'Action Tunisienne (23 November 1932), reproduced in Histoire, I, see 124.

[89] "Le 'Durellisme' ou le Socialisme boiteux", in La Voix du Tunisien (19 January 1929); see Histoire, I, 19.

[90] Dimassi, Habib, 268, quoting Bourguiba. Bourguiba, "Le Budget Tunisien" and "Répartition et Restitution", in L'Action Tunisienne of 1 November 1932 and 4 April 1933 respectively; see Histoire, I, 100-2 and 276-81.

[91] Dimassi, Habib, 281.

[92] Mahjoubi, Origines, 489, quoting El-Ghoul, Naturalisation, 130.

[93] "Une Dangereuse équivoque: Le statu quo?", in L'Action Tunisienne (24 April 1933); see Histoire, I, 325-6.

[94] Mahjoubi, Origines, 492 and 499, based on El-Ghoul, Naturalisation, 144 and 157-8 quoting M'Hamed Bourguiba, "Le Peuple chez S.A. le Bey", in L'Action Tunsienne, (18 April 1933).

[95] "La Voix du peuple s'est fait entendre", in L'Action Tunsienne (19 April 1933); see Histoire, I, 317. Also see Bourguiba, Ḥayâtî, 69-70 and Dimassi, Habib, 163.

[96] "Un Congrès historique: Regroupement des forces tunisiennes", in L'Action Tunsienne (15 May 1933); see Histoire, I, 357-8.

[97] Mahjoubi, Origines, 502-3, quoting La Voix du Peuple (20 May 1933) and Dimassi, Habib, 263.

[98] Bourguiba, Ḥayâtî, 74-5. The text of Habib Bourguiba's letter of resignation, addressed to Ahmed Essafi, Secretary General of the Executive Commission of the Destour Party, is published in Histoire, II, 20-22.

[99] Mahjoubi, Origines, 514 and 522; Bourguiba, Ḥayâtî, 77-8. Other opinions hold that Peyrouton had first presented a liberal attitude with promises of reform; see Jacques Berque, Le Maghreb entre les deux guerres, (Paris: Seuil, 1962), 262.

[100] Mahjoubi views the Néo-Destour option of tactics as heir to the C.G.T.T. of M'Hamed Ali during the 1920s; see Origines, 515. He also considers them to be based on the lessons learned from the Communist and Fascist parties in the Europe of the late 1920s; ibid., 518 n.31. Also see Noureddine Sraieb, "Note sur les dirigeants politiques et syndicalistes tunisiens de 1905 à 1934", in Revue de l'Occident musulman et de la Méditerranée 9 (1971), 91-118.

[101] See Mahjoubi, Origines, 258-261 and 529, and L.C. Brown, "Tunisia under", 81-2. Also seeJulien L'Afrique, 80. According to Mahjoubi, Origines, 518 n.31, the tactics and mode of actions of the dissident group were based on the lessons learned from the Communist and the Fascist parties in Europe.

[102] Hermassi, Leadership, 93-97.

[103] Mahjoubi, Origines, 519.

[104] L.C. Brown, Tunisia under, 94.

[105] Bourguiba, "Le 'Durellisme' ou le Socialisme boiteux", in La Voix du Tunisien (1 February 1929), reproduced in Histoire, I, 12. This explains the decision to use Tunisian Arabic and the lack of hesitation to use religious themes in order to mobilize the masses.

[106] Dimassi, Habib, 233.

[107] Bégué, Message, 51 and 44.

[108] Ferchiou, Techniques, 25, and Boubaker Azaiez, Tels Syndicalistes, tels syndicats ou les Péripéties du Mouvement syndical Tunisien (Tunis: STEAG, 1980), 31.

[109] Bourguiba, Ḥayâtî, 78. All Quranic citations given in English are from The Holy Quran; Text, Translation and Commentary by Abdullah Yusuf Ali (Washington, D.C.: Khalil al-Rawaf, 1946).

[110] Histoire, II, 19, claims that this was the first time in Tunisian history that the base membership, the people, was asked to judge between differences among the leadership.Also Bourguiba, Ḥayâtî, 84. Dimassi, Habib, 309, gives the figure of 12 delegations from Tunis and 36 from the rest of the country, with about 1,000 persons attending.

[111] Bourguiba, Ḥayâtî, 83. Also see Dimassi, Habib, 309-13. A slight difference is to be noted between Bourguiba's version of the Congress, where he occupies center-stage, and that painted by Dimassi, where the main role is played by Tahar Sfar.

[112] Dimassi, Habib, 299.

[113] Histoire, II, 30. The government of the period in France was led by Doumergue, following the riots of 7 February 1934 and included many Néo-Socialiste deputies; see Greene, From, 75-6. The French translation of the Arabic text of Bourguiba's speech as published in Al-Nahḍah (10-15 March 1934) is to be found in Histoire, II, 26-32.

[114] Julien, L'Afrique, 80.

[115] Dimassi, Habib, 315, goes into great detail to show the importance of this gesture in view of the fact that Materi was known to have refused to swear on the Qur'ân at the March 1933 meeting.

CHAPTER 4

[1] Lejri, Evolution, II, 93.

[2] Julien, L'Afrique, 79, holds a different view, stating that the rival parties were "d'origine sociale et de conceptions opposées."

[3] Histoire, VI, 204.

[4] Histoire, II, 203, translated from an article published by the Arabic newspaper, Al-Nahḍah [The Renaissance] (heir to Guellaty's Al-Burhân] based on a letter, dated 8 February 1935, writen by Bourguiba.

[5] Lejri, Evolution, II, 249 n. 502, quoting Bourguiba. Also see ibid., 242-243, on "bourguibism" as tactics rather than ideology.

[6] Julien, L'Afrique, 81.

[7] Histoire, VI, 255, from graffitti found on the prison walls; ibid., VII, 197, from a tract posted 7 July 1938; ibid., 199, from a tract posted 10 August 1938; ibid., 200 and 303, from a pamphlet posted 15 October 1939; ibid., VIII, 251, from a tract dated 21 October 1941; ibid., IX, 124, from Bourguiba's famous speech on Radio Bari on 6 April

1943 -- in order of citation.

[8] Ibid., VI, 259.

[9] Septembre 1934: Répression et Résistance, edited by Moncef Dellagi (Tunis: Maison tunisienne de l'Edition, n.d.), 275, 310, 405, 420-1. Also see G. Zawadowski, "Situation de l'Islam dans la Tunisie d'entre les deux guerres (1918-1939)", En Terre d'Islam (Lyon) XVII/ 22 (1943), 78-100.

[10] Histoire, VII, 348-349, from a Confidential Report prepared by Longobardi, Commandant des Affaires Musulmanes, dated 31 January 1940.

[11] Julien, L'Afrique, 154. But see Mohamed Maamouri, "The Linguistic Situation in Independent Tunisia", The American Journal of Arabic Studies I (1973), 53. The use of "variant" rather than "dialect" is due to the influence of Jean-Claude Corbeil, "Culture et Société: Questions linguistiques et identité culturelle; de la francisation à l'arabisation", propos recueillis par Clément Trudel, Le Devoir (Montreal) 8 May 1982, 27. Also see his "Eléments d'une théorie de la régulation linguistique" (Unpublished paper, April 1981). Although there are no documentary or other records of these early speeches, there are enough reports to enable us to describe the style of Bourguiba; see in particular, Dimassi, Habib, 323.

[12] Paris: Bibliothèque des langues orientales vivantes. Also see the Preface by George Marçais of William Marçais' Articles et Conférences (Paris: Adrien-Maisonneuve, 1961).

[13] Bourguiba, Ma Vie, 119-120. There is some inconsistency with the Arabic version, Ḥayâtî, 83-84, where the sentence "et je retournais à ma faveur les situations les plus conpromises" is missing.

[14] Habib Thameur who was later accused of holding a pro-Axis position, addressed Bourguiba as "leader". See Dimassi, Habib, 513 and Lejri, Evolution, II, 133.

[15] In a letter addressed to Chedly Khairallah and dated 23 January 1935, Bourguiba himself used the French phrase "le bon combat"; see Lejri, Evolution, II, 117 n. 223.

[16] Histoire, IV, 255; ibid., VI, 260, from the Report prepared by Jacques-Henry, dated January-April 1938 and ibid., VII, 271, from a Police Report dated 30 July 1939.

[17] Dimassi, Habib, 375 and 376-378. Also see Histoire, II, 262 for the Declaration made by Guillon on his arrival in Tunis, published in La Dépêche Tunisienne, 23 April 1936.

[18] Septembre, 8, preface by Moncef Dellagi.

[19] Histoire, II, 220-221; Bourguiba, Ḥayâtî, 89-90.

[20] Histoire, IV, 188, from Bourguiba's article "Mise au Point" published in L'Action Tunisienne, 8 January 1938 and ibid., II, 255, from "Nouvelle manifestation à Tunis", published in La Dépêche Tunisienne on 24 February 1936.

[21] Dimassi, Habib, 379; Lejri, Evolution, II, 45.

[22] Histoire, III, 81, from the article "31 mai 1933-16 décembre 1936" by Habib Bourguiba in L'Action Tunisienne, 16 December 1936. Ibid., 88-89, from a letter by Habib Bourguiba to Hédi Nouira, dated 17 October 1936. Also see Dimassi, Habib, 412.

[23] See Histoire, V, 90-91, from Nouira's letter to Bourguiba, 7 December 1936.

[24] See Dimassi, Habib, 385, quoting from a letter written on 1 June 1936. Also see the version published in Histoire, III, 29.

[25] See Julien, L'Afrique, 85. Also see Jean Nouschi, "La Politique coloniale du Front Populaire: le Maghreb", Les Cahiers de Tunisie XXVII/109-110 (1979), 143-160.

[26] See Mathilde Bourguiba's many letters to Madame Challaye where she often refers to their common friend, Eve Noelle, the sister of Duran-Angliviel and the founder of the socialist club, "L'Essor"; Histoire, II, 165 n. 1. Félicien Challaye wrote the preface to Bourguiba's position paper, Le Destour et la France, published in 1937.

[27] Histoire, III, 51, from the article "Déclaration de Bourguiba" published in the newspaper Libération in July 1936.

[28] Ibid., 14, 56 and 77,from the article "Le Destour et la France" by Habib Bourguiba, published in L'Action Tunisienne, 23 December 1936; Dimassi, Habib, 391.

[29] Histoire, V, 81, from Nouira's letter to Bourguiba dated 25 November 1936 and ibid., III, 205, from Bourguiba's article, "De Paul Lambert à Duran-Angliviel", published in L'Action Tunisienne, 27 February 1937.

[30] Ibid., 71, from "Interview avec M. Viénot", published in Annales Coloniales, November 1936 and cited by Dimassi, Habib, 404.

[31] Histoire, IV, 125, quoting from an article published in L'Action Tunisienne, 23 May 1937. Also see Dimassi, Habib, 422ff and Lejri, Evolution, II, 185-186 n.367.

[32] Histoire, IV, 82.

[33] Ibid., 103 and ibid., 78, from "La 'Parole Décisive' du Cheikh Thaâlbi sur le différend entre les Néo-destouriens et les 'Archéos'", published in Arabic in Al-Irâdah, 3 October 1937.

[34] Histoire, III, 102, from Habib Bourguiba's letter to Hédi Nouira, dated 22 November 1936. Ibid., 366, from Bourguiba's article "La C.G.T.T. et Nous", published in L'Action Tunisienne, 19 November 1937. Also see Dimassi, Habib, 429.

[35] Julien, L'Afrique, 89-90.

[36] Ibid., IV, 150, from Bourguiba's article, "Pour dissiper une équivoque", published in L'Action Tunisienne, 19 November 1937. Also see Dimassi, Habib, 429.

[37] Histoire, IV, 269-278, from Duran-Angliviel's article, "Sa collusion avec Mussolini" published in Tunis-Socialiste, 1 April 1938; "Démenti" in L'Action Tunisienne, 2 April 1938; "Duran-Angliviel maintient ses accusations contre les 'crapulards' du Néo-Destour", Tunis-Socialiste, 4 April 1938; and "Double Trahison" in L'Avenir Social, 9 April 1938.

[38] Ibid., IV, 279, from "En marge des évènements" in L'Avenir Social, 9 April 1938. Also see Dimassi, Habib, 436-440.

[39] See Histoire, V, 59. The ensuing results are estimated at nine million francs in material losses, 109 Tunisians and 5 Frenchmen wounded according to Dimassi, Habib, 446-447; or 122 dead and 62 wounded according to Mohammed Sayah in his preface to Histoire, V, 9; or 22 dead and 150 wounded, according to Julien, L'Afrique, 90.

[40] Dimassi, Habib, 451-473.

[41] Ibid., 477 and 474.

[42] Actually, the Jerba link is fascinating but there is not enough documentation to give more than just the broad outlines of the phenomenon. Because Tunisia lacks the type of refuge that mountains give, practically the only place of rufuge for dissidents, historically, has been the island of Jerba. It has served as the refuge of the Khârijî and of the Jewish minorities. Although the Khârijî religious difference is not emphasized, the Jerbians still keep to themselves and have, thus, established a monopoly of the grocery-store business throughout Tunisia, spreading through North Africa and even in France. It is quite possible that Salah Ben Youssef, himself from Jerba, was able to plug into this network for the financial backing crucial during this period of repression. Bourguiba himself

attests to the fact that a system had been worked out whereby the families of the imprisoned Party members (in the order of thousands) were provided for by agreement with these corner grocers; see Dimassi, Habib, 516.

[43] Ibid., 482-489. Also see Histoire, VII, 31 and ibid., VI, 37. According to Histoire, VIII, 137, from a Police Report dated 26 September 1939, Thameur's action was based on the Zaytûnah students.

[44] The ambiguity lay in a certain incriminating letter written by one Anfuso and addressed to Bourguiba, whose authenticity was considered doubtful and which has anyway disappeared from his file; see Histoire, VII, 47 preface by Mohamed Sayah, and Dimassi, Habib, 498. The Germans did free Bourguiba and the remaining prisoners. The seven Néo-Destour leaders including Bourguiba spent almost a year in Rome and were invited to negotiate in view of "liberating Tunisia from French domination". The Axis powers did return them to Tunisia at a critical moment of the War, in early 1943, when the Allies were making their North African push. Finally, there is the letter Bourguiba wrote to the Grand Mufti of Jerusalem, Shaykh Ḥusaynî, which seems to have been the subject of differing interpretations; see Dimassi, Habib, 512. But see Histoire, IX, 108-9, for Bourguiba's letter to Alberto Mellini, Italian Minister of Foreign Affairs dated 19 January 1943, where he rejects any negotiations except through the Bey.

[45] Bourguiba, Ḥayâtî, 53. Also see Histoire, 94-95 from Bourguiba's letter to Habib Thameur, dated 8 August 1942.

[46] Ibid., 101, from Casemajor's book, L'Action Nationaliste en Tunisie, du Pacte fondamentale de M'Hamed Bey à la mort de Moncef Bey, 1857-1948, published in very limited numbers (200) for circulation among French government functionaries. The version offered by the Histoire series differs somewhat in also giving credit for "neutralizing" Axis sympathy to other Néo-Destour leaders such as Ben Yahmed and Mahmoud Messadi; Histoire, VII, 57-58, preface by Mohamed Sayah.

[47] Touchard, Gauche, 246-247 and 255.

[48] Histoire, VII, 60; Dimassi, Habib, 510; Julien, L'Afrique, 96-97 and Histoire, VII, 56, preface by Mohamed Sayah.

[49] Ibid., 64.

[50] Ibid., X, 35-37.

[51] Dimassi, Habib, 524.

[52] Julien, l'Afrique, 98-99; LeTourneau, L'Afrique, 105; Histoire, IX, 137-139.

[53] Julien, L'Afrique, 175.

[54] Histoire, X, 16-9.

[55] Ibid., 157-8 and Julien, L'Afrique, 179. Surprisingly, the Histoire collection does not include the full text of this manifesto but only an extract to indicate that Habib Bourguiba attended two of the preparatory meetings. The Jewish member was Me Albert Bessis. The documentation available shows that Jewish Tunisians began to participate in the nationalist movement to some degree following the War; for example, we note several members of the Jewish community in the welcoming party which met Bourguiba on his return from Egypt in 1949; see Histoire, X, 545.

[56] Ibid., 463 and Kassab, Histoire, 454.

[57] Sebag, Tunisie, 220, characterizes this congress as an attempt at rapprochement between the two Destours but the religious symbolism inherent in "laylat al-qadr" lends greater credence to Ibn ʿAshûr's view; see his Ḥarakah, 201, 205-6. Also see Histoire, XI, 23 and 313 from Henri de Montéty's article, "La Tunisie à la croisée des chemins" published in Le Monde on 15-18 July 1950.

[58] Dimassi, Habib, 589-599; LeTourneau, L'Afrique, 115. A good short description of the rise of the U.G.T.T. and of its relations with the C.G.T. and the F.S.M. is found in Sebag, Tunisie, 221-227.

[59] According to Wilfrid Knapp, North-West Africa: A Political and Economic Survey, 3rd edition (Oxford: Oxford University Press, 1977), 361, the link with the United States was forged mainly through the connections between the U.G.T.T. and the A.F.L., later the A.F.L.-C.I.O. Also see Julien, L'Afrique, 180.

[60] Histoire, XI, 7.

[61] Julien, L'Afrique, 178-179.

[62] Dimassi, Habib, 566. For an account of this harrowing trip, see Bourguiba, Ḥayâtî, 65; Tunisia, Habib, 70; Histoire, X, 201-234; Dimassi, Habib, 535-569.

[63] Ibid., 567, 569-575 and Histoire, X, 48

[64] Histoire, X, 46-47.

[65] Dimassi, Habib, 576-7. Also see Histoire, X, 52-4.

[66] Ibid., 57-61 and Dimassi, Habib, 578-85. For the text of the memorandum on Palestine, see Histoire, X, 257-264.

[67] See photograph in Kassab, Histoire, 458. Also see Dimassi, Habib, 576, 583, 590.

[68] These letters are supposed to have been published in the newspaper Al-Ḥurriyyah; see Dimassi, Habib, 586-587.

[69] Histoire, X, 331 and 75; Dimassi, Habib, 592; Touchard, Gauche, 274.

[70] Histoire, X, 344-346. Stuart E. Brown, "Tunisia and the Arab League (1956-1966)", (Unpublished M.A. thesis, Institute of Islamic Studies, McGill University, Montreal, Quebec, 1969), 2-10.

[71] Histoire, XI, 315-316.

[72] Ursel Clausen, Tunisie: Notes Biographiques (Hamburg: Deutsches Orient-Institut, 1976), 310.

[73] Dimassi, Habib, 604-605.

[74] Ibid., 600; Histoire, X, 511.

[75] Ibid., 548 from the article, "Réunion extraordinaire du conseil national du Néo-Destour" in Mission, 4 August 1949.

[76] Ibid., XI, 109. Also see Dimassi, Habib, 607 and Bourguiba, Ḥayâtî, 124.

[77] Kassab, Histoire, 458.

[78] Dimassi, Habib, 613.

[79] Ibid., 619 and Histoire, XI, 264-265.

[80] Ibid., 268. We have here a typical example of Bourguiba's ability to cover himself before history. During the National Council meeting of the Party on 4 August 1950, he went to the extent of supporting the Néo-Destour participation in the Chenik government while in a letter "to a friend" dated 9 August 1950 he considered the concessions made to the Chenik government as "disappointing" (ibid., 337 and 345).

[81] Dimassi, Habib, 627. Also see Histoire, XI, 365-403.

[82] Ibid., 448 and Dimassi, Habib, 630. Also see Histoire, XI, 448.

[83] Ibid., 638.

[84] Ibid., 643; Histoire, XIII, 22.

[85] Ibid., 119 and Dimassi, Habib, 667; also see Histoire, XIII, 119.

[86] Dimassi, Histoire, 359.

[87] Ibid., 691. Also see Histoire, XIII, 13, 402, 459.

[88] Julien, L'Afrique, 228.
[89] Histoire, XIV, 317.
[90] Dimassi, Habib, 741.
[91] Histoire, XIV, 364, 381 and 453.
[92] Ibid., 465 and 547-548.
[93] Lejri, Evolution, II, 246, quoting Bourguiba.
[94] Histoire, XIV; Dimassi, Habib, 753.

CHAPTER 5

[1] For a good discussion of the consensual basis of legitimacy and of the Weberian theory, see J.G. Merquior, Rousseau and Weber, Two Studies on the Theory of Legitimacy (London: Routledge and Kegan Paul, 1980).
[2] The use of "historical" rather than "traditional" may be justified for cultures possessing written literatures; see the works of Jurgen Habermas, particularly the following: Communication and the Evolution of Society, translated by Thomas McCarthy (Boston: Beacon Press, 1979); Knowledge and Human Interests, translated by Jeremy J. Shapiro (Boston: Beacon Press,1971); Legitimation Crisis, translated by Thomas McCarthy (Boston: Beacon Press, 1975); and Theory and Practice, translated by John Viertel (Boston: Beacon Press, 1973).
[3] Bourguiba, Ḥayâtî, 66; Dimassi, Habib, 243.
[4] "Le Voile" in L'Etendard Tunisien (11 January 1929); see Histoire, I, 1-6.
[5] "'Le Durellisme' ou le Socialisme boiteux" in L'Etendard Tunisien (19 January 1929); see Histoire, I, 13.
[6] Ibid., 14.
[7] Ibid., 15.
[8] Mahjoubi, Origines, 530, quoting from "Note de la Direction de la Sûreté à la Direction de l'Intérieur, Tunis, 29 July 1931, Archives du Gouvernement Tunisien, Carton 12 bis.
[9] Bourguiba, "Voile", Histoire, I, 5.
[10] Michel Barlow, Le Socialisme d'Emmanuel Mounier (Paris: Privat, 1971), 72 n.3.
[11] "Personnalité", in La Grande Encyclopédie (Paris: Larousse, 1886-1902), 487.
[12] Dictionnaire Encyclopédique Quillet (Paris: Librairie Aristide Quillet, 1970), 5123. The Vocabulaire Juridique, sous la direction de Henri Capitant (Paris: Presses universitaires de France, 1936), 374, gives the following definition:

"Personnalité (Lat. personalitas de persona v. personne): Aptitude à être sujet de droit". Other legal reference works do not differ much from this definition; e.g. the Lexique des termes juridiques sous la direction de Raymond Guillien et Jean Vincent (Paris: Dalloz, 1978), 288, gives "Personnalité juridique: Dr.civ. Qualité d'une personne juridique" and "Personne juridique: Dr. civ. Etre titulaire de droits et d'obligations et qui de ce fait a un rôle dans l'activité juridique".

[13] Dictionnaire, 5123.

[14] Thus, the 1886-1902 edition of La Grande Encyclopédie devoted a large percentage of space allotted the entry "personnalité" to the juridical facet of the term but the 1975 edition separates the juridical from the psychological facet by considering the first under the separate entry of "personne morale" while "personnalité" is then considered only in its psychological facet. This psychological facet has been particularly developed in the United States so that there exists at least one journal devoted to the subject, The Journal of Personality, published by the Psychology Department of Duke University.

[15] See, for example, Hichem Djait, La Personnalité et le Devenir Arabo-Islamique (Paris: Seuil, 1974); Béchir Ben Slama, Al-Shakhṣiyyah al-tûnisiyyah: Khaṣâʾiṣuhâ wa-muqawwimâtuhâ [The Tunisian Personality: Its Characteristics and its Constituents] (Tunis: ʿAbd al-Karîm Ibn ʿAbd Allâh, 1974); and Identité Culturelle et Conscience Nationale en Tunisie: Actes du Colloque de Tunis, 1974 (Tunis: Centre d'Etudes et de Recherches Economiques et Sociales, 1979). Also see the collection of papers delivered at the first colloquium of Egyptian and Tunisian professors in Tunis, Al-Dhâtiyyah al-ʿarabiyyah bayn al-waḥdah wa-al-tanawwuʿ [The Arab Self between Unity and Multiplicity] (Tunis: Centre d'Etudes et de Recherches Economiques et Sociales, 1979); Al-Sayyid Yâsîn, Al-Shakhṣiyyah al-ʿarabiyyah bayn al-mafhûm al-isrâʾîlî wa-al-mafhûm al-ʿarabî [The Arab Personality between the Israeli Concept and the Arab Concept] (Cairo: Center for Political and Strategic Studies, 1974); and Mirît B. Ghâlî, "Mawqiʿ al-shakhṣiyyah al-miṣriyyah min al-qawmiyyah al-ʿarabiyyah" (The Position of the Egyptian Personality with reference to Arab Nationalism), Al-Siyâsah al-dawliyyah, [International Politics] 36 (April 1974), 6-25.

[16] On the importance of a common education as the means for creating a common socialization process among the élite, see Jose Murilo de Carvalho, "Political Elites and State Building: The Case of Nineteenth Century Brazil", Comparative Studies in Society and History 24/2 (July 1982), 378-99.

[17] Pierre Kayser, "Les Droits de la Personnalité: Aspects théoriques et pratiques", in Revue Trimestrielle de Droit civil (1971), 446.

[18] Barthélémy Goudy, De la Personnalité juridique (Paris: Librairie de la Société du recueil général des lois et des arrêts et du journal du palais, 1896), 7 and also 25-7.

[19] René Clemens, Personnalité morale et personnalité juridique (Paris: Librairie du Recueil Sirey, 1935), 36-7; also see Goudy, Personnalité, 46, 93, 103.

[20] Nouveau Répertoire de Droit, 2ème édition sous la direction de Emmanuel Vergé et Roger de Ségogne (Paris: Jurisprudence Générale Dalloz, 1964), 614 paragraph 1.

[21] On ḥabûs, see the article "waḳf" by Heffening in E.I.[1]

[22] Goudy, Personnalité, 18-9, states that Heise was the first to hold that a purpose was necessary to the "personnalité" and that Savigny held this superior purpose to bestow juridical capacity. Brinz asserted that juridical capacity may thus be attached to other than human individuals; e.g. to property itself. French legal thinking, on the whole, rejected this position; see ibid., 133. Also see S. Pufendorf, Le droit de la nature et des gens ou Système général des principes les plus importants de la morale, de la jurisprudence et de la politique (1672), translated from German into French by Barbeyrac (Basle, 1771); A. Heise, Grundriss eines Systems des gemeinen Civilrechts zum Behilf von Pandekten, Vorlesungen (1807); A. Brinz, Lehrbuch der Pandekten (Erlangen, 1860); E.J. Bekker, "Zur Lehre vom Rechtssubjekt", in Jahrbucher fur die Dogmatik (1873); R. Savigny, Système du Droit Romain, translated from German by Meulenacre, 2nd ed. (Paris, 1888); M. Bluntschli, Le Droit international codifié, translated from German by M. de Riedmaten (Paris, 1881).

[23] J.L. Talmon, Romanticism and Revolt: Europe, 1815-1848 (New York: Harcourt, Brace and World, 1967), 125. Also see Clemens, Personnalité, xi and 60.

[24] Bernard Gilson, L'Individualité dans la Philosophie de Bergson (Paris: J. Vrin, 1978), 65ff.
[25] Fr. Laurent, Principes de droit civil (Bruxelles, 1876); Gabriel Marquis de Vareilles-Sommières, Les Personnes morales (Paris: Librairie générale de droit et de jurisprudence, 1919); R. Saleilles, De la Personnalité juridique, Histoire et Théories, 2ème édition (Paris: Rousseau, 1922) and L. Michoud, La Théorie de la Personnalité morale et son application au droit français, 2ème édition (Paris: Pichon, 1924).
[26] Clemens, Personnalité, 73.
[27] Nouveau, 614 paragraph 2.
[28] Clemens, Personnalité, 153. Also see Maurice Hauriou, "De la Personnalité comme élément de la réalité sociale", in Revue générale du Droit, de la Législation et de Jurisprudence (1898) and Georges Renard, La Théorie de l'Institution (Paris: Sirey, 1930).
[29] Clemens, Personnalité, 152.
[30] Nouveau, 614 paragraph 12.
[31] Vocabulaire, 374.
[32] Nouveau, 614 paragraph 2. Also see F. Lemeunier, Dictionnaire juridique, économique et financier (Paris: Delmas, 1969), 256.
[33] On the legal considerations of the status of Protectorate, see Alfred M. Kamanda, A Study of the Legal status of Protectorates in Public International Law (Ambilly-Annemasse: Presses de Savoie, 1961).
[34] See Hubert Deschamps, Roi de la Brousse: Mémoires d'autres Mondes (Paris: Berger-Levrault, 1975), for a left-of-center justification of the policies of assimilation, based on the rejection of racism and on the belief that backward people yet had the possibility of achieving equality with Europeans as long as they relinquished their backward cultures and assimilated themselves to European culture.
[35] Kamanda, Study, 195 and 307 respectively.
[36] But see Mohamed A. Lahbabi, Le Personnalisme Musulman, 2nd ed. (Paris: Presses universitaires de France, 1967).
[37] Abdelwahab Bouhdiba, "Dawr al-muʾmin fî daʿm ḫuqûq al-insân" (The Role of the Believer in upholding Human Rights), opening speech at "Al-Multaqâ al-islâmî al-masîḫî al-thâlith: Al-Islâm wa-al-Masîhiyyah wa-ḫuqûq al-insân" (The Third Muslim-Christian Meeting: Islam, Christianity and Human Rights), Amilcar-Carthage, 24 May 1982. For the Prophetic traditions, see Muslim, Chapter

"Al-Imân" (Faith), 78 and Al-Bukhârî, "Al-Ẓâlim" (The Tyrant), 5, respectively, as quoted by ibid. The English version is my translation.

[38] Bourguiba, Khuṭab, XIV, 271.

[39] Moncef Chenoufi, "Maṣâdir ʿan riḥlatây al-ustâdh al-imâm al-shaykh Muḥammad ʿAbduh ilâ tûnis" (The Sources for the two Trips to Tunisia undertaken by Muḥammad ʿAbduh), Ḥawliyyât al-jâmiʿah al-tûnisiyyah [University of Tunis Annual Papers] 4 (1966). To my mind, Bourguiba comes closest to the Egyptian nationalist Muṣṭafâ Kâmil but the analogy can only be made for the young Bourguiba since Kâmil died when he was 34 years old (1874-1908).

[40] Clemens, Personnalité, 137, quoting Hauriou. Also see ibid., 130.

[41] Bluntschli, Droit, 61.

[42] Bourguiba, "L'Evolution d'un Protectorat", Histoire, I, 24-5.

[43] Henri Bergson, "La Personnalité: Conférence prononcée à l'Athénée de Madrid le 6 mai et prise en sténographie par l'hebdomadaire 'Espana', traduite en espagnol par M.G. Morente et retraduite en français par M. Gauthier in Les Etudes Bergsonniennes, Volume IX (Paris: Presses universitaires de France, 1970),80-1. Also see André Decocq, Essai d'une Théorie générale des droits sur la Personne (Paris: Librairie générale de droit et de jurisprudence,1960), 5.

[44] See, for example, P. Janet, L'Evolution psychologique de la Personnalité (Paris: Collège de France, 1929), where the author attempts to construct a psychology of the human being as subject. A good survey of theories of personality in the field of psychology, particularly as they were developed in the United States may be found in Yâsîn, Shakhṣiyyah, 37-75.

[45] "Personnalité", Grande, (1886-1902), 488.

[46] Knapp, North-West, 394.

[47] Grande (1886-1902), 488.

[48] Gilson, L'Individualité, 66.

[49] Grande (1975), 9302.

[50] Ibid., 9303.

[51] Ibid. Also see Mikel Dufrenne, La Personnalité de Base: Un Concept Sociologique (Paris: Presses universitaires de France, 1953), 277.

[52] Grande (1975),9303.

[53] See Note 15 above.

[54] C. Wright Mills and Hans Gerth, Character and Social Structure: The Psychology of Social Institutions (New York: Harcourt, Brace and Company, 1953), 294 and 430; also see pages 195 and 286-287.

[55] See, among other speeches, Bourguiba, "Madkhal ilâ târîkh al-ḥarakah al-qawmiyyah" (Introduction to the History of the Nationalist Movement), Khuṭab, XIV (1962), 233-71, and "ʿIbrat thalâthîn sanah min al-kifâḥ" (Lesson from Thirty Years of Struggle), ibid., XVII (1964), 87-123.

[56] Howard C. Reese, Area Handbook for the Republic of Tunisia (Washington, D.C.: United States Government, 1970), 237. On mass parties and charisma in the Arab world, see Enver M. Koury, The Patterns of Mass Movements in Arab Revolutionary Progressive States (The Hague: Mouton, 1970).

[57] Gilson, L'Individualité, 74. For Mills, Character, 106, "person" is more than just an individual as it refers to the "variations of roles which compose the person and the person's way of reacting to these roles".

[58] Cf. Histoire, XV, 9, where Mohamed Sayah states that dissension set in after rather than before the signing of the accords and explains the phenomenon by referring to the shallowness of public opinion in underdeveloped countries where the masses are easily swayed one way or the other.

[59] Histoire, XV, 13 and 33.

[60] Ibid., XV, 28.

[61] Ezzeddine Guellouz, during the conference held by the Ministère de l'Education Supérieure et de la Recherche Scientifique, "Les Réactions à l'occupation française de la Tunisie en 1881", Sidi Bou Said, 30 May 1981.

[62] Histoire, XV, 81-2, from the article "Retour de Salah Ben Youssef à Tunis", published in Le Petit Matin, 14 September 1955.

[63] Ibid., 38 and 166.

[64] Although his Friday noon "sermon" lasted until the prayers of the maghrib, the Histoire collection has only a one-page account of this historic challenge.

[65] There seems to be some confusion on the actual chain of events during the following few days. Histoire, XV, 39-40, states that Bourguiba was at Kalaa Seghira on 7 October and that he returned to Tunisia the following day for the Bureau Politique meeting at which Ben Youssef was excluded. According to Khuṭab, I and to Index, 9, Bourguiba was in Kalaa Kbira on 7 October and in Kalaa Seghira on 9 October 1955. According to Index, 9, on 13

October he was in Monastir where he made a declaration following the exclusion of Salah Ben Youssef from the Party. Also see Histoire, XV, 40-41.

[66] Ibid., 150-155; Dwight L. Ling, Tunisia: From Protectorate to Republic (Bloomington: Indiana University Press, 1967), 177; Knapp, North-West, 364.

[67] Lacouture, "Options", 166. Between 17 and 25 September 1955, Bourguiba made at least five speeches in Sfax; see Khuţab, I, 59-81.

[68] See Histoire, XV, 382 and 12.

[69] Ibid., 135 from the article, "Le conflit Bourguiba-Ben Youssef" published in Tunis-Socialiste, 14 October 1955.

[70] Khuţab, I, 65. Interestingly enough, Mendès-France himself was of Jewish background.

[71] See Khuţab, I, 8-58, for some fifteen speeches Bourguiba made during this period.

[72] Mohamed Sayah accuses Ben Youssef of a demagogic "amalgame voulu du religieux et du politique", see Histoire, XV, 143 and 140-146.

[73] See Histoire, XV, 156, where Mohamed Sayah, in his eagernes to prepare for a justification of the reversal of the socialist experience of the 1960s which has been largely identified with Ben Salah, tries to demonstrate that the U.G.T.T., instead of helping Bourguiba, created trouble; see ibid., 155-159 and 216ff.

[74] Ibid., 165-166 from Bourguiba's speech in commemoration of Hédi Chaker on 22 September 1955; also see Khuţab, I, 80.

[75] Khuţab, I, 128 and 125-126; Histoire, XV, 269.

[76] My underlines. Ibid., XV, 360-1 and 365-366.

[77] Ibid., 297.

[78] Ibid., 388 specifically, but also see 386-390.

[79] Ibid., 389 and 437 n.18.

[80] Ibid., 399.

[81] Ibid., 400-12. Also see Ling, Tunisia, 179. According to Knapp, North-West, 365, the police raid was undertaken with the help of French security forces.

[82] Histoire, XV, 477-8, 483-5 and 503.

[83] Lacouture, "Options", 167.

[84] Histoire, XV, 651.

[85] Ibid., 659, from an editorial published in Le Monde. Though Tunisia became independent de jure, certain aspects of the treaty signed with France still limited its independence. The two main points were economic as Tunisia remained within the franc zone, and military, as France retained the right to maintain military bases on Tunisian soil.

[86] Ling, Tunisia, 180, based on the account given in The New York Times, 15 August 1961 which indirectly accuses Bourguiba. If it was indeed a "death penalty", the assassination of Ben Youssef is out of character with Bourguiba's usual behavior towards political opponents as he stands out among political leaders in the Arab world for his ability to remove rivals from power and to reconcile them again. But see Bourguiba, Ḥayâtî, 115, where he accepts responsibility.

[87] Histoire, XV, 634-9 and 643-7.

[88] Ibid., 666.

[89] Ling, Tunisia, 188.

[90] Knapp, North-West, 361. LeTourneau, L'Afrique, 141 and Debbasch, République, 48-52 and, particularly, Zghal, "Retour".

[91] Knapp, North-West, 361. Also see Debbasch, République, 5; LeTourneau, L'Afrique, 148 and Histoire, XV, 676 and 679.

[92] Lacouture, "Options", 174-5 and Ling, Tunisia, 157 and 193, quoting from The New York Times, 17 December 1956.

[93] Lacouture, "Options", 180.

[94] Ling, Tunisia, 201.

[95] Ibid. Interestingly enough, it was also during this period that a flurry of books on Tunisia was published in the United States. Most of these books were based on the prevalent theory of modernization whose basic premises were that "development" could be accomplished through planning and that a strong, unified, central government was necessary in order to carry out the Plan. Among this flurry of books are the following: Charles A. Micaud with L. Carl Brown and Clement H. Moore, Tunisia: The Politics of Modernization (New York: Frederick A. Praeger, 1964); Clement H. Moore, Tunisia since Independence: The Dynamics of One-Party Government (Berkeley: University of California Press, 1965); Douglas E. Ashford, Morocco-Tunisia: Politics and Planning (Syracuse: Syracuse University Press, 1965) and National Development and Local Reform: Political Participation in Morocco, Tunisia and Pakistan (Princeton: Princeton University Press, 1967); and

Dwight L. Ling, Tunisia: From Protectorate to Republic (Bloomington: Indiana University Press, 1967). Though published in Great Britain, the book by Lars Rudebeck, Party and People: A Study of Political Change in Tunisia 2nd edition (London: C. Hurst, 1967, 1969) follows in the same tradition. Following the retrenchment in United States foreign policy and the reversal of the Ben Salah experiment in 1969, there was an abrupt fall-off of books published in the United States on Tunisia. Perhaps the book by James Allman, Social Mobility, Education and Development in Tunisia (Leiden: Brill, 1979) signals a renewed interest in North Africa in general and in Tunisia in particular.

[96] Norma Salem,"Islam and the Status of Women in Tunisia",in Muslim Women, edited by Freda Hussain (London: Croom Helm, forthcoming).

[97] Abdel-Moula, Université, 54.

[98] Knapp, North-West, 365.

[99] Yadh Ben Achour, "Islam perdu, Islam retrouvé", Annuaire de l'Afrique du Nord (1979), 68-69.

[100] Debbasch, République, 39.

[101] See the above definition of "personnalité" in the field of psychology.

[102] Knapp, North-West, 368 and Debbasch, République, 39.

[103] Debbasch, République, 68.

[104] Michel Camau, "Religion politique et Religion d'état en Tunisie", in Vatin and Gellner, Islam, 229.

[105] Souhayr Belhassen, "Femmes tunisiennes islamistes", Annuaire de l'Afrique du Nord (1979), 77 and "L'Islam contestataire en Tunisie", Jeune Afrique No. 949 (14 March 1979). Also see Ben Achour, "Islam", 73; Mark A. Tessler, "Political Change and the Islamic Revival in Tunisia", The Maghreb Review I/1 (January - February 1980); Waterbury, "Légitimation", 414 and 421-422; Zghal and Chérif, "Reactivation", and Zghal, "Retour".

CHAPTER 6

[1] The Conclusion is heavily influenced by Joseph R. Levenson, Liang Ch'i-Cha'o and the Mind of China (Berkeley: University of California Press, 1970). Specifically, I owe him the credit for formulating the problem of how to conceive of ideas in history. An early interest in the transmission of political culture and behavior patterns owes

something to the concept of ideological "generations" as postulated by Erik H. Erikson, Life History and the Historical Moment (New York: Norton, 1975) and William B. Quandt, Revolution and Political Leadership: Algeria, 1954-1968 (Cambridge: Massachusetts Institute of Technology, 1969).

[2] What Mills, Character, 153, wrote about memory for an individual may be also applied to history, the collective memory, as "past experience regained by an act of attention".

[3] See Chapter V, Note 48.

[4] David C. Gordon, North Africa's French Legacy, 1954-1962 (Cambridge: Harvard University Press, 1962), 56.

[5] Gunter Lewy, Religion and Revolution (New York: Oxford University Press, 1974), 583-584. Also see Peter L. Berger, The Sacred Canopy (New York: Doubleday, 1967); Donald E. Smith, Religion and Political Development: An Analytic Study (Boston: Little, Brown, 1970) and Religion and Political Modernization (New Haven: Yale University Press, 1974).

[6] Berger, Sacred, 22.

[7] As cited by Lewy, Religion, 542.

[8] Ibid., 556, 566, 572-573, 582.

[9] Mahjoubi, Origines, 625-629. Also see André Nouschi, "La Crise de 1930 en Tunisie et les débuts du Néo-Destour", Revue de l'Occident Musulman et de la Méditerrané (1970), 113-123.

[10] Mustapha Kraiem and Carmel Sammut, "Introduction" to Kraiem, Classe, 7ff. Also see Carmel Sammut, "L'Expression des symboles nationalistes par les premiers nationalistes tunisiens dans le contexte colonial français", Revue d'Histoire du Maghreb, 7-8 (1977), 201-20.

[11] Ibid., 9, citing J.P. Charnay and J. Berque, Normes et Valeurs dans l'Islam contemporain (Paris: Payot, 1966), 7.

[12] Berque, Maghreb, 76 and 78 respectively.

[13] Kraiem, Classe, 29.

[14] Ibid., 31 and also 30.

[15] Robert Musil, The Man Without Qualities; translated from the German by Eitline Wilkins and Ernst Kaiser (London: Secker and Warburg, 1953).

[16] The legal dimension still crops up from time to time. For example, the following statement was found in a discussion about the origins of the modern corporation, "The corporate form was known to exist in the Roman Empire although the notion of its legal personality was not fully developed"; see John D. Daniels, Ernest W. Ogram, Jr. and Lee H.

Radebaugh, International Business: Environments and Operations (3rd edition, Reading: Addison-Wesley Publishing Company, 1982), 15.

[17] Even Khumaynî himself states that the divine will, source of all legitimacy from a purely religious perspective, expresses itself through the will of the people; see his Al-Ḥukûmah al-islâmiyyah [The Islamic Government] (Najaf: n.p., 1969).

[18] See Barakat, "Tunisian".

[19] Ben Slama, Naẓariyyah, 110 but also 7.

[20] Ibid., 112ff, particularly 130. This position recalls the German school of legal thought where each "personnalité" is viewed as an eternal entity and is widespread among many nationalist movements in the Arab world; see, for example, ʿAllâl al-Fâsî, Al-Ḥarakât al-istiqlâliyyah fî al-maghrib al-ʿarabî [The Independence Movements in the Arab Maghrib], 4th ed. (Rabat: Al-Risâlah, 1980),vii.

[21] A la Recherche des Normes perdues (Tunis: Maison tunisienne de l'Edition,1973), 18-9. This position implicitly incorporates the view that each "personnalité" achieves juridical capacity only through continuous action. Also see Ben Slama, Naẓariyyah, 34 and Hermassi, Leadership, 54.

[22] Ben Slama, Naẓariyyah, 39, 41-42.

[23] Ibid., 25.

[24] Ibid., 59.

[25] Ibid.

[26] Ibid., 70.

[27] Ibid., 64-66.

[28] Djait, Personnalité, 52-3.

[29] Ibid., 51.

[30] Ibid., 272-275.

[31] See his "Islam et Politique" in Vatin and Gellner, Islam, 144 and 149.

[32] Ben Slama, Naẓariyyah, 89. Also see Hermassi, Leadership, 72, who noted the inseparability between culture and politics, at least during the colonial period in Tunisia, and his The Third World Reassessed (Berkeley: University of California Press, 1980), 197, where he noted that, following independence, there was a tendency to invoke the Tunisian "personnalité" as a way of detaching the country from the Arab world as a whole. On the official cultural policies of independent Tunisia, see Rafik Said, La Politique culturelle en Tunisie (Paris: U.N.E.S.C.O., 1970); Abdelaziz Kacem, "La Politique culturelle en Tunisie", Annuaire de l'Afrique du Nord (1973), 29-44 and Jean-Claude Vatin, "Questions culturelles

et questions à la culture?", Annuaire de l'Afrique du Nord (1973), 3-16. I believe that the developments of the 1980s represent a search for an equilibrium in Tunisia between the pull of the Arab "East" and that of the French "West". The difficulties inherent in the process of asserting a "Tunisian" identity were demonstrated in a study conducted in 1970. Only 23 percent of the female students and 18.7 percent of the male students held that they belonged to a Tunisian culture. See Tahar L. Djedidi, "Culture et Société", Annuaire de l'Afrique du Nord (1973), 19-27.

[33] Pierre-Robert Baduel, "Gafsa comme Enjeu", Annuaire de l'Afrique du Nord (1980), 485-511.

[34] Zghal, "Retour", 43 and 63.

[35] Camau,"Religion", in Vatin and Gellner, Islam, 228

[36] Abdallah Laroui, Al-ʿArab wa-al-fikr al-târîkhî [The Arabs and Historical Thought], 3rd ed. (Beirut: Dâr al-ḥaqîqah, 1980), 7 and 10.

[37] See Hélé Béji, Désenchantement national: Essai sur la décolonisation (Paris: Maspéro, 1982).

BIBLIOGRAPHY

ʿAbd al-Bâqî, Ibrâhîm. Al-Jinsiyyah fî qawânîn duwal al-maghrib al-ʿarabî al-kabîr; dirâsah muqâranah [Nationality in the Laws of the States of the Great Arab Maghrib: A Comparative Study]. Cairo: Maṭbaʿat al-Jabalâwî,1971

ʿAbd Allâh, al-Ṭâhir. Al-Ḥarakah al-waṭaniyyah al-tûnisiyyah; ruʾyah shaʿbiyyah qawmiyyah jadîdah, 1830-1956. [The Tunisian Patriotic Movement: A New Populist Nationalist Perspective, 1830-1956]. n.p.: n.p., n.d.

ʿAbd al-Raḥmân, Asʿad. Al-Inmâʾ al-siyâsî fî al-tajribatayn al-nâṣiriyyah wa-al-burqîbiyyah [Political Development in the Two Experiences: The Nasirite and the Bourguibite]. Kuwait: MERG Incorporated, 1981

Abdel-Malek, Anouar. "La reconquête de l'identité", Chapter 4 in La Pensée politique arabe contemporaine. Paris: Seuil, 1970

Abdel-Moula, Mahmoud. L'Université Zaytounienne et la Société tunisienne. Tunis: Abdel-Moula, 1971

Abdessalam, Ahmed. Sadiki et les Sadikiens. Tunis: Cérès Productions, 1975

Ajami, Fouad. The Arab Predicament: Arab Political Thought and Practice since 1967. Cambridge: Cambridge University Press, 1981

Allman, James. Social Mobility, Education and Development in Tunisia. Leiden: Brill, 1979

Amin, Samir. L'Accumulation à l'échelle mondiale: Critique de la Théorie du sous-développement. Paris: Anthropos, 1970

---. Sociétés précapitalistes et capitalisme. Paris: Anthropos, 1978

Apter, David. The Politics of Modernization. Chicago: Chicago University Press, 1965

Bibliography

Ashford, Douglas E. Morocco-Tunisia: Politics and Planning. Syracuse: Syracuse University Press, 1965

---. National Development and Local Reform: Political Participation in Morocco, Tunisia and Pakistan. Princeton: Princeton University Press, 1967

Azaiez, Boubaker L. Tels Syndicalistes, tels syndicats ou les Péripéties du Mouvement syndical tunisien. Tunis: STEAG, 1980

Baduel, Pierre-Robert. "Gafsa comme Enjeu", Annuaire de l'Afrique du Nord (1980), 485-511.

Barakat, Halim. "The Tunisian Al-Fikr: Polarities of the East and the West," Paper delivered at the Conference on "North Africa Today: Issues of Development and Integration," Georgetown University, 22-23 April 1982

Barlow, Michel. Le Socialisme d'Emmanuel Mounier. Paris: Privat, 1971

Barnes, Harry E. The New History and the Social Studies. New York: Century, 1926

Basset, Alfred et al. Initiation à la Tunisie. Paris: Adrien-Maisonneuve, 1950

Basso, Keith H. and Henry A. Selby (eds.). Meaning in Anthropology. Albuquerque: University of New Mexico Press, 1976

Bégué, Camille. Le Message de Bourguiba: Une Politique de l'Homme. Paris: Hachette, 1972

Béji, Hélé. Désenchantement national: Essai sur la décolonisation. Paris: Maspéro, 1982

Belhaouane, Ali. Tûnis al-thâʾirah [Revolutionary Tunisia]. Cairo: Lajnat taḥrîr al-maghrib al-ʿarabî, 1954

Belhassen, Souhayr. "Femmes tunisiennes islamistes", Annuaire de l'Afrique du Nord (1979), 77-87

---. "L'Islam contestataire en Tunisie", Jeune Afrique No.949 (14 March 1979)

Ben Achour, Yadh. "Islam perdu, Islam retrouvé", Annuaire de l'Afrique du Nord (1979), 68-69

Ben Slama, Béchir. Al-Naẓariyyah al-târîkhiyyah fî al-kifâḥ al-taḥrîrî al-tûnisî [The Historical Theory in the Tunisian Liberation Struggle]. Part I. Tunis: ʿAbd al-Karîm Ibn ʿAbd Allâh, 1977

---. Al-Shakhṣiyyah al-tûnisiyyah: khaṣâʾiṣuhâ wa-muqawwimâtuhâ [The Tunisian Personality: Its Characteristics and its Constituents]. Tunis: ʿAbd al-Karîm Ibn ʿAbd Allâh, 1974

Berger, Peter L. The Sacred Canopy. New York: Doubleday, 1967
Bergson, Henri. Les Etudes Bergsonniennes. Paris: Presses universitaires de France, 1970
Berque, Jacques. Le Maghreb entre les deux guerres. Edition revue et augmentée. Paris: Seuil, 1962
Berry, Thomas E.(ed.). The Biographer's Craft. New York: Odyssey Press, 1967
Besnier, Maurice et al. La Tunisie au début du XXe siècle. Paris: de Rudeval, 1904
Betts, Raymond F. Assimilation and Association in French Colonial Theory, 1890-1914. New York: Columbia University Press, 1961
Bluntschli, A. Allgemeines Staatsrecht (1851), traduit par M. de Riedmaten, 2e ed. Paris: Guillaumin, 1881
Bouhdiba, Abdelwahab. A la Recherche des Normes perdues. Tunis: Maison tunisienne de l'Edition, 1973
---. "Dawr al-muʾmin fî daʿm ḥuqûq al-insân" [The Role of the Believer in upholding Human Rights]. Conference given at "Al-Multaqâ al-islâmî al-masîḥi al-thâlith: Al-Islâm wa-al-masîḥiyyah wa-ḥuqûq al-insân" [The Third Muslim-Christian Meeting: Islam, Christianity and Human Rights], Amilcar-Carthage, 24 May 1982
---. Raisons d'Etre. Tunis: Centre d'Etudes et de Recherches économiques et sociales, 1980.
Bourguiba, Habib. Citations choisies par l'Agence Tunis-Afrique-Presse. Preface by Chedli Klibi. Tunis: Editions Dar el-amal, 1978
---. Le Destour et la France. Paris: Epernay-Sur-Seine, 1937
---. Ḥadîth al-jumʿah: ʿArḍ likul al-khuṭab wa-al-kalimât al-khâlidah allatî alqâhâ al-raʾîs al-jalîl Habib Bourguiba bayn 8 afrîl 1956 wa 20 mâris 1957 [Friday Speeches: A Presentation of all the Speeches and Eternal Words delivered by His Excellency President Habib Bourguiba between 8 April 1956 and 20 March 1957]. Part I collected and edited by Aḥmad al-Râṭînî. Tunis: Al-ʿAmal, 1957
---. Ḥayâtî, Arâʾî, Jihâdî [My Life, My Opinions, My Struggle]. Tunis: Ministère de l' Information, 1978. Translated into French under the title, Ma Vie, Mes Idées, Mon Combat. Tunis: Ministère de l'Information, 1977
---. Khuṭab [Speeches]. 20 volumes from 1955 to 1965. Tunis: Ministère de l'Information, 1974-1981

---. Khuṭab mawlidiyyah [Speeches made on the occasion of the Prophet's Birthday]. 1957-1968 and 1972-1976. Tunis: Ministère de l'Information, 1979

---. La Tunisie et la France; Vingt-cinq ans de lutte pour une coopération libre. Tunis: Maison tunisienne de l'Edition, c.1954

Bowen, Catherine D. Biography: The Craft and the Calling. Boston: Little and Brown, 1968

Brenner, Paul. "The Origins of Capitalist Development: a Critique of Neo-Smithian Marxism". New Left Review 104 (1977),25-92

Brown, L. Carl. The Tunisia of Aḥmad Bey, 1837-1855. Princeton: Princeton University Press, 1974

---. "The Tunisian Path to Modernization," Paper written in April 1971, Princeton, New Jersey

---. "Tunisia under the Protectorate: A History of Ideological Change." Ph.D. dissertation, Harvard University, Cambridge, Massachusetts, 1962

Brown, Stuart E. "Tunisia and the Arab League (1956-1966)." M.A. thesis, Institute of Islamic Studies, McGill University, Montreal, Quebec, 1969

---. "The Young Tunisians." Ph.D. dissertation, Institute of Islamic Studies, McGill University, Montreal, Quebec, 1976

Cahen, Claude. "L'Evolution de l'Iqṭâʿ du IXe au XIIIe siècle," Annales Economies, Sociétés, Civilisations VIII/1 (janvier-mars 1953)

Camau, Michel."Religion politique et Religion d'état en Tunisie", in Vatin and Gellner, Islam

Cambon, Henri. Histoire de la Régence de Tunis. Paris: Berger-Levrault, 1948

Carvalho, José Murilo de. "Political Elites and State-Building: The Case of Nineteenth-Century Brazil," Comparative Studies in Society and History 24/2 (July 1982),378-99

Casemajor, Roger. L'action nationaliste en Tunisie, du pacte fondamental de M'Hamed Bey à la mort de Moncef Bey (1857-1949). Tunis: n.p., 1949

Cayci, Abdurrahman. La Question tunisienne et la Politique ottomane, 1881-1913. Erzurum: Ataturk Universitesi, 1963

Centre de Recherches et d'Etudes sur les Sociétés méditerranéennes (C.R.E.S.M.). La Formation des Elites politiques maghrébines par Lhachmi Berrady et al. Paris: Librairie générale de droit et de jurisprudence, 1973

Challaye, Félicien. Péguy socialiste. Paris: Amiot-Dumont, 1954

Charnay, J.P. et Jacques Berque (eds.). Normes et Valeurs dans l'Islam contemporain. Paris: Payot, 1966

Chatelain, Yves. La Vie littéraire et intellectuelle en Tunisie de 1900 à 1937. Paris: Geuthner, 1937

Chater, Khalifa. Insurrection et Répression dans la Tunisie du XIXe siècle: La Mehaila de Zarrouk au Sahel (1864). Tunis: Publications de l'Université de Tunis, 1978

Chenoufi, Moncef. "Maṣâdir ʿan riḥlatay al-ustâdh al-imâm al-shaykh Muḥammad ʿAbduh ilâ Tûnis" [Sources for the Two Trips to Tunisia undertaken by Muḥammad ʿAbduh]. Ḥawliyyât al-jâmiʿah al-tûnisiyyah [University of Tunis Annual Papers] 4 (1966)

Chirot, Daniel. Social Change in the 20th Century. New York: Harcourt, Brace, Jovanovich, 1977

Clausen, Ursel. Tunisie: Notes Biographiques. Hamburg: Deutsches Orient-Institut, 1976

Clemens, René. Personnalité morale et personnalité juridique. Paris: Sirey, 1935

Clifford, James L. From Puzzles to Portraits; Problems of a Literary Biographer. Chapel Hill: University of North Carolina Press, 1970

Cockshut, A.O.J. Truth to Life: The Art of Biography in the Nineteenth Century. New York: Harcourt, Brace, Jovanovich, 1974

Cole, G.D.H. A History of Socialist Thought. Volume IV, Part II, Communism and Social Democracy, 1914-1931. London: MacMillan, 1958

Conte, Arthur. La Légende de Bourguiba. Paris: Editions Media, 1978

Corbeil, Jean-Claude. "Culture et Société: Questions linguistiques et identité culturelle; de la francisation à l'arabisation." Propos recueillis par Clément Trudel, Le Devoir, Montreal, 8 mai 1982, 27

---. "Eléments d'une théorie de la régulation linguistique." Unpublished paper, April 1981

Dabbab, Mohammed. Les Délégations destouriennes à Paris ou la "Question tunisienne" dans les années 1920; Revendications, Manoeuvres, Polémiques, Scission. Textes et documents. Tunis: Maison tunisienne de l'Edition, 1980

Davidson, Alastair. Antonio Gramsci: Towards an Intellectual Biography. London: Merlin Press, 1977

Debbasch, Charles. La République Tunisienne. Paris: Librairie générale de droit et de jurisprudence, 1962

Decocq, André. Essai d'une Théorie générale des droits sur la Personne. Paris: Librairie générale de droit et de jurisprudence, 1960

Dellagi, Moncef. "Bibliographie de l'Histoire du Mouvement National Tunisien," Revue d'Histoire Maghrébine 13 (1979),27-50

Demeerseman, André. "Catégories sociales en Tunisie au XIXe siècle d'après la chronique de Ahmad ibn Abi al-Diyaf," Institut des Belles Lettres Arabes XXX/117 (1967),1-12;XXXII/123 (1969),17-36, 124, 241-72; XXXIII/125-41 (1970),69-101

Deschamps, Hubert. Roi de la Brousse, Mémoires d'autres Mondes. Paris: Berger-Levrault, 1975

Al-Dhâtiyyah al-ʿarabiyyah bayn al-waḥdah wa-al-tanawwuʿ [The Arab Self between Unity and Multiplicity]. Tunis: Centre d'Etudes et de Recherches Economiques et Sociales, 1979

Dictionnaire Encyclopédique Quillet. Paris: Librairie Aristide Quillet, 1970

Dimassi, Ali. Habib Bourguiba; l'Apôtre de la Liberté tunisienne. Tunis: Ali Dimassi, 1979

Djait, Hichem. La Personnalité et le Devenir arabo-islamique. Paris: Seuil, 1974

---."Islam et Politique", in Vatin and Gellner, Islam

Djedidi, Tahar L. "Culture et Société en Tunisie", Annuaire de l'Afrique du Nord (1973), 19-27

Dolgin, Janet L. with David S. Kennitzer and David M. Schneider (eds.). Symbolic Anthropology: A Reader in the Study of Symbols and Meanings. New York: Columbia University Press, 1977

Droz, Jacques (ed.). Histoire générale du socialisme. 4 volumes. Paris: Presses universitaires de France, 1972

Dufrenne, Mikel. La Personnalité de Base: un Concept Sociologique. Paris: Presses universitaires de France, 1953

Duguit, Léonard. Traité de droit constitutionnel. 2nd ed. Paris: de Boccard, 1921

Durkheim, Emile. The Elementary Forms of Religious Life (1915). Translated from the French by Joseph W. Swain. London: Allen and Unwin, 1964

Durupty, Michel. Institutions administratives et droit administratif tunisiens. Paris: Centre national de Recherche scientifique, 1973

Duvignaud, Jean. "Classes et Conscience de Classe dans un Pays du Maghreb: la Tunisie," Cahiers Internationaux de Sociologie XXXVIII (1965),185-200

Emmanuel, Arghiri. L'Echange inégal. Paris: Maspéro, 1969

Entelis, John P. Comparative Politics of North Africa: Algeria, Morocco, and Tunisia. Syracuse: Syracuse University Press, 1980

Erikson, Eric H. Life History and the Historical Moment. New York: Norton, 1975

Faruki, Kemal A. The Evolution of Islamic Constitutional Theory and Practice from 610 to 1926. Karachi: National Publishing House, 1971

Al-Fâsî, ʿAllâl. Al-Ḥarakât al-istiqlâliyyah fî al-maghrib al-ʿarabî [The Independence Movements in the Arab Maghrib](1948). 4th edition. Rabat: Al-Risâlah, 1980

Ferchiou, Sophie. Techniques et Sociétés: Exemple de la Fabrication des Chéchias en Tunisie. Paris: Mémoires de l'Institut d'Ethnologie, VII, 1971

Firth, Raymond. Symbols, Public and Private. London: George Allen and Unwin, 1973

Frye, Northrop. Anatomy of Criticism; Four Essays Princeton: Princeton University Press, 1957

Ganiage, Jean. L'Expansion coloniale de la France sous la Troisième République (1871-1914). Paris: Payot, 1962

---. Les Origines du Protectorat Français en Tunisie, 1861-1881. Paris: Presses universitaires de France, 1959

---. "La Population de la Tunisie vers 1860: Essai d'évaluation d'après les registres fiscaux," Etudes Maghrébines: Mélanges Charles-André Julien. Paris: Presses universitaires de France, 1964

Garas, Félix. Bourguiba et la Naissance d'une Nation. Paris: René Julliard, 1956

Ghâlî, Mirît B. "Mawqiʿ al-shakhṣiyyah al-miṣriyyah min al-qawmiyyah al-ʿarabiyyah" [The Position of the Egyptian Personality with reference to Arab Nationalism], Al-Siyâsah al-dawliyyah [International Politics] 36 (April 1974), 6-25

El-Ghoul, Yahya. "Naturalisation française et mouvement national tunisien." Unpublished thesis, University of Tunis, 1973

Gibb, Sir Hamilton. "Islamic Biographical Literature," Historians of the Middle East, edited by Bernard Lewis and P.M. Holt. London: Oxford University Press, 1962

Gilson, Bernard. L'Individualité dans la philosophie de Bergson. Paris: J. Vrin, 1978

Gittings, Robert. The Nature of Biography. Seattle: University of Washington Press, 1978

Goldstein, Daniel. Libération ou Annexion: Aux chemins croisés de l'histoire tunisienne, 1914-1922. Tunis: Maison tunisienne de l'Edition, 1978

Gordon, David C. North Africa's French Legacy, 1954-1962. Cambridge: Harvard University Press, 1962

Goudy, Barthélemy. De la Personnalité juridique. Paris: Librairie de la Société du recueuil général des lois et des arrêts et du journal du palais, 1896

Gran, Peter. The Islamic Roots of Capitalism in Egypt, 1760-1840. Austin: University of Texas Press, 1979

Grandchamp, Pierre. Etudes d'histoire tunisienne, XVIIIe-XXe siècle. Paris: Presses universitaires de France, 1966

Green, Arnold H. The Tunisian 'Ulama, 1873-1915; Social Structure and Response to Ideological Currents. Leiden: Brill, 1978

Greene, Nathanael. From Versailles to Vichy; The Third French Republic, 1919-1940. New York: Thomas Y. Crowell, 1970

Gunder-Frank, André. L'Accumulation dépendante. Paris: Anthropos, 1978

Habermas, Jurgen. Communication and the Evolution of Society (1968), translated by Thomas McCarthy. Boston: Beacon Press, 1979

---. Knowledge and Human Interests, translated by Jeremy J. Shapiro. Boston: Beacon Press, 1971

---. Legitimation Crisis, translated by Thomas McCarthy. Boston: Beacon Press, 1975

---. Theory and Practice, translated by John Viertel. Boston: Beacon Press, 1973

Habib Bourguiba: Index Chronologique des Discours, Interviews, Declarations et Conférences, 1955-1971. Tunis: Ministère de l'Information, n.d.

Al-Ḥaddâd, al-Ṭahir. Imraʾatunâ fî al-sharîʿah wa-al-mujtamaʿ [Our Woman in the Law and in Society] (1930). 2nd edition. Tunis: Al-Dâr al-tûnisiyyah li-al-nashr, 1972

---. Al-ʿUmmâl al-tûnisiyyûn wa-ẓuhûr al-ḥarakah al-niqâbiyyah fî tûnis [The Tunisian Workers and the Beginnings of the Labor Movement in Tunisia] (1927). 3rd edition. Tunis: Al-Dâr al-tûnisiyyah li-al-nashr, 1972

Harber, C.C. "Tunisian land tenure in the early French Protectorate," The Muslim World 63(1973), 307-15

Harris, Marvin. The Rise of Anthropological Theory: A History of Theories of Culture. New York: Thomas Crowell, 1968

Harvey, André. Bergson, maître de Péguy. Paris: Elzévir, 1948

Haupt, Georges et Madeleine Rébérioux (eds.). La Deuxième internationale et l'Orient. Paris: Editions Cujas, 1967

Hauriou, Maurice. "De la personnalité comme élément de la Réalité sociale," Revue générale du droit, de la législation et de Jurisprudence (1898)

Hermassi, Elbaki. Leadership and National Development in North Africa: A Comparative Study Berkeley: University of California Press, 1972 Translated into French under the title, Etat et Société au Maghreb; Etude Comparative. Paris: Anthropos, 1975

---. The Third World Reassessed. Berkeley: University of California Press, 1980

Histoire du Mouvement National Tunisien, edited by Mohamed Sayah and translated into Arabic under the general title Târîkh al-ḥarakah al-waṭaniyyah al-tûnisiyyah [History of the Tunisian Patriotic Movement] Tunis: Ministère de l'Information.

Vol.I Habib Bourguiba: Articles de Presse, 1929-1934, edited by Chedli Klibi (1967), translated into Arabic as Habib Bourguiba: Maqâlât ṣaḥafiyyah 1929-1934 [Habib Bourguiba: Newspaper Articles, 1929-1934] (March 1979);

Vol.II Le Néo-Destour face à la Première Epreuve, 1934-1936 (January 1969) translated into Arabic as Al-Dustûr al-jadîd izâʾ al-miḥnah al-ûlâ, [The New Destour faced with the first test of strength] (April 1979);

Vol.III Le Néo-Destour et le Front Populaire en France. 1. Le Dialogue, 1936-38 (April 1969) translated into Arabic Al-Dustûr al-jadîd wa-al-jabhah al-shaʿbiyyah fî Faransah, 1936-1938. 1. Al-Ḥiwâr [The New Destour and the Popular Front in France, 1936-1938. 1. Dialogue] (November 1979);

Vol.IV Le Néo-Destour et le Front Populaire en France. 2. La Rupture, 1936-38.

(May 1969);
Vols.V,VI 9 Avril 1938. Le "Procès" Bourguiba (2nd edition, March 1970);
Vols.VII, VIII,IX Le Néo-Destour face à la Deuxième Epreuve,1938-1943: Cinq ans de Résistance. (January 1970);
Vol.X Pour Préparer la Troisième Epreuve 1. Le Néo-Destour brise le Silence, 1944-1949. (January 1972);
Vol.XI, XII Pour Préparer la Troisième Epreuve. 2 and 3. Le Néo-Destour engage un ultime Dialogue, 1950-1951. (February 1973);
Vol.XIII Le Néo-Destour face à la Troisième Epreuve,1952-1956. 1. L'Echec de la Répression (May 1979);
Vol.XIV Le Néo-Destour face à la Troisième Epreuve, 1952-1956. 2. La Victoire. (June 1979);
Vol.XV Le Néo-Destour face à la Troisième Epreuve, 1952-1956. 3.L'Indépendance (July 1979).

"Historical Population Studies." Special issue of Daedalus (Spring 1968)

Hook, R.H. (ed.). Fantasy and Symbol: Studies in Anthropological Interpretation. London: Academic Press, 1979

Hook, Sidney. The HERO in History: A Study in Limitation and Possibility. New York: John Day, 1943

Hopkins, Nicholas S. "Traditional Tunis and Its Transformations," in S. Benet et al., The Impact of Modernization on Peasant Societies. New York: New York Academy of Sciences, 1974

Hudson, Michael C. Arab Politics: The Search for Legitimacy. New Haven: Yale University Press, 1977

Ibn ʿAshûr, Muḥammad al-Fâḍil. Al-Ḥarakah al-adabiyyah wa-al-fikriyyah fî Tûnis [The Literary and Intellectual Movement in Tunisia]. Cairo: Dâr al-Hanâʾ, 1956

Ibn Mîlâd, Maḥjûb. Habib Bourguiba fî subul al-ḥurriyyah al-tûnisiyyah [Habib Bourguiba in the Paths of Tunisian Liberty]. Tunis: Al-Dâr al-tûnisiyyah li-al-nashr, 1968

Identité culturelle et Conscience nationale en Tunisie: Actes du Colloque de Tunis, 1974. Tunis: Centre d'Etudes et de Recherches Economiques et Sociales, 1979

Izutsu, Toshihiko. The Concept of Belief in Islamic Theology: A Semantic Analysis of Iman and Islam. Tokyo: Keio Institute of Cultural and Linguistic Studies, 1966-67

---. Ethico-Religious Concepts in the Quran. Montreal: McGill University Press, 1966

---. God and Man in the Koran: Semantics of the Koranic Weltsanschauung. Tokyo: Keio Institute of Cultural and Linguistic Studies, 1964

---. The Structure of Ethical Terms in the Koran. Tokyo: Keio Institute of Philological Studies, 1959

Jambu-Merlin, Robert. Le Droit Privé en Tunisie. Paris: Librairie générale de droit et de jurisprudence, 1960

Janet, Pierre. L'Evolution psychologique de la Personnalité. Paris: Collège de France, 1929

Johnstone, Ronald. Religion and Society in Interaction. Englewood Cliffs: Prentice-Hall, 1975

Julien, Charles-André. L'Afrique du Nord en Marche: Tunisie, Algérie, Maroc. Paris: Payot, 1964

---. "Colons français et jeunes tunisiens, 1882-1921," Revue française d'Histoire d'Outre-Mer LIV (1967)

Kacem, Abdelaziz. "La Politique culturelle en Tunisie", Annuaire de l'Afrique du Nord (1973), 29-44

Kamanda, Alfred M. A Study of the Legal Status of Protectorates in Public International Law. Ambilly-Annemasse: Presses de Savoie, 1961

Kassab, Ahmed. Histoire de la Tunisie; L'Epoque contemporaine. Tunis: Société tunisienne de Diffusion, 1976

Kayser, Pierre. "Les Droits de la Personnalité: Aspects théoriques et pratiques," Revue Trimestrielle de Droit civil (1971),445-93

Keddie, Nikki R. An Islamic Response to Imperialism: Political and Religious Writings of Sayyid Jamal ad-Din "al-Afghani". Berkeley: University of California Press, 1968

Khairallah, Chedly. Le Mouvement Evolutionniste Tunisien (Notes et documents), Tôme III. Tunis: Editions Cujas, 1967

Khalfah, Muḥammad A. Bourguiba wa-al-jânib al-nafsânî min khiṭṭatih aw-al-istrâtîjiyyah al-nafsâniyyah [Bourguiba and the Psychological Side of his Plan or the Psychological Strategy]. Tunis: Al-Sharikah al-tûnisiyyah li-funûn al-rasm, 1971

Khâlid, Aḥmad. "Jidâl ḥawl al-ḥijâb bayn Habib Bourguiba wa-Mohamed Nomane sanat 1929" [Debate about the Veil between Habib Bourguiba and Mohamed Nomane in the year 1929] in his Aḍwâʾ min al-bayʾa al-tûnisiyyah ʿalâ al-Ṭâhir al-Ḥaddâd wa-niḍâl jîl [Highlights from the Tunisian Environment on Tahir Haddad and the Struggle of a Generation]. Tunis: Al-Dâr al-tûnisiyyah li-al-nashr, 1979

Khumaynî, Rûḥ Allâh al-Mûsawî. Al-Ḥukûmah al-islâmiyyah [The Islamic Government]. Najaf: n.p., 1969

Knapp, Wilfrid. North-West Africa: A Political and Economic Survey, 3rd ed. Oxford: Oxford University Press, 1977

Koury, Enver M. The Patterns of Mass Movements in Arab Revolutionary-Progressive States. The Hague: Mouton, 1970

Kraiem, Mustapha. La Classe Ouvrière Tunisienne et la Lutte de Libération Nationale, (1939-1952). Tunis: Mustapha Kraiem, 1980

---. Nationalisme et syndicalisme en Tunisie, 1918-1929. Tunis: U.G.T.T., 1976

---. "Le Parti Réformiste Tunisien (1920-1926)," Revue d'Histoire Maghrébine (1975),150-62

---. La Tunisie Précoloniale. Tome I: Etat, Gouvernement, Administration. Tome II: Economie, Société. Tunis: Société tunisienne de Diffusion, 1973

Lacouture, Jean. "Les Options d'Habib Bourguiba," in his Cinq Hommes et la France. Paris: Seuil, 1961

Lahbabi, Mohamed A. Le Personnalisme Musulman, 2nd ed. Paris: Presses universitaires de France, 1967

Laitman, Leon. Tunisia Today: Crisis in North Africa. New York: Citadel Press, 1954

Laroui, Abdallah. Al-ʿArab wa-al-fikr al-târîkhî [The Arabs and Historical Thought], 3rd ed. Beirut: Dâr al-Ḥaqîqah, 1980

---. Les Origines Sociales et Culturelles du Nationalisme marocain, 1830-1912 Paris: Maspéro, 1977.

Laslett, Peter. The World We Have Lost. New York: Charles Scribner's Sons, 1965

Lasswell, Harold. Politics: Who gets What, When and How. New York: Meridian Books, 1958

Lejri, Mohamed-Salah. L'Evolution du Mouvement National Tunisien des origines à la deuxième guerre mondiale, 2 volumes. Tunis: Maison tunisienne de l'Edition, 1974

Lemeunier, François. Dictionnaire juridique, économique et financier. Paris: Delmas, 1969
LeTourneau, Roger. Evolution Politique de l'Afrique du Nord musulmane, 1920-1961. Paris: Armand Colin, 1962
Levenson, Joseph R. Liang Ch'i-Cha'o and the Mind of China. Berkeley: University of California Press, 1970
Lewy, Gunter. Religion and Revolution. New York: Oxford University Press, 1974
Lexique de termes juridiques, sous la direction de Raymond Guillien et Jean Vincent. Paris: Dalloz, 1978
Liauzu, Claude. Salariat et mouvement ouvrier en Tunisie: Crises et mutations (1931-1939). Paris: Centre national de la Recherche scientifique, 1978
Ligou, Daniel. Histoire du socialisme en France (1871-1961). Paris: Presses universitaires de France, 1962
Ling, Dwight L. Tunisia: From Protectorate to Republic. Bloomington: Indiana University Press, 1967
Linton, Ralph. The Cultural Background of Personality. New York: Appleton-Century-Crofts, 1945
Maamouri, Mohamed. "The Linguistic Situation in Independent Tunisia," The American Journal of Arabic Studies, I (1973), 50-65
Mahjoubi, Ali. Les Origines du Mouvement Nationaliste en Tunisie, 1904-1934. Tunis: Publications de l'Université de Tunis, 1982
Mantran, Robert. "L'Evolution des relations entre la Tunisie et l'Empire Ottoman du XVIe au XIXe siècle," Cahiers de Tunisie, 26-27 (1959), 319-33
Marçais, William. Articles et Conférences. Paris: Adrien-Maisonneuve, 1961
--- with Abderrahman Guiga. Textes arabes de Takrouna. Paris: Bibliothèque des langues orientales vivantes, 1925
Memmi, Albert. La Dépendance: esquisse pour un portrait du dépendant. Paris: Gallimard, 1979
---. Statue de sel (1966), préface d'Albert Camus, édition revue et corrigée. Paris: Gallimard,1972
Merad, Ali."L'Idéologisation de l'Islam dans le monde musulman contemporain", in Vatin and Gellner. Islam

Merquior, J.G. Rousseau and Weber, Two Studies on the Theory of Legitimacy. London: Routledge and Kegan Paul, 1980
Micaud, Charles A. with L. Carl Brown and Clement H. Moore. Tunisia: The Politics of Modernization. New York: Frederick A. Praeger, 1964
Michoud, L. La Théorie de la Personnalité morale et son application au droit français. 2nd ed. Paris: Pichon, 1924
Mills, C. Wright and Hans Gerth. Character and Social Structure: The Psychology of Social Institutions. New York: Harcourt, Brace and Company, 1953
Montety, Henri de. "Les Données du problème tunisien," Politique Etrangère 17(March 1952), 447-466
---. "Old Families and New Elites in Tunisia," translated from "Enquête sur les vieilles familles et les nouvelles élites en Tunisie" (mimeo; Paris 1939) and from "Vieilles familles et nouvelle élite en Tunisie," Documents sur l'évolution du Monde musulman, no.3 (8 August 1940), in Man, State and Society in the Contemporary Maghrib, edited by I. William Zartman. London: Pall Mall Press, 1973 .
Moore, Clement H. Tunisia since Independence: The Dynamics of One-Party Government. Berkeley: University of California Press, 1965
Musil, Robert. The Man without Qualities; translated from the German by Eitline Wilkins and Enrst Kaiser. London: Secker and Warburg, 1953
Mzali, Mohamed-Salah. Au Fil de ma Vie: Souvenirs d'un Tunisien. Tunis: Editions H. Mzali, 1972
Naṣr, Mârlîn. Al-Taṣawwur al-qawmî al-ʿarabî fî fikr Jamâl ʿAbd al-Nâṣir (1952-1970): Dirâsah fî ʿilm al-mufradât wa-al-dalâlah [The Arab Nationalist Conception in the Thought of Jamâl ʿAbd al-Nâṣir (1952-1970): A Study in Lexicology and Semantics]. Beirut:Markaz dirâsât al-waḥdah al-ʿarabiyyah, 1981
Al-Niẓâm al-bûrqîbî: al-azmah al-siyâsiyyah wa-al-iqtiṣâdiyyah [The Bourguiba System: The Political and Economic Crisis]. Beirut: Dâr Ibn Khaldûn, 1980
Nouschi, André "La crise de 1930 en Tunisie et les débuts du Néo-Destour", Revue de l'Occident Musulman et de la Méditerranée (1970), 113-123
---. "La Politique coloniale du Front Populaire: Le Maghreb", Les Cahiers de Tunisie XXVII/109-110 (1979), 143-160

Nouveau Répertoire de Droit, 2ème édition sous la direction de Emmanuel Vergé et Roger de Ségogne. Paris: Jurisprudence Générale Dalloz, 1964

Owen, Roger E. and Thomas Naff (eds.). _Studies in Eighteenth Century Islamic History_. Carbondale: South Illinois University Press, 1977

Partner, Peter. "Bourguiba: a Different Kind of Arab," _Harper's Magazine_ (October 1957),1-6

Pautard, André. _Bourguiba_. Paris: Editions Média, 1978

Peacock, James L. _Consciousness and Change: Symbolic Anthropology in Evolutionary Perspective_. Oxford: Basil Blackwell, 1975

Poncet, Jean. _La Colonisation et l'Agriculture européennes en Tunisie depuis 1881: Etudes de géographie historique et économique_. Paris: Mouton, 1961

---. _La Tunisie à la Recherche de son Avenir; Indépendance ou néocolonialisme?_ Paris: Editions Sociales, 1974

Al-Qâḍî, Fârûq. _Mâdhâ yurîd Bourguiba?_ [What does Bourguiba want?]. Cairo: Dâr al-Fikr, 1958

Quandt, William B. _Revolution and Political Leadership: Algeria, 1954-1968_. Cambridge: Massachusetts Institute of Technology Press, 1969

Qur'ân. _The Holy Quran_; Text, Translation and Commentary by Abdullah Yusuf Ali. Washington, D.C.: Khalil al-Rawaf, 1946

Rabbath, Edmond. _Unité syrienne et devenir arabe_. Paris: Librairie Marcel Rivière, 1937

Raymond, André and Jean Poncet. _La Tunisie_. 2nd ed. Paris: Presses universitaires de France, 1971

Reese, Howard C. _et al_. _Area Handbook for the Republic of Tunisia_. Washington, D.C.: United States Government, 1970

Renard, Georges. _La Théorie de l'Institution_. Paris: Sirey, 1930

Renaud, Paul E. "De la Personnalité; esquisse d'une théorie d'ensemble." 3 volumes. Unpublished thesis: McGill University, Law Faculty, Montreal, Quebec,1922

Rivlin, Benjamin. "The Tunisian Nationalist Movement: Four Decades of Evolution," _The Middle East Journal_ VI/2 (Spring 1952)

Roberts, Stephen. _History of French Colonial Policy, 1870-1925_. London: Frank Cass and Company, 1963

Robinet, André. Péguy entre Jaurès, Bergson et l'Eglise; métaphysique et politique. Paris: Seghers, 1968
Romeril, Paul E.A. "Tunisian Nationalism - A Bibliographical Outline," The Middle East Journal XV (1960),206-15
Rosenthal, Franz. A History of Muslim Historiography. 2nd revised ed. Leiden: Brill, 1968
---. Knowledge Triumphant: The Concept of Knowledge in Medieval Islam. Leiden: Brill, 1970
Rossi, Pierre. La Tunisie de Bourguiba. Tunis: Editions Kahia, 1967
Rouissi, Moncer. Population et Société au Maghreb. Tunis: Cérès, 1977
Rous, Jean. Habib Bourguiba, l'homme d'action de l'Afrique. Paris: Jean Didier, 1969
---. Tunisie ... Attention! Paris: Deux Rives, 1952
Rudebeck, Lars. Party and People: A Study of Political Change in Tunisia (1967). 2nd ed. London: C. Hurst and Company, 1969
Said, Edward. Covering Islam; How the Media and the Experts determine how We see the Rest of the World. New York: Pantheon, 1981
Said, Rafik. La Politique culturelle en Tunisie. Paris: U.N.E.S.C.O., 1970
Salama, Bice. L'Insurrection de 1864 en Tunisie. Tunis: Maison tunisienne de l'Edition, 1967
Saleilles, Robert. De la Personnalité juridique, Histoire et Théories. 2nd ed. Paris: Rousseau, 1922
Salem, Norma. "Islam and the Status of Women in Tunisia", in Muslim Women, edited by Freda Hussain (London: Croom Helm, forthcoming)
---. "Michel ʿAflaq: A Biographical Sketch," Arab Studies Quarterly II/2 (Spring 1980), 162-174
---. "Michel ʿAflaq: A Biographical Study of His Approach to Arabism." M.A. thesis, Institute of Islamic Studies, McGill University, Montreal, Quebec, 1975
---. "A Partial Reconstruction of Michel ʿAflaq's Thought: The Role of Islam in the Formulation of Arab Nationalism," The Muslim World LXVII/4 (October 1977),280-94
---. "The Sacred and the Profane: Sadat's Speech to the Knesset," The Middle East Journal 34/1 (Winter 1980),13-24
Sammut, Carmel. "L'Action des Jeunes tunisiens: Réformisme d'Assimilation ou nationalisme d'émancipation?," Revue d'Histoire Maghrébine

10-11 (1978),67-153
---. "L'Expression des symboles nationalistes par les premiers nationalistes tunisiens dans le contexte colonial français," Revue d'Histoire Maghrébine 7-8 (1977),201-20
Sapir, Edward. Culture, Language and Personality, selected essays edited by David G. Mandelbaum. Berkeley: University of California Press, 1964
Sayadi, Mohamed. "Le Discours bourguibien". Mémoire de Maitrise, Sociology, Université de Montréal, Montreal, Quebec, 1974
Sayadi, Mongi. La Première association nationale moderne en Tunisie: Al-Jam'iyya al-Khalduniyya (1896-1958). Tunis: Maison tunisienne de l'Edition, 1974
Sebag, Paul. La Tunisie; Essai de Monographie. Paris: Editions Sociales, 1951
Septembre 1934; Répression et Résistance. Synthèse des rapports des contrôleurs civils établie par la Résidence Générale sur les évènements survenus en septembre-octobre 1934, edited by Moncef Dellagi. Tunis: Maison tunisienne de l'Edition, n.d.
Smida, Mongi. l'Enseignement supérieur en Tunisie: (Structures - Régimes - Bourses). Tunis: Société tunisienne de Diffusion, 1974
Smith, Donald E. Religion and Political Development: An Analytic Study. Boston: Little, Brown, 1970
---. Religion and Political Modernization. New Haven: Yale University Press, 1974
Sourdel, Dominique. La Civilisation de l'Islam classique. Paris: Arthaud, 1968
Sraieb, Noureddine. "Enseignement, Elites et Systèmes de valeur: Le Collège Sadiki de Tunis," Annuaire de l'Afrique du Nord (1971),104-135
---. "Note sur les dirigeants politiques et syndicalistes tunisiens de 1905 à 1934," Revue de l'Occident musulman et de la Méditerranée 9 (1971),91-118
Talmon, J.L. Romanticism and Revolt: Europe, 1815-1848. New York: Harcourt, Brace and World, 1967
Tessler, Mark. "Political Change and the Islamic Revival in Tunisia", The Maghreb Review I/1 (January-February 1980)
Tibi, Bassam. Arab Nationalism: A Critical Inquiry, edited and translated from the German by Marion Farouk-Sluglett and Peter Sluglett. New York: St.Martin's Press, 1981

Tlatli, Salah-Eddine. Tunisie Nouvelle: Problèmes et Perspectives. Tunis: Imprimerie SEFAN, 1957
Tlili, Béchir. Crises et Mutations dans le Monde Islamo-méditerranéen contemporain (1907-1918). Tunis: Publications de l'Université de Tunis, 1978
---. "La grande guerre et les questions tunisiennes; le groupement de la 'Revue du Maghreb' (1916-1918)," Les Cahiers de Tunisie XXVI/101-102 (1978),31-108
---. Socialistes et Jeunes Tunisiens à la veille de la Grande Guerre (1911-1913). Tunis: Publications de l'Université de Tunis, 1974
Touchard, Jean. La Gauche en France depuis 1900 Paris: Seuil, 1977.
Ţûbâl, Ibrâhîm. Al-Badîl al-thawrî fî tûnis [The Revolutionary Alternative in Tunisia]. Beirut: Dâr al-Kalimah, 1979
Al-Tûnisî, Khayr al-Dîn. The Surest Path: The Political Treatise of a Nineteenth Century Muslim Statesman, A Translation of the Introduction to the Surest Path to Knowledge concerning the Condition of Countries, tranlated with a commentary by L. Carl Brown. Cambridge: Harvard University Press, 1967
Tunisie. Ministère de l'Enseignement Supérieur et de la Recherche Scientifique. Commission d'histoire du Mouvement National. Premier séminaire d'histoire du mouvement national: "Les Réactions à l'occupation française de la Tunisie en 1881," Sidi Bou Said, Tunisia, 28-31 May 1981
Tunisie. Ministère de l'Information. Habib Bourguiba; Ḥayâtuh, Jihâduh [Habib Bourguiba: His Life, His Struggle]. Tunis: Ministère de l'Information, 1966
Turner, Bryan S. Marx and the End of Orientalism. London: George Allen and Unwin, 1978
Vareilles-Sommières, Gabriel Marquis de. Les Personnes morales. Paris: Librairie générale de droit et de jurisprudence, 1919
Vatin, Jean-Claude. "Questions culturelles et questions à la culture", Annuaire de l'Afrique du Nord (1973), 3-16
--- et al. Culture et Société au Maghreb. Paris: Centre National de Recherche Scientifique, 1975
--- and Ernest Gellner. Islam et Politique au Maghreb. Paris: Editions du C.N.R.S., 1981
Vigneault, Robert. L'Univers féminin dans l'oeuvre de Charles Péguy. Paris: Déclés de Brower, 1967

Vigny, Alfred de. Oeuvres complètes, préface, présentation et notes de Paul Viallaneux. Paris: Seuil, 1965

Vocabulaire juridique, article "Personnalité". Rédigé par des Professeurs de Droit, des Magistrats, et des Juriconsultes sous la direction de Henri Capitant. Paris: Presses universitaires de France, 1936

Wallerstein, Immanuel. The Modern World System: Capitalist Agriculture and the Origins of the European World Economy in the 16th Century. New York: Academic Press, 1964

Waterbury, John. "La Légitimation du Pouvoir au Maghreb: Tradition, Protestation et Répression", Annuaire de l'Afrique du Nord (1977), 411-422

Weber, Max. The Sociology of Religion (1922), translated by Ephraim Fischoff. Boston: Beacon, 1963

Yâsîn, Al-Sayyid. Al-Shakhṣiyyah al-ʿarabiyyah bayn al-mafhûm al-isrâʾîlî wa-al-mafhûm al-ʿarabî [The Arab Personality between the Israeli Concept and the Arab Concept]. Cairo: Center for Political and Strategic Studies, 1974

Yinger, John M. Religion, Society and the Individual; An Introduction to the Sociology of Religion. New York: MacMillan, 1957

Zartmann, William I. (ed.). Man, State and Society in the Contemporary Maghrib. New York: Praeger, 1973

Zawadowski, Gabriel. "Situation de l'Islam dans la Tunisie d'entre les deux guerres (1918-1939), En Terre d'Islam (Lyon) XVII/22 (1943),78-100

Zghal, Abdelkader. "Les Effets de la Modernisation de l'Agriculture sur la Stratification sociale dans les Campagnes tunisiennes," Cahiers Internationaux de Sociologie XXXVII (1965),201-206

---. "Mouvements paysans en Tunisie," Cahiers int. hist. écon. soc. 8 (n.d.),337-45

---. "Nation-building in the Maghreb," International Social Science Journal 23 (1971),435-51

---. "Le Retour du sacré et la nouvelle demande idéologique des jeunes scolarisés: le cas de la Tunisie", Annuaire de l'Afrique du Nord (1979), 41-64

--- and Mohamed Chérif. "The Reactivation of Tradition in a post-traditional society," Daedalus 102i (1973),225-37

Bibliography

Ziadeh, Nicola A. Origins of Nationalism in Tunisia. Beirut: American University of Beirut, 1962

Zmerli, Sadok. Figures Tunisiennes: Les Précurseurs. Tunis: Bouslama, c.1964

---. Figures Tunisiennes: les Successeurs. Tunis: Maison tunisienne de l'Edition, 1967

COMMON USAGE TO TRANSLITERATED FORM

Abdel-Malek, Anouar	ʿAbd al-Malik, Anwar
Abdel-Moula, Mahmoud	ʿAbd al-Mawlâ, Maḥmûd
Abdel Nasser, Gamal	ʿAbd al-Nâṣir, Jamâl
Ali, Abdullah Yusuf	ʿAlî, ʿAbd Allâh Yûsuf
Abdessalam, Ahmed	ʿAbd al-Salâm, Aḥmad
Ajami, Fouad	ʿAjamî, Fuʾâd
Amin, Samir	Amîn, Samîr
Antonius, Rachad	Antonius, Rashâd
El-Aouina	Al-ʿUwaynah
Azaiez, Boubaker	ʿAzâʾiz, Abû Bâqir
Badra, Madani	Badrâ, Madanî
Barakat, Halim	Barakât, Ḥalîm
Bardo	Bardû
Bash Hanba, Ali	Bâsh Ḥanbah, ʿAlî
Béji, Hélé	Bâjî, Hâlah
Belhaouane, Ali	Ibn al-Hawân(?), ʿAlî
Ben Achour, Fadhel	Ibn ʿAshûr, Fâḍil
Ben Achour, Yadh	Ibn ʿAshûr, Yâdh (?)
Ben Ammar, Taher	Ibn ʿAmmâr, Ṭâhir
Ben Ammar, Wassila	Ibn ʿAmmâr, Wasîlah
Ben Ayed, Farhat	Ibn ʿAyyâd, Farḥât
Ben Bella, Ahmed	Ibn Bi-Allâh (?), Aḥmad
Ben Hassein, Lakhdar	Ibn Ḥusayn, al-Akhḍar
Ben Milad, Mahjoub	Ibn Milâd, Maḥjûb
Ben Salah, Ahmed	Ibn Ṣalâḥ, Aḥmed
Ben Salem	Ibn Sâlim
Ben Slama, Béchir	Ibn Salâmah, Bashîr
Ben Slimane, Slimane	Ibn Sulaymân, Sulaymân
Ben Yahmed, Béchir	Ibn Yaḥmad, Bashîr
Ben Youssef, Salah	Ibn Yûsuf, Ṣalâḥ
Berrady, Lhachmi	Barrâdî, al-Hâshimî
Bessis, Albert	Basîs, Albert
Bey	Bây
Bizerte	Banzart
Borj LeBoeuf	Burj al-Thawr
Bouhajeb, Ali	Abû Ḥâjib, ʿAlî

Bouhdiba, Abdelwahab	Abû Ḥudaybah, ʿAbd al-Wahhâb
Boullata, Issa J.	Bullâṭah, ʿIsâ Y.
Bourguiba, Ahmed	Abû Ruqaybah, Aḥmad
Bourguiba, Ḥabîb	Abû Ruqaybah, Ḥabîb
Bourguiba, M'Hamed	Abû Ruqaybah, Muḥammad
Bourguiba, Mahmoud	Abû Ruqaybah, Maḥmûd
Bourguiba, Mohamed	Abû Ruqaybah, Muḥammad
cadhi	qâḍî
caid	qâʾid
Cap Bon	Al-Waṭan al-Qiblî
chahada	shahâdah
Chaker, Hédi	Shâkir, Hâdî
charaa	sharʿ, sharîʿah
Chater, Khalifa	Shâtir, Khalîfah
Chenik, Mohamed	Shiniq, Muḥammad
Chenoufi, Moncef	Shanûfî, Munṣif
Ech-Cherif, Idriss	Al-Sharîf, Idrîs
Cherif, Mohamed	Sharîf, Muḥammad
Chewki, Ahmed	Shawqî, Aḥmad
Cohen-Hadria, Elie	Kâhin-Ḥadriyyah, Elie
Coran	Qurʾân
Dabbab, Mohammed	Dabbâb, Muḥammad
Dellagi, Moncef	Dallajî, Munṣif
Dessouki, Ali H.	Dasûqî, ʿAlî H.
Dimassi, Ali	Dimâsî(?), ʿAlî
Djait, Hichem	Jaʿîṭ, Hishâm
Djellaz	Jallâẓ
Djerid	Jarîd
djihad	jihâd
Driss, Rachid	Idrîs, Rashîd
Enfida	Al-Nafîḍah
Fahs	Faḥṣ
Faruki, Kemal	Fârûqî, Kamâl
fellagas	fallâqah
Ferchiou, Sophie	Farshîʾu (?), Ṣâfiyyah
Ferhat, Salah	Farḥat, Ṣalâḥ
fetwa	fatwâ
Gabes	Qâbis
Gafsa	Qafṣah
Galite	Jalṭah
El-Ghoul, Yahya	Al-Ghûl, Yaḥyâ
Gnaoui	Jinnâwî
Guellaty, Hassen	Qallâtî, Ḥasan
Guiga, Abderrahman	Qîqah, ʿAbd al-Raḥmân
Guiga, Bahri	Qîqah, Baḥrî
Hached, Ferhat	Ḥâshid, Farḥat
Hadj, Messali	Ḥâjj, Muṣallî(?)
Hammam-Sousse	Ḥammâm-Sûsah
Al-Hammi, M'Hamed Ali	Al-Ḥammî, Muḥammad ʿAlî
Hermassi, Elbaki	Hirmâsî(?), al-Bâqî
Hourani, Cecil	Ḥawrânî, Cecil

Jerba	Jirbah
Kairouan	Qayrawân
Kalaa-Kbira	Qalʿah Kabîrah
Kalaa-Seghira	Qalʿah Şaghîrah
Kassab, Ahmed	Qaşşâb, Aḫmad
Le Kef	Al-Kâf
Kerkenneh	Qarqanah
Kheireddine	Khayr al-Dîn
Klibi, Chedli	Qulaybî, Shadhilî
Khairallah, Chedly	Khayr Allâh, Shadhilî
Koran	Qurʾân
Kraiem, Mustapha	Kurayyim, Muşţafâ
Ksar Hellal	Qaşr Hilâl
Ladgham, Bahi	Al-Aḑgham, Bâhî
Ladjimi, Chams-Eddine	Al-ʿAjamî(?), Shams al-Dîn
Lahbabi, Mohamed	Al-Aḫbâbî, Muḫammad
Lamine Bey	Al-Amîn Bây
Laroui, Abdallah	Al-ʿArwî, ʿAbd Allâh
Lasram, M'Hamed	Al-Asram, Muḫammad
Lejri, Mohamed-Salah	Al-Âjirî(?), Muḫammad-Şalâḫ
Al-Madani, Ahmed Tewfik	Al-Madanî, Aḫmad Tawfîq
Mahdiya	Mahdiyyah
Mahjoubi, Ali	Maḫjûbî, ʿAlî
Mahomet	Muḫammad
makhzen	makhzan
La Marsa	Al-Marsâ
Masmoudi, Mohamed	Maşmûdî, Muḫammad
Materi, Mahmoud	Mâţirî, Aḫmad
Mekki, Chedli	Makkî, Shadhilî
Memmi, Albert	Mammî(?), Albert
Messadi, Mahmoud	Masʿadî, Aḫmad
Mestiri, Ahmed	Mistîrî, Aḫmad
Metlaoui	Mitlâwî
Mohamed V	Muḫammad al-Khâmis
Moknine	Muknîn
Monastir	Munastîr
Moncef Bey	Munşif Bây
Msaken	Masâkin
mufti	muftî
Musa, Salamah	Mûsâ, Salâmah
Mzali, Mohamed	Mizâlî, Muḫammad
Mzali, Mohamed-Salah	Mizâlî, Muḫammad Şalâḫ
En-Naceur, Mohamed	Al-Nâşir, Muḫammad
Enneifer, Salah	Al-Nayfar, Şalâḫ
Nomane, Mohamed	Nuʿmân, Muḫammad
Nouira, Hédi	Nuwayrah, Hâdî
oulémas	ʿulamâʾ
Pasha	Bâshâ
Raad, Raymond	Raʿd, Raymond
Rabbath, Edmond	Rabbâţ, Edmond
Al-Rawaf, Khalil	Al-Rawâf, Khalîl

Redif.	Raḑif
Rouissi, Moncer.	Ruʾîsî(?), Munşir(?)
Sadiki	Al-Şâdiqiyyah
Essafi, Ahmed.	Al-Şâfî, Aḫmad
Sahel.	Sâḫil
Saidi, Hédi.	Şaʿîdî, Hâdî
Sakiet Sidi Youssef. . .	Sâqiyyat Sayyidî Yûsuf
Sakka, Ahmed	Saqqâ, Aḫmad
Salama, Bice	Salâmah, Bice
Salem, Norma	Sâlim, Norma
Sammut, Carmel	Şammût, Carmel
Sayadi, Mohamed.	Şayyâdî, Muḫammad
Sayadi, Mongi.	Şayyâdî, Munjî
Sayah, Mohamed	Şayyâḫ, Muḫammad
Sbih, Missoum.	Şubayḫ, Maʿsûm
Sebag, Paul.	Şabbâgh, Paul
Sfar, Béchir	Safar, Bashîr
Sfar, Tahar.	Safar, Ţâhir
Sfax	Şifâqis
Sfia, Mohamed-Salah. . .	Şafiyyah, Muḫammad Şalâḫ
Siala.	Siyâlah
Sidi Bou Said.	Sayyidî Abû Saʿîd
Slim, Taieb.	Salîm, Ţayyib
Smida, Mongi	Şumaydah (?), Munjî
Sousse	Sûsah
Sraieb, Noureddine . . .	Surayyib, Nûr al-Dîn
Taalbi	Thaʿâlibî
Takrouna	Takrûnah
Thaalbi, Abdelaziz . . .	Thaʿâlibî, ʿAbd al-Azîz
Thameur, Habib	Thâmir, Ḫabîb
Tibi, Bassam	Ţîbî, Bassâm
Tlatli, Salah-Eddine . .	Tulatlî (?), Şalâḫ al-Dîn
Tlemcen.	Tilmisân
Tlili, Béchir.	Talîlî, Bashîr
Triki, Hassine	Ţarîqî, Ḫusayn
Zarg Layoun.	Azraq al-ʿUyûn
Zaytouna	Zaytûnah
Zeitouna	Zaytûnah
Zghal, Abdelkader. . . .	Zaghal, ʿAbd al-Qâdir
Ziadeh, Nicola A.. . . .	Ziyâdah, Nicola A.
Zmerli, Sadok.	Zumarlî, Şâdiq
Zouaves.	Zawâf

TRANSLITERATED FORM TO COMMON USAGE

ʿAbd al-Malik, Anwar. . .	Abdel-Malek, Anouar
ʿAbd al-Mawlâ, Maḫmûd . .	Abdel-Moula, Mahmoud
ʿAbd al-Nâşir, Jamâl. . .	Abdel Nasser, Gamal
ʿAbd al-Salâm	Abdessalam, Ahmed
Abû Ḫâjib, ʿAlî.	Bouhajeb, Ali
Abû Ḫudaybah, ʿAbd al-Wahhâb. . . .	Bouhdiba, Abdelwahab

Abû Ruqaybah, Aḥmad	Bourguiba, Ahmed
Abû Ruqaybah, Ḥabîb	Bourguiba, Habib
Abû Ruqaybah, Maḥûd	Bourguiba, Mahmoud
Abû Ruqaybah, Muḥammad	Bourguiba, M'Hamed
	Bourguiba, Mohamed
Al-Aḍgham, Bâhî	Ladgham, Bahi
Al-Aḥabâbî, Muḥammad	Lahbabi, Mohamed
ʿAjamî, Fuʾâd	Ajami, Fouad
Al-ʿAjamî, Shams al-Dîn	Ladjimi, Chams-Eddine
Al-Ajirî(?), Muḥammad-Ṣalâḥ	Lejri, Mohamed-Salah
ʿAlî, ʿAbd Allâh Yûsûf	Ali, Abdullah Yusuf
Amîn, Samîr	Amin, Samir
Al-Amîn Bây	Lamine Bey
Antonius, Rashâd	Antonius, Rachad
Al-ʿArwî, ʿAbd Allâh	Laroui, Abdallah
Al-Aṣram, Muḥammad	Lasram, M'Hamed
ʿAzaʾiz, Abû Bâqir	Azaiez, Boubaker
Azraq al-ʿUyûn	Zarg Layoun
Badrâ, Madanî	Badra, Madani
Bâjî, Hâlah	Béji, Hélé
Banzart	Bizerte
Barakât, Ḥalîm	Barakat, Halim
Bardû	Bardo
Barrâdî, al-Hâshimî	Berradi, Lhachmi
Bâshâ	Pasha
Basîs, Albert	Bessis, Albert
Bây	Bey
Bullâṭah, ʿIsâ J.	Boullata, Issa J.
Burj al-Thawr	Borj LeBoeuf
Dabbâb, Muḥammad	Dabbab, Mohamed
Dallâjî, Munṣif	Dellagi, Moncef
Dasûqî, ʿAlî H.	Dessouki, Ali H.
Dimâsî(?), ʿAlî	Dimasi, Ali
Faḥṣ	Fahs
fallâqah	fellagas
Farḥat, Ṣalâḥ	Ferhat, Salah
Fârûqî, Kamâl	Faruki, Kemal
Farshîʾu(?), Ṣafiyyah	Ferchiou, Sophie
fatwâ	fetwa
Al-Ghûl, Yaḥyâ	El-Ghoul, Yahya
Ḥâshid, Farḥat	Hached, Ferhat
Hâjj, Muṣallî	Hadj, Messali
Ḥammâm-Sâsah	Hammam-Sousse
Al-Ḥammî, Muḥammad ʿAlî	Al-Hammi, Mohamed Ali
Ḥawrânî, Cecil	Hourani, Cecil
Hirmâsî(?), al-Bâqî	Hermassi, Elbaki
Ibn ʿAmmâr, Ṭahir	Ben Ammar, Tahar
Ibn ʿAmmâr, Wasîlah	Ben Ammar, Wassila
Ibn ʿAshûr, Fâḍil	Ben Achour, Fadil
Ibn ʿAshûr, Yâdh(?)	Ben Achour, Yadh

Ibn Ayyâd, Farḫat	Ben Ayed, Farhat
Ibn Bi-Allâh(?), Aḫmad	Ben Bella, Ahmed
Ibn al-Hawân (?), ʿAlî	Belhaoune, Ali
Ibn Ḫusayn, al-Akhḑar	Ben Hassein, Lakhdar
Ibn Milâd, Maḫjûb	Ben Milad, Mahjub
Ibn Şalâḫ, Aḫmad	Ben Salah, Ahmed
Ibn Salâmah, Bashîr	Ben Slama, Béchir
Ibn Sâlim	Ben Salem
Ibn Sulaymân, Sulaymân	Ben Slimane, Slimane
Ibn Yaḫmad, Bashîr	Ben Yahmed, Béchir
Ibn Yûsuf, Şalâḫ	Ben Youssef, Salah
Idrîs, Rashîd	Driss, Rachid
Jaʿîţ, Hishám	Djait, Hichem
Jallâz	Djellaz
Jalţah	Galite
Jarîd	Djerid
jihâd	Djihad
Jinnâwî	Gnaoui
Jirbah	Jerba
Al-Kâf	Le Kef
Kâhin-Ḫadriyyah, Elie	Cohen-Hadria, Elie
Kurayyim, Muşţafâ	Kraiem, Mustapha
Al-Madanî, Aḫmad Tawfîq	Al-Madani, Ahmed Tewfik
Mahdiyyah	Mahdiya
Maḫjûbî, ʿAlî	Mahjoubi, Ali
makhzan	mahkzen
Makkî, Shadhilî	Mekki, Chedli
Mammî(?), Albert	Memmi, Albert
al-Marsâ	La Marsa
Masʿadî, Aḫmad	Messadi, Mahmoud
Masâkin	Msaken
Maşmûdî, Muḫammad	Masmoudi, Mohamed
Mâţirî, Aḫmad	Materi, Ahmed
Mistîrî, Aḫmad	Mestiri, Ahmed
Mitlâwî	Metlaoui
Mizâlî, Muḫammad	Mzali, Mohamed
Mizâlî, Muḫammad-Şalâḫ	Mzali, Mohamed-Salah
muftî	mufti
Muḫammad	Mahomet
Muḫammad al-Khâmis	Mohamed V
Muknîn	Moknine
Munastîr	Monastir
Munşif Bây	Moncef Bey
Mûsâ, Salâmah	Musa, Salamah
Al-Nafîḑah	Enfida
Al-Nâşir, Muḫammad	En-Naceur, Mohamed
Al-Nayfar, Şalâḫ	Enneifer, Salah
Nuʿmân, Muḫammad	Nomane, Mohamed
Nuwayrah, Hâdî	Nouira, Hédi

Qâbis	Gabes
qâdî	cadhi
Qafṣah	Gafsa
qâʾid	caid
Qalʿah Kabîrah	Kalaa-Kbira
Qalʿah Ṣaghirah	Kalaa- Seghirah
Qallâtî, Ḥasan	Guellaty, Hassen
Qarqanah	Kerkenna
Qaṣr Hilâl	Ksar Hellal
Qaṣṣâb, Aḥmad	Kassab, Ahmed
Qayrawân	Kairouan
Qîqah, Baḥrî	Guiga, Bahri
Qulaybî, Shâdhilî	Klibi, Chedly
Qurʾân	Coran
	Koran
Raʿd, Raymond	Raad, Raymond
Rabbâṭ, Edmond	Rabbath, Edmond
Radîf	Redif
Al-Rawâf, Khalîl	Al-Rawaf, Khalil
Rîf	Rif
Ruʾîsî(?), Munṣir	Rouissi, Moncer
Ṣabbâgh, Paul	Sebag, Paul
Al-Ṣadiqiyyah	Sadiki
Ṣafar, Bashîr	Sfar, Béchir
Ṣafar, Ṭahir	Sfar, Tahar
Al-Ṣâfî, Aḥmad	Essafi, Ahmed
Ṣafiyyah,Muḥammad-Salâh	Sfia, Mohamed-Salah
Sâḥil	Sahel
Ṣaʿîdî, Hâdî	Saidi, Hédi
Salâmah, Bice	Salama, Bice
Sâlim, Norma	Salem, Norma
Salîm, Ṭayyib	Slim, Taieb
Ṣammût(?), Carmel	Sammut, Carmel
Sâqiyyat Sayyidî Yûsuf	Sakiet Sidi Youssef
Saqqâ, Aḥmad	Sakka, Ahmed
Ṣayyâdî, Muḥammad	Sayadi, Mohamed
Ṣayyâdî, Munjî	Sayadi, Mongi
Ṣayyâḥ, Muḥammad	Sayah, Mohamed
Sayyidî Abû Saʿîd	Sidi Bou Said
shahâdah	chahada
Shâkir, Hâdî	Chaker, Hédi
Shanûfî, Munṣif	Chenoufi, Moncef
sharʿ, sharîʿah	charaa
Al-Sharîf, Idrîs	Ech-Cherif, Idriss
Sharîf, Muḥammad	Cherif, Mohamed
Shâṭir, Khalîfah	Chater, Khalifa
Shawqî, Aḥmad	Chewki, Ahmed
Shinîq, Muḥammad	Chenik, Mohamed
Ṣifâqis	Sfax
Siyâlah	Siala
Ṣumaydah(?), Munjî	Smida, Mongi

Surayyib, Nûr al-Dîn . .	Sraeib, Noureddine
Sûsah.	Sousse
Takrûnah	Takrouna
Talîlî, Bashîr	Tlili, Béchir
Ţarîqî, Ḩusayn	Triki, Hassine
Thaʿâlibî, ʿAbd al-ʿAzîz.	Taalbi
. .	Thaalbi, Abdelaziz
Thâmir, Ḩabîb.	Thameur, Habib
Ţîbî, Bassâm	Tibi, Bassam
Tilmisân	Tlemcen
Tulatlî,Şalâh al-Dîn. .	Tlatli, Salah-Eddine
Al-Tûnisî, Khayr al-Dîn.	Kheireddine
ʿulamâʾ.	oulémas
Al-ʿUwayna	El-Aouina
Al-Waţan al-Qiblî. . . .	Cap Bon
Zaghal, ʿAbd al-Qâdir. .	Zghal, Abdelkader
Zaytûnah	Zaytouna
. . . .	Zeitouna
Zawâf.	Zouaves
Ziyâdah, Nicola A. . . .	Ziadeh, Nicola A.
Zumarlî, Şâdiq	Zmerli, Sadok

Index

ʿAbduh, Muḥammad 28, 60, 62, 144
acculturation, active-syncretic 4, 7, 26
action 7,18,53;clandestine 104-5; disciplined 117; graduatlist 60-2, 99-100, 130-1; mass 19,38-39,41,45,63-4;terrorist 111,124,127,129,158;and faith 95,143-4;also see dialogue, Islam, Néo-Destour
L'Action Tunisienne 75,79, 87,89,143
Al-Afghânî, Jamâl al-Dîn 144
ʿAflaq, Michel 6-7, 17-18, 134, 182
ʿamal see action
Arab League see League of Arab States
Arab Maghrib Office 120, 121,152
Archéo-Destour Party, Congress (1933) 88-9, 94,98;differences with Reformists 62-3; establishment of 47,48,53, 56;leadership of 56-7; membership of 64-6; program of 26,55,57,59; tactics of 91; and Communism 58; and land-tenure 57;and Socialism 58,80; and Thaalbi 54, 57; and Young Tunisians 54-5,57; also see Néo-Destour
assimilation, policies of 41, 43, 107
association, policies of 42-3, 107
Association des Anciens du Sadiki (1905) 42
Association of Zaytûnah Mosque Students see Zaytûnah
Ataturk 52, 126
autonomy 26, 127, 131, 151-8
awqâf see land-tenure

Bardo, Treaty of 27,63, 130, 157, 160
basic personality see personnalité de base
Bégué, Camille 13,85-6
Belhaoune, Ali 110
Ben Ammar, Wassila 113
Ben Salah, Ahmed 37, 154, 156, 163; and failure of socialism 163-4
Ben Slama, Béchir 183-5, 187-8, 190 also see personnalité
Ben Youssef 122, 125-6, 137, 160; also see Islam, personnalité
Benedict, Margaret see personnalité de base

Bergson, Henri 72-3,139,168
biography as method 1,7-10,19, 167-8; types of 8, 9, 18; also see history
Bizerte crisis (1961) 162
Black Eleven see action, terrorist
Black Hand see action, terrorist
Blum, Léon 106
Bouhajeb, Ali 81, 88, 89
Bouhdiba, Abdelwahab 183
boundary conditions see limits
Bourguiba, Ahmed 29, 31, 39, 40, 89
Bourguiba, Habib, birth of (1903) 20,29;Combattant Surprême 103; father of 33-4;flight to Egypt 118-22;marriages of 32, 73,113; mother of 29, 31-32;primary school of 29,39-40,48-9;secondary school of 48-51,66-68; sibling order of 29-30; testicle of 50; tuberculosis 49,50-1; and action 91-4,97-8, 113; and ʿAflaq 134, 182; and Arab Maghrib Office 120-1; and Ben Youssef 122-3, 130-2, 151-60; and Béchir Sfar funeral 39, 68, 70; and Bergson 72;and Bey 68,70,160-1; and de Vigny 72; and Destour Party 88-90; and direct contact 95, 101-3,124;and Djellaz riots 68, 70; and economics 85-6, 154-6, 163-4; and heroes 70, 72-3; and Jaurès 69-70;and journalism 74-5,80,87-8; and language 16-7,102; and law 68, 136-45,153;and national unity 156-7,163-4; and socialism 85-6, 133-4, 155,163-4; and Thaalbi 56,70,99-100, 111;and tramway boycott 68, 70; and U.G.T.T.152,154,156-7; and United States 113-5, 117-9, 121, 162; as al-mujâhid al-akbar; 102-3; as Secretary General of Néo-Destour 96; in France 68-72; also see Islam, legitimacy, Néo-Destour, personnalité, religion
Bourguiba, Mahmoud 29, 31, 40, 50
Bourguiba, M'Hamed 29,31, 39,40,60,73,75,90,96
Bourguiba, Mohamed 29, 31, 50,60
Brown, L. Carl 93
Bureau Politique see Néo-Destour

capitalism, world 23,36-7
Carnot, Lycée 49,51
Cartel des Gauches (1924-1926) 54,64-6,106
cause see factor
C.G.T. - Confédération Générale du Travail 64-5, 109
C.G.T.T. - Confédération Générale Tunisienne du Travail 53,65,109-10
Challaye, Félicien 55,73, 106, 107
Chenik, Mohamed 81,89,96, 113, 115, 125-6
C.I.S.L. - Confédération Internationale des Syndicats Libres 117
class,alliances 3,22,43-44, 85, 91, 97, 122; -fractions 3, 43; definitions of 1-3; fractions 3,43;lumpenproletariat 38, 84, 91, 117; or ṭabaqah 3; types of 21-3,25-6,35,
Collège Sadiki see Sadiki

colonialism, effects of 83-7; progressive 55; and education 41-2; and land-tenure 36-7; and nationalism 23, 45-6; also see Protectorate
Combattant Suprême see Bourguiba, Habib
Comte, Auguste 70, 140
Confédération Générale du Travail see C.G.T.
Confédération Générale Tunisienne du Travail see C.G.T.T.
Confédération Internationale des Syndicats Libres see C.I.S.L.
Congrès Colonial (1906) 43
Congrès sur l'Afrique du Nord (1908)43
consciousness see class, personnalité, religion
constitution(1861) 23-6; (1959) 165; also see Destour Party, Néo-Destour Party,Socialist Destour Party
contact direct see Bourguiba, Habib
Convention de la Marsa see Marsa, Convention de la
co-sovereignty 58, 107-9, 125, 126

de Vigny, Alfred 72
de-legitimation see Islam, religion
décrets scélérats 66,90
delegations 58, 64,69
demonstrations see action, mass
dependency 37, 70, 191; theories of 23; andsocial injustice 190,193
Destour see Archéo-Destour, Néo-Destour
dialogue 7, 53, 53,118,121; first 105-9; renewed, with France 122-7, 129-31, 152; and compromise 100-1; and mass action 99-101
Dimassi, Ali 14, 15
dîn see religion
direct contact see Bourguiba, Habib
discourse, classical Islamic 6; political 1, 7, 135, 181; also see language, legitimacy, religion
dissonance 165, 190
Djellaz riots 45-7
Djait, Hichem 185-90
Durkheim, Emile 4-5, 140
dustûr see constitution; also see Archéo-Destour Party; Néo-Destour Party;Socialist Destour Party

economic crisis (1922) 15; (1930s) 83-6
emic see language categories
épreuve de force see test of strength
étapes see action, gradualist
L'Etendard, Tunisien 74,77
etic see language categories
Eucharistic Congress 74-8

factor, types of 9-10, 15
fallâqah see action, terrorist
Fascism 81, 110
Faure, Edgar 127, 130
Fédération des Syndicats Mondiale see F.S.M.
Fédération Socialiste de Tunisie 53, 62-3
Free Constitutional Party see Archéo-Destour Party, establishment of
Front Populaire (1936-1938) 54, 106-10
Frontist Party see Parti Frontiste
F.S.M. - Fédération des Syndicats Mondiale 117

Gafsa 190
generative function see religion
Guellaty, Hassen 46,59-63
Guiga, Bahri 73,79,88,89, 90, 96,104, 113

ḥabûs see land-tenure
Hached, Ferhat 116, 117, 125, 128, 131; also see U.G.T.T.
Al-Ḥaddâd, al-Ṭâhir 176
Al-Ḥammi, M'Hamed Ali 65
ḥanshîr see land-tenure
Hermassi, Elbaki 2
history, continuity ofTunisian 24,144,161,183; official school of 13, 14, 27, 91; history as collective memory 11, 167, 177; also see biography, legitimacy, politics
Al-Ḥizb al-dustûrî al-ḥurr al-tûnisî see Archéo-Destour Party, establishment of
holy war 102, 103, 186
Hugo, Victor 48

identity see personnalité
independence 159
institution see personnalité
insurrection (1864) 23-4, 33-5, 39
integrative function see religion
interlocuteur 42-3,96,98-131, 152
International Financial Commission (1868) 24
iṣlâḥ see reform
Islam, "official" 175-6, 178; "popular" 175-6, 178; and action 61-2; and Ben Youssef 153-5; and Bourguiba 1, 155; and consciousness 100; and dominant ideology 175; as communication 92-3,100-1;as component of Tunisian personnalité 178; as de-legitimizing factor 77,82, 166;as legitimizing 77, 188-93; as nation and state 178-9; as preserver of Tunisian personnalité 76-7 also see language, religion

Jam'iyyat al-Awqâf see land-tenure
Jam'iyyat al-Ḥabûs see land-tenure
Jam'iyyat talâmidhat jâmi' al-zaytûnah see Zaytûnah
Jaurès, Jean 55,70,72,73
Jeunes Tunisiens see Young Tunisians
Jews, Tunisian 53, 56, 67, 82, 115, 155
jihâd see holy war
Julien, Charles-André 25, 106, 114

Kardiner, Abram see personnalité de base
key terms 7, 18, 132;also see action,dialogue, personnalité, réalisme
Khairallah, Chedly 73, 74, 78, 104
Khaldûniyyah 41, 42
Khayr al-Dîn see al-Tûnisî, Khayr al-Dîn
Kraiem, Mustapha 16, 175-9
Ksar Hellal 93-4; also see Néo-Destour Party

labor, free 36; union 15; also see C.G.T., C.G.T.T., U.G.T.T.
land-tenure 34-8, 42; and nationalism 38;in Sahel 38-9; also see Archéo-Destour, colonialism, personnalité
language, Arabic 16-7; categories 4; and

politics 11; and religion and politics 6; as component of personnalité 75; of the masses 19; also see Bourguiba, interlocuteur, religion, symbol
Laroui, Abdallah 192-3
laylat al-qadr (1946) 116; (1975) 166
League of Arab States 116, 118-22, 152
Lefras, Mathilde see Louvain, Mathilde
legitimacy, charismatic 132, 151-2; historical 12,15,16,132,145-51; institutional 14; legal 14,132-145; search for 18; and history 10-11; and political discourse 7; and politics and religion 4, 9; and social consensus 5, 7; and success 105, 159, 161; of the Bey 57, 160-1; also see language, personnalité, religon, women
Lejri, Mohamed-Salah 14, 15
limits 4, 9-10, 141, 172
Linton, Ralph see personnalité de base
Louvain, Mathilde 32,73,119
lumpen-proletariat see class
Lycée Carnot, see Carnot Lycée

Mahjoubi, Ali 14,15, 173-5
La Main Rouge 160; also see action, terrorist
Marsa, Convention de la 27, 62, 130
Masmoudi, Mohamed 122
Materi, Mahmoud 44,73,74, 88,90,96,110,113,115
Mead, Margaret see personnalité de base
Mendès-France, Pierre 107 125, 129-30
Messadi, Mahmoud 128,154
Mestiri, Ahmed 12
M'Hamed Ali see Al-Hammi, M'Hamed Ali
military rule (1912) 46; (1938) 111; (1952) 127; in South 27
milk see land-tenure
mobility see society, mobility in
mobilization see action, mass
Monastir 32, 33, 89
Monastir Congress 12
Moncef Bey 113-4
Al-Mujâhid al-akbar see Bourguiba, Habib
Mustafa Kemal see Ataturk
Mzali, Mohamed 183
Mzali, Mohamed-Salah 128-9

National Council see Néo-Destour structure
National Union see Union Nationale
nationalism, characteristics of Tunisian 53; periodization of Tunisian 25-7; religious dimension of 15, 46; theoretical bases of Tunisian 43; types of, in the Arab world 182, 189; and class structure 23; and state-building 14, 23-4, 160; as independence movement 14; as nation-building 14, 23-5, 161-3; also see personnalité
nation-building see nationalism as
naturalization see religion; also see personnalité
Néo-Destour Party, 14, 15, 17; establishment of 26, 84, 93-7; Bureau Politique, first 104, second 104, third 104-5, fourth 111, fifth 111-2, sixth 112-

3; Congress, Ksar Hellal (1934) 95,98,105, second (1946) 116,third (1948) 123,fourth(1952) 129, fifth (1955) 153, 156-7; leadership of 56-7; membership of 65-6; program of 102; structure of 96,98,103; tactics of 53, 91-3,97-8, 113; and Allies 113; and Archéo-Destour 91-3, 96-7, 99-100, 111; and Axis 111-4, 120;and Islam 97,101;and masses 109;and Reformist Party 111; and U.G.T.T. 94, 117-8, 130; and Young Tunisians 98; and Zaytûnah 104-5;also see Archéo-Destour Party, Socialist Destour Party
Néo-Socialistes (1933) 80-81
New Destour see Néo-Destour
Nomane, Mohamed 46,60-63
Nouira, Hédi 106,110

Old Destour see Archéo-Destour
Orientalism 172
Ottoman Empire 22,47,52-4

Palestine 120
Parti de la Liberté 54
Parti Frontiste 107, 125
Parti Libéral Constitutionnel see Archéo-Destour, establishment of
Parti Libre Tunisien see Archéo-Destour,establishment of
Parti Socialiste 53, 80; also see S.F.I.O.
Parti Tunisien 54
Péguy, Charles 55, 73
personal status 68; Code of 163;and naturalization 82; also see religion
personnalisme 146-7, 171
personnalité 7, 18, 53, 59; Arab-Islamic 11, 14,16,116-7,153;Habib Bourguiba's 31; definition of 135, legal, 136-45,153, psycho-sociological 144-50, 153;organ of 141;Tunisian 11,14-5,43-4,47-8,54,75,78,80,116-7;and action 140,143-4; and association 137,141;and Ben Slama 183-5,187-8; and Bergson 139,145-6, 147;and Bourguiba,Habib 72, 150-1, 156, 168-71, and consciousness 140-1; and Djait 185-8;and dependence and social injustice 193;and land-tenure 138, 142; and legitimacy 14-6, 117, 169; and naturalization 88; and Protectorate 142, 144-5; and société 137, 139, 141, 145-6; and the State 141-3, 144; de base 148-9, 186-also see religion, women
politics, definition of3-4; and history 11; of presence 124
Popular Front see Front Populaire
populist see action, mass
Protectorate, establishment of 24,26

Qur⁾ân 94-5,110,143

réalisme 7, 53, 54, 61
reform 21, 23, 28; constitutional 62;Islamic 22, 60,62,144;and Protectorate 28;in Tunisia 21-4, 46, 96; also see Sadiki, Al-Tûnisî
Reformist Party 53, 59-63
religion, ambiguity of 172,

192; definition of 3-4; generative function of 5; integrative function of 5; and consciousness 175-9, 188-9; and economics 173-5,188-9; and language 19, 82,98-104, 169,172;and legitimacy 26;and nationalism 26; and naturalization 15, 83-94; and personal status 82; and politics 1,5,12,17-8,166,171-9; as collective representation 4-7, 171;as component of personnalité 13,191,67,75,82,102,134; as opium of masses 171, 172; also see Islam, personnalité, symbols
Renouvier, Charles 146-7; also see personnalisme
Republic of Tunisia (1957) 18, 159
revolt see insurrection

Sâdât, Anwar 6,7
Sadiki, creation of 21,40-42; also see Bourguiba
Sahel 22, 39, 41, 42
Sakiet Sidi Youssef 162
Salafiyyah see reform, Islamic
Sammut, Carmel 175-9
Sayah, Mohamed 11-3
Schuman, Robert 127
Section Fédérale Internationale Communiste see S.F.I.C.
Section Française de l'Internationale Ouvrière seeS.F.I.O
self-determination 47,52
semantics 6-7, 135
Sfar, Béchir 7,33,38,42, 51,69,96;funeral of 39, second father of the reawakening 43; speech (1906) 43
Sfar, Tahar 73-4,90,96, 104,134
S.F.I.C. - Section Fédérale Internationale Communiste 53
S.F.I.O.-Section Française de l'Internationale Ouvrière 53,60,81
shakhŝiyyah see personnalité
shâshiyyah industry see women
signs, systems of see symbols
siyâsah see politics
Socialist Destour Party 16, 24
Socialist Party see Parti Socialiste
society, homogeneity of Tunisian 20; mobility in traditional 21-4, 39,41,44; mobility of Bourguiba family in 31-4,39
sovereignty see co-sovereignty, personnalité and state
specificity see personnalité
state-builiding see nationalism and
symbol 5; action of 5; codes of 5; complex of 5; dynamics of 5, 6; Islamic 45; religious 1,6,66,75-6,100; spheres 149; also see religion, collective representation
ţabaqah see class
ţaqm see Néo-Destour structure
terrorism see action, terrorist
test of strength, first 91,99-100;second 109-112; third 126,127-9
Thaalbi, Abdelaziz 46, 50,97, 108, 144; also see Archéo-Destour, Bourguiba
theatre 30,31,48,50,69,136

time, independent factor 3, 5, 8
Tours Congress (1920) 53, 58, 60
tramway boycott 46,47,51
Tunis Congress 107-8
Al-Tûnisî, Khayr al-Dîn 21, 22, 23, 36, 40, 43, 72, 96
La Tunisie Martyre 50,54
Le Tunisien 25, 26, 43

U.G.A.T.-Union Générale des Agriculteurs Tunisiens 124, 127, 152, 154
U.G.E.T.-Union Générale des Etudiants Tunisiens 164
U.G.T.T.-Union Générale des Travailleurs Tunisiens 16,94,116-8,127, 152; also see Néo-Destour
U.N.A.T.-Union Nationale des Agriculteurs Tunisiens 154
U.N.F.T.-Union Nationale des Femmes Tunisiennes 164
Union Française 122,124, 153
Union Générale des Agriculteurs Tunisiens see U.G.A.T.
Union Générale des Travailleurs Tunisiens see U.G.T.T.
Union Nationale 54
Union Nationale des Agriculteurs Tunisiens see U.N.A.T.
U.T.A.C.-Union Tunisienne de l'Artisanat et du Commerce 124, 127,152, 154

Viénot, Pierre 106-7,109, 122, 125
violence see action
La Voix du Tunisien 74-5, 77-9

women, Bourguiba 31; and legitimacy 133, 165-6; and mass action 111; and personnalité 132-3; and shâshiyyah industry 31-4;and social mobility 31-2

Young Tunisians 25,26,43, 46, 53, 117

Zarg Layoun see action terrorist
Zaytûnah,charter for 21; in independence movement 44, 104-5; student associations